"FISHING HOT SPOTS: RHINELANDER AREA" (Book 7 of North Central Series) is published by Fishing Hot Spots, Inc. Reproduction in whole or in part without written permission from Fishing Hot Spots, Inc. is prohibited.

LAKES ALPHABETICALLY

Alice Lake	122	Flag Lake	122
Alva Lake	17	Flannery Lake	37
Bass Lake (S8, T37N, R9E)	69	Fourth Lake	77
Beaver Lake	19	Fox Lake	140
Bertram Lake	69	Garland Lake	140
Birchrock Lake	44	George Lake	91
Bob's Lake	44	Goodyear Lake	42
Boggy Lake	29	Green Bass Lake	121
Boom Lake	54	Gross Lake	107
Bowles Lake	140	Gudegast Creek	87
Box Lake	69	Hancock Lake	124
Buck Lake (S19, T36N, R9E)	98	Hanson Lake	111
Buck Lake (S33, T38N, R7E)	29	Hat Rapids Flowage (Wisconsin R.)	101
Bullhead Lake	88		
Cherry Lake	44	Heal Lake	107
Clear Lake (S10, T36N, R9E)	90	Hess Lake	107
Clear Lake (S24, T37N, R7E)	33	Hixon Lake	96
Clear Lake (S8, T37N, R9E)	69	Hodag Lake	43
Cook Lake	122	Hoist Lake	122
Coon Lake	36	Hook Lake	44
Corner Lake	14	Indian Lake	140
Crescent Lake	116	Jennie Raisen Lake	88
Crystal Lake	68	John Lake	122
Cuenin Lake	95	Josie Lake	23
Davis Lake	107	Julia Lake	99
DeMarce Lake	107	Lake Creek Lake	64
Dollar Lake	88	Landberg Lake	107
Douglas Lake	68	Langley Lake	109
Doyle Lake	69	Liege Lake	20
East Horsehead Lake	26	Lily Lake (Lily Bass Lake)	112
Elna Lake	30	Little Bertram Lake	69
Emden Lake	88	Long Lake (S3, T37N, R7E)	15
Emma Lake	114	Long Lake (S11, T36N, R9E)	88
Faust Lake (Foss Lake)	89	Long Lake (S30, T36N, R8E)	140
Fetke Lake	69	Loon Lake	122
Fifth Lake	77	Maud Lake	32
Finger Lake	140	Mazy Lake	140

1

Lake	Page	Lake	Page
Midget Lake	107	Simmons Lake	29
Mildred Lake	33	Snowden Lake	81
Minnow Lake	88	Soo Lake	42
Mirror Lake	121	South Pine Lake	64
Moen Lake	70	Spruce Lake (S22, T37N, R7E)	22
Mud Lake (S7, T37N, R9E)	69	Spruce Lake (S16, T36N, R8E)	122
Mud Lake (S11, T37N, R9E)	88	Spur Lake	122
Netties Lake (Sylvan Lake)	67	Squash Lake	135
Newbold Lake	44	Sunset Lake	80
Newbold Springs	44	Swamp Lake	29
Nose Lake	140	Tenderfoot Lake	88
O'Day Lake	29	Third Lake	75
Ole Lake	44	Thompson Lake	82
Oneida Lake	127	Thunder Lake	61
Pelican River	105	Timber Lake (S15, T37N, R7E)	21
Perch Lake (S5, T36N, R8E)	122	Timber Lake (S12, T36N, R8E)	107
Perch Lake (S10, T36N, R9E)	107	Townline Lake	40
Perch Lake (S2, T36N, R7E)	131	Twin Lakes (North and South)	110
Pine Lake	65	Tyler Lake	29
Pritch Lake	140	Velvet Lake	39
Prune Lake	122	Vicks Lake	122
Rhinelander Flowage (Wisconsin R.)	47	Washburn Lake	133
Roby Lake	140	West Horsehead Lake (Little Horsehead Lake)	23
Round Lake	122	Whitey Lake	29
Rudy Lake	140	Wildwood Lake	45
Ruth Lake	29	Wolf Lake	140
Samway Lake	108	Wood Curt Lake	69
Second Lake	74		
Shadow Lake	122		
Shepard Lake	86		
Silverbass Lake	44		

Copies of "FISHING HOT SPOTS: RHINELANDER AREA" and other books in the North Central Series may be obtained by writing:

**FISHING HOT SPOTS
1999 RIVER STREET
RHINELANDER, WI 54501
(715) 369-5555**

Keeping Up-to-Date With
Help From Our Friends

This book was published to help fishermen decide on where to fish. We have stressed factual, organized data on 129 lakes... information that you will find most important in enjoying your "time on the water."

Some of the material is continously subject to change by the forces of mother nature or man. As you come across these discrepancies in the book, please take a moment and let us know of your findings.

Much of the information presented in this book came from fishermen like yourselves. If when fishing in the Rhinelander area you find a new access... an access improvement... a service facility... a "Hot Spot"... or a new fishing pattern, please let us know.

Drop us a line at Fishing Hot Spots, 1999 River Street, Rhinelander, WI, 54501. The more detailed and specific your comments, the better. Thank you and good 'fishin'.

Bob Knops

Drafting and Cartography - DuWayne Wiles

Copyright ©, 1988
Fishing Hot Spots, Inc.
ISBN 0-939314-20-7

PLEASE NOTE: Despite our efforts to provide current factual data, certain of the information herein is necessarily intended as a general guide only, the publisher not being responsible for variances existing at the time of publication, nor those found to occur from time to time, regarding rights of public access, roads, boat ramps, parking, and available services and map data as illustrated.

The maps shown in this book are not intended for use as navigational charts. Although various marker buoys and standards might be shown, others might not be included. The publisher is not responsible for omissions or location changes in any navigational aids.

TABLE OF CONTENTS

Preface 6
Introduction to Rhinelander Area 9

SECTION 1

Corner Lake 14
Long Lake (S3, T37N, R7E) 15
Alva Lake 17
Beaver Lake 19
Liege Lake 20
Timber Lake (S15, T37N, R7E) 21
Spruce Lake (S22, T37N, R7E) 22
Josie Lake 23
West Horsehead Lake
   (Little Horsehead Lake) 23
East Horsehead Lake 26
Boggy Lake 29
Buck Lake (S33, T38N, R7E) 29
O'Day Lake 29
Ruth Lake 29
Simmons Lake 29
Swamp Lake 29
Tyler Lake 29
Whitey Lake 29

SECTION 2

Elna Lake 30
Maud Lake 32
Clear Lake (S24, T37N, R7E) 33
Lake Mildred 33
Coon Lake 36
Flannery Lake 37
Velvet Lake 39
Townline Lake 40
Soo Lake 42
Goodyear Lake 42
Hodag Lake 43
Birchrock Lake 44
Bob's Lake 44
Cherry Lake 44
Hook Lake 44
Newbold Lake 44
Newbold Springs 44
Ole Lake 44
Silverbass Lake 44

SECTION 3

Wildwood Lake 45
Rhinelander Flowage 47
Boom Lake 54
Thunder Lake 61
Lake Creek Lake 64
South Pine Lake 64
Pine Lake 65
Netties Lake (Sylvan Lake) 67

Crystal Lake 68
Douglas Lake 68
Bass Lake (S8, T37N, R9E) 69
Bertram Lake 69
Box Lake 69
Clear Lake (S8, T37N, R9E) 69
Doyle Lake 69
Fetke Lake 69
Little Bertram Lake 69
Mud Lake (S7, T37N, R9E) 69
Wood Curt Lake 69

SECTION 4

Moen Lake 70
Second Lake 74
Third Lake 75
Fourth Lake 77
Fifth Lake 77
Sunset Lake 80
Snowden Lake 81
Lake Thompson 82
Shepard Lake 86
Gudegast Creek 87
Bullhead Lake 88
Dollar Lake 88
Emden Lake 88
Jennie Raisen Lake 88
Long Lake (S11, T36N, R9E) 88
Minnow Lake 88
Mud Lake (S11, T37N, R9E) 88
Tenderfoot Lake 88

SECTION 5

Faust Lake (Foss Lake) 89
Clear Lake (S10, T36N, R9E) 90
Lake George 91
Cuenin Lake 95
Hixon Lake 96
Buck Lake (S19, T36N, R9E) 98
Lake Julia 99
Hat Rapids Flowage (Wisconsin R.) .. 101
Pelican River 105
Davis Lake 107
DeMarce Lake 107
Gross Lake 107
Heal Lake 107
Hess Lake 107
Landberg Lake 107
Midget Lake 107
Perch Lake (S10, T36N, R9E) 107
Timber Lake (S12, T36N, R8E) 107

SECTION 6
Samway Lake 108
Langley Lake 109
Twin Lakes (North and South) 110
Hanson Lake................... 111
Lily Lake (Lily Bass Lake) 112
Emma Lake 114
Crescent Lake.................. 116
Green Bass Lake 121
Mirror Lake 121
Alice Lake 122
Cook Lake 122
Flag Lake 122
Hoist Lake 122
John Lake 122
Loon Lake 122
Perch Lake (S5, T36N, R8E) 122
Prune Lake.................... 122
Round Lake 122
Shadow Lake 122
Spruce Lake (S16, T36N, R8E) 122

Spur Lake..................... 122
Vicks Lake 122

SECTION 7
Hancock Lake.................. 124
Oneida Lake 127
Perch Lake (S2, T36N, R7E) 131
Washburn Lake 133
Squash Lake................... 135
Bowles Lake 140
Finger Lake 140
Fox Lake 140
Garland Lake 140
Indian Lake.................... 140
Long Lake (S30, T36N, R8E) 140
Mazy Lake 140
Nose Lake 140
Pritch Lake.................... 140
Roby Lake 140
Rudy Lake 140
Wolf Lake..................... 140

Glossary 141
Tips on Releasing Fish 143

ACKNOWLEDGEMENTS

Publication of FISHING HOT SPOTS — "RHINELANDER AREA" would not have been possible without the cooperation of several organizations, agencies, and individuals. Special thanks are due to the following members of the Northwoods Fishing Club for providing much of the fishing information.

Bob Aylesworth
Art Barlow Jr.
Art Barlow Sr.
Bob Bastian
Lee Bastian
Rollie Bessett

Dick Bourcier
Bob Bruso
Curt Ebert
Fred Hoerchler
Dan Jerzak
Mel Lange

Emmit Lawonn
'Butch' Marquardt
Dave McCarty
Charlie Ross
Lambert Saal
Denny Spencer
Al Wyland

These other local fishermen also provided valuable information — Harry Antonuk, Scott Bradley, Steve Huber, Lloyd LeClair, and Rich Reinert.

Additional thanks are extended to the Wisconsin Department of Natural Resources, Oneida County Courthouse personnel, and many area residents for their assistance.

Fishing Hot Spots also thanks LOWRANCE ELECTRONICS for supplying the depth sounding equipment used for the map revisions contained in this book.

PREFACE

An extensive amount of research has gone into the compilation of data that makes up this series of books. Factual information was gathered from material published by the State of Wisconsin, lake files of the area Fish Management Office in Woodruff, interviews of DNR Fish Management personnel, area residents, and local guides. Additionally, wherever possible, lake research was conducted by the Fishing Hot Spots staff. Fishing Hot Spots, Inc. presents this detailed information to you, the fisherman, for one reason; to help you to catch more fish in the Northern Wisconsin lakes region. Our books will show you WHERE to catch fish and WHAT kinds of fish are available.

Each book, like this one, describes the lakes and fishing within a 65 to 220 square mile area. The areas are geographically located around a Northern Wisconsin city or town which can provide fishermen with a variety of angling needs.

As most fishermen know, some lakes are "good" fishing lakes and others are not. Of course, there are many variables that make up a lake's character. A "good" bass lake might be a below average walleye lake. A lake might excel in sustaining several kinds of fish, just one kind of fish, or none at all. If a fisherman is spending his time on a lake angling for the wrong species of fish, he might reach the erroneous conclusion that the lake is "no good"; or he might be spending his valuable fishing time working a lake that supports few, if any, quality fish. We want to help you avoid this.

A big factor in a lake's fish productivity is its fertility. If a lake is infertile it may not sustain a reasonable fish community due to a limited forage base. If it is extremely fertile an imbalance could be created where excessive weed growth can pose the threat of winterkill or where pollution creates poor water quality better suited for rough fish rather than desirable fish species. A lake in proper balance is able to sustain a fishery characterized by desirable size fish, good growth rates, and levels of natural reproduction sufficient to maintain gamefish populations without stocking.

Another important factor is the nature of the lake's bottom, including both its shape and composition. Bottom composition refers to the type of material on the lake's floor. The different materials of muck, sand, gravel or rubble will greatly influence what species of fish can naturally reproduce within a lake. Some species require gravel spawning habitat, some sand, and others the matted vegetation on a muck bottom. Bottom composition will also effect the abundance and variety of the lake's food supply.

But perhaps the most obvious aspect of a lake's bottom is its shape or contour. This is an important characteristic to consider when you decide WHERE on a lake to fish. Remember that fish will relate to a variety of features within a lake such as islands, humps, bars, and holes. The edges of these structures are often preferred by fish...and fishermen too.

Also a key in fishing success is the time that the lake is fished.

Fishing success on a particular lake can vary greatly from year to year or perhaps even longer cycles. For example, year class strength for a particular species of fish can vary considerably from one year to the next. This affects not only its own status, but will also impact the many interrelated organisms within a lake, including other fish. It is also well known that fishing success varies greatly with the time of year or day the lake is fished. This discussion would merit an entire book by itself.

Other factors to keep in mind include water clarity, oxygen level, water temperature, and the size and depth of the lake.

These and still other elements are important to you, the fisherman, in determining what lake to fish, when to fish it, and ultimately where exactly on the lake to direct your efforts.

You will notice each lake report included in this, and other Fishing Hot Spots books, gives you a complete profile of each body of water in an easy to use outline form. The outline format is the same for all lakes covered in the entire FHS series of books. This enables the reader to obtain answers quickly, and to effectively compare data on various lakes. In the lake outline, "Location" descriptions can be checked on the book's back cover map. Under "Fishery" there are, on occasion, different species of fish that are listed in parentheses. This indicates that a particular species is present in extremely limited numbers.

We also want to provide you with details on the many services anglers require. Under the "Related Services" heading of the outline, the availability of campgrounds, resorts, bait shops, guides, and other services are provided.

Another important heading in the FHS outline is "Access" under which the location, type, and features of any access sites are described. To avoid repetition, an Access Classification Chart is shown following the introduction. This system will be used to denote accesses throughout the entire book.

The type and location of the access to any lake is very important to you the fisherman. You must be able to get on the lake. Many maps and brochures omit some boat landings and most of them do not indicate any of the Type III or Type IV accesses. We have tried to give you up-to-date access information on every lake within the Rhinelander Area.

Most of the public access sites described in this book are owned by either the State of Wisconsin, Oneida County, or one of the eight townships within the area. Some of the town landings are operated in cooperation with a paper company or a local sportsmans club.

If a lake does not have public access, the State can not engage in any form of fish management. Private concerns may upgrade the lake's fishery, however permission from the State is still required.

Included in this book are a number of lake survey maps. These are very useful tools to use when learning to fish a lake. There is nothing difficult about using one of these maps. Basically, it shows the shape of the bottom by a series of contour lines roughly parallel to one another. Each line represents an indicated depth of water. Obviously, these lines never cross one another.

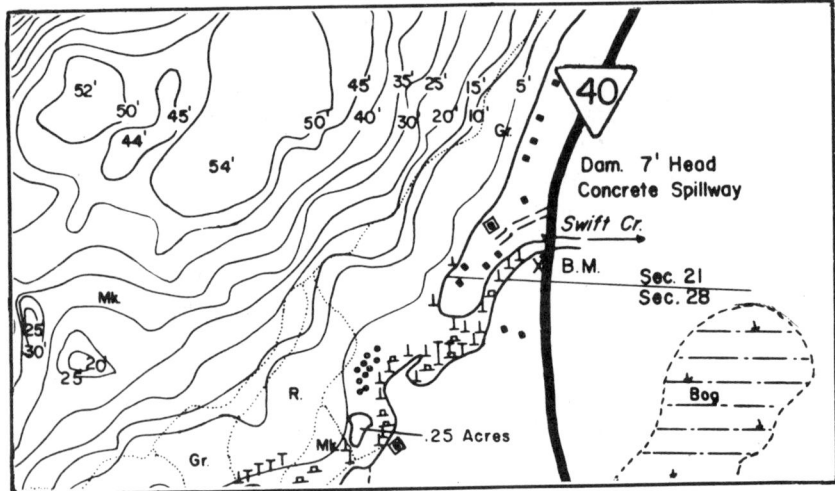

By using the map you will be able to locate many of the underwater islands, shoals, bars, and drop-offs. Closely spaced contour lines indicate a steep drop, while widely spaced lines indicate a flatter, more gradually sloping bottom. The more irregular the series of contour lines, the more uneven the bottom. This means you will find smaller breaks along the main structure or drop-off. These breaks can often hold fish. A straight series of contour lines indicates a uniform drop-off. Fish tend to scatter and suspend over this type of bottom.

The map also shows the bottom material in the littoral zone and areas of weed growth. The type of bottom material is of great interest because of the food preference and habitat requirements of various fish. For example, smallmouth bass prefer a rocky bottom since they feed on the crayfish, insects, and minnows that live in and around the rocks. However, largemouth bass are found in the shallow warmer waters often in heavy vegetation. They are cosmopolitan feeders - utilizing everything from minnows to frogs.

The location of weedbeds is also vital information for fishermen. Probably the most consistent fishing you will do is on the deep water edge of a weedbed, especially if there is also a break in the bottom contour. All of this information is important to you in fishing any lake.

You will now be able to go out on the lake with a map and find these areas of fishing interest. The easiest way of finding "Hot Spots" is with an electronic depthfinder, but a weighted line or marked anchor rope will do nicely. Once you have found a few structures or weedbeds and have caught a few fish, be sure to mark the spot. This "spot" will more than likely produce fish again and again.

A good method of location to use is the "rifle sight" method. Here is how it works. From your "spot," line up two objects on shore, one behind the other. Do this twice so the lines are in different directions. In the future you will move your boat onto one line of sight and then move along this line until you hit the second one. You will then be over your "spot." Jot down these intersecting lines on a map or piece of paper for future reference. Probably the best way of marking a good spot is with a small buoy but this is not always feasible.

Very often the shoreline will give you a clue as to the contour of the lake bottom. This is helpful when there is no lake survey map available. If the shoreline is a steep bank, chances are that the lake bottom has a steep drop-off. A wetland shoreline would indicate a flat lake bottom. A point of land might denote a continuing underwater bar.

In bringing all of this information together in an easy to use and understandable format, Fishing Hot Spots intends to answer the one question asked by every fisherman - "Where should I fish?" By putting to use Fishing Hot Spots many years of fishing research experience you will know where and when to fish in this area.

INTRODUCTION TO RHINELANDER AREA

As part of the Fishing Hot Spots North Central Series, the Rhinelander Area book covers 220 square miles surrounding this Northern Wisconsin community. A total of 129 named lakes are covered plus two rivers. All 129 lakes are discussed, but the larger and more popular waters are treated in much greater detail than the smaller unknown lakes.

Centrally located within the area, Rhinelander offers a variety of services for fishermen. Overnight lodging is available at the many motels within the vicinity. Several bait and tackle shops are located in town and offer a wide range of live bait and other fishing supplies. A number of local boat dealers offer parts and service for most major brands of boats, motors, and trailers. Fuel, oil, ice, and beverages are all available at several outlets throughout the area. Guide service can be obtained on many lakes and may be arranged by contacting bait shops, resorts, or the Rhinelander Chamber of Commerce. Boat and motor rental is also supplied by many of the resorts.

A number of federal, state, and county highways provide major transportation routes throughout the area. In the east-west direction, U.S. Highway 8 passes through town and runs across the entire book area. County Highways K and C are also popular east-west routes. Highway K extends to the west of Rhinelander, while Highway C runs to the east. State Highway 47 and Highway 17 are the main north-south thoroughfares in the Rhinelander area. Once off the main highways, a system of town roads will lead to most of the lakes.

The 129 lakes contained in this book represent a total of nearly 10,000 acres of water. Of these lakes, 55 have some form of public access. Access sites span a full range of development and quality...from the many first rate facilities, usually located on the larger lakes, to some difficult wilderness types. All accesses presented in this book have been personally visited by a member of the Fishing Hot Spots staff. Some lakes have access areas that have

RHINELANDER AREA MAP

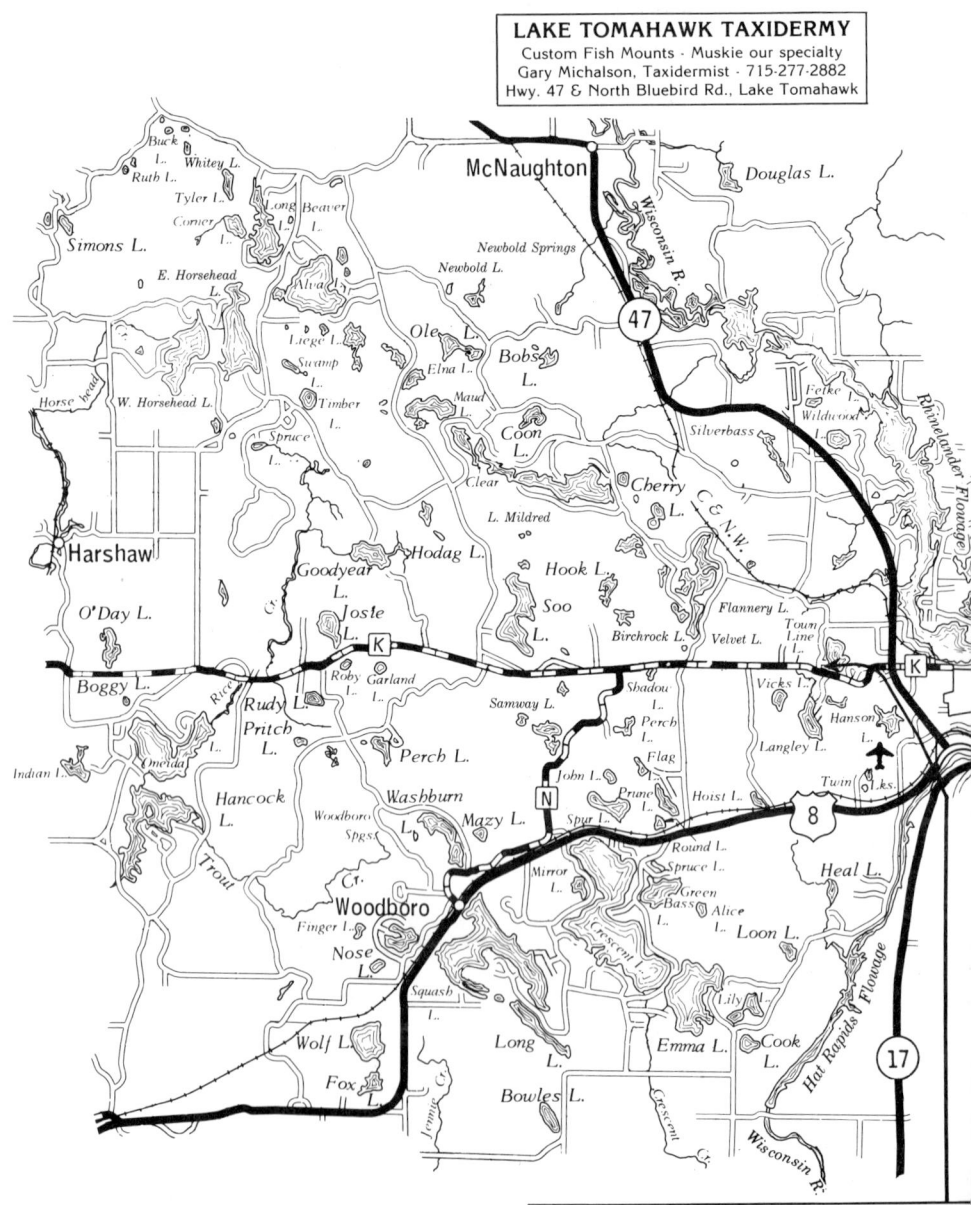

RHINELANDER AREA GUIDES
- ROLLIE BESSETT — All species, spec. in muskie - (715) 369-5884
- CHARLIE ROSS — Spec. in muskie - (715) 362-3816
- DENNY SPENCER — Spec. in muskie, Boom & Wis. River - (715) 369-1054
- TOM URBAN — "If it swims, we catch it" - (715) 362-3618

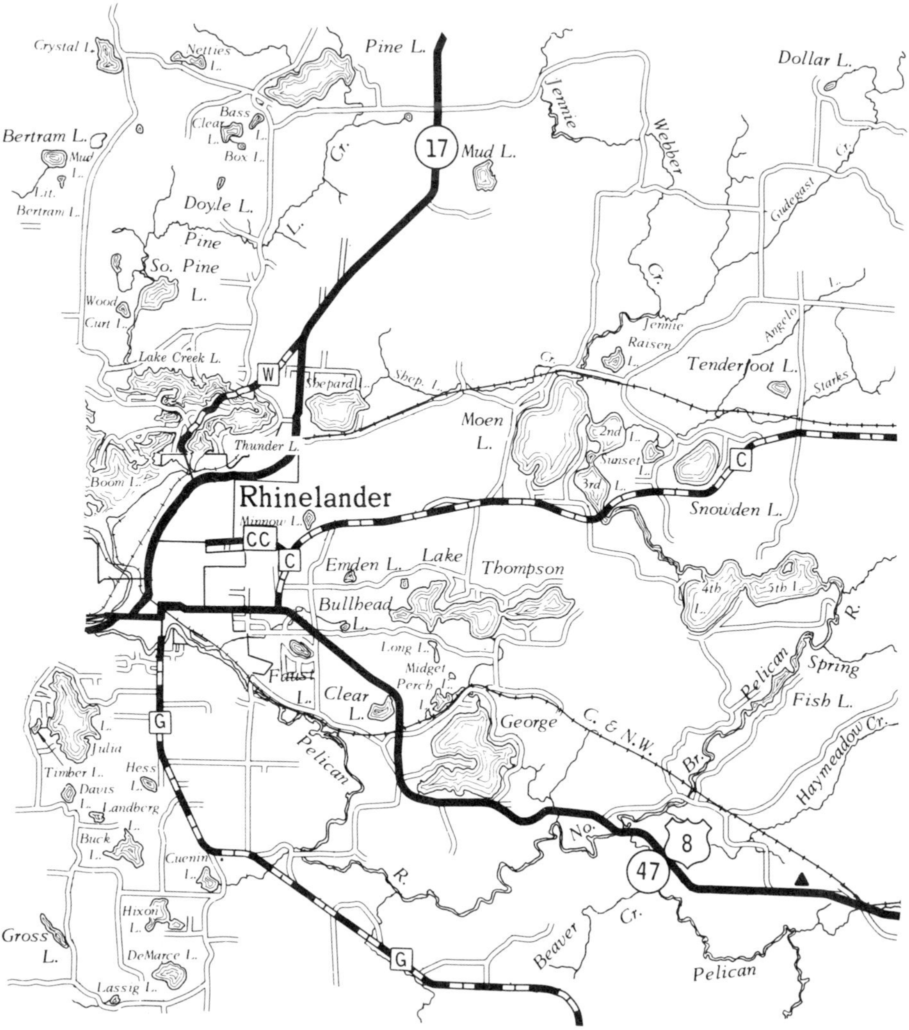

CATCH A GREAT VACATION!
Rhinelander Area Chamber of Commerce
P.O. Box 795
City Hall
Rhinelander, WI 5450
(715) 362-7464

CENTURY 21 - DAY & ASSOCIATES
P.O. Box 816, Rhinelander, WI 54501
715-369-1223   1-800-472-7334 (WI)

been used by the public for many years. However, during the preparation of this book these areas where found to be private and have not been included in our access listings. Conversely, there were some situations where legitimate public access points were thought to be private. Our research proved otherwise and these sites are now included as public access locations.

Following each section in the book is a listing entitled "Lakes Limited in Access or Fishery...." The vast majority of these lakes were found to be completely private, but a few have extremely difficult public access. Additionally, most of these lakes are small infertile waters that offer little fishing potential. Because these lakes offer little to the fishing public they have been treated as a group so that more space within the book could be devoted to lakes of greater appeal.

Of great interest to many anglers is the Boom Lake - Rhinelander Flowage complex. In addition to Boom Lake and the Rhinelander Flowage, this large impoundment of the Wisconsin River also forms both Thunder Lake and Lake Creek Lake. This system totals 2,100 acres and supports one of the most diverse and premier fisheries in the area. Other featured lakes within the area include Crescent Lake, Lake George, Thompson Lake, Hancock Lake, Oneida Lake, Squash Lake, and the Moen Chain. All of these lakes are quite popular with anglers and provide excellent fishing opportunities.

Besides the featured lakes, there are numerous small lakes in the

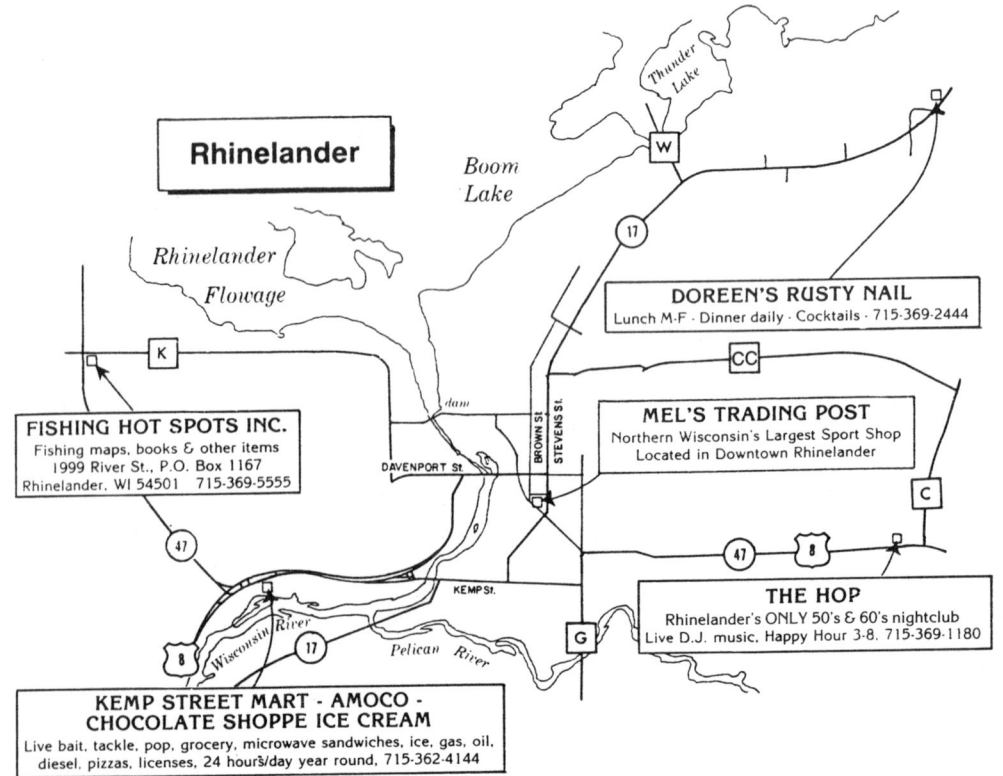

area, most less than 100 acres in size. These lakes are generally bass/bluegill fisheries and can provide good fishing in out-of-the-way locations. To best fish these lakes, small boats or canoes are recommended since often times accesses are undeveloped. Some of these waters can also be fished by wading the shoreline or with the use of a 'belly boat'.

Many of these smaller lakes within the area are seepage lakes with water of low fertility. The nature of the surrounding bedrock and the influence of many areas of bog account for the infertility. The low fertility results in lakes of limited productivity that are quite sensitive to excessive angler harvest. The bigger predatory fish such as largemouth bass are especially sensitive, since they are the fish that help maintain a balanced fish community. Removing too many of these larger fish can cause a lake to become dominated by stunted panfish. To help avoid the loss of quality fishing provided by many of the smaller waters, catch and release is suggested.

As a final note, trout fishermen have a number of opportunities available to them. Perch Lake, in the western part of the area, is the most popular and productive trout water. It is a small lake that is stocked annually with catchable size rainbow trout. Goodyear Springs has a native population of brook trout and can be accessed via Goodyear Creek. The stocking of brown trout in Squash Lake will add to this area's trout fishery. Stream anglers are limited to Gudegast Creek which is also stocked annually by the State.

LAKE ACCESS CLASSIFICATIONS

TYPE I
DIRECT ACCESS TO WATER; BOAT LANDING RAMP, WITH PARKING.

TYPE II
DIRECT ACCESS TO WATER; BOAT LANDING RAMP, WITHOUT PARKING.

TYPE III
UNIMPROVED OR DIFFICULT ACCESS; ANY TYPE ROAD WITHIN 200 FT. OF SHORE, BUT NO DIRECT ACCESS TO WATER.

TYPE IV
WILDERNESS ACCESS; NO ROADS WITHIN 200 FT. OF SHORE.

TYPE V
NAVIGABLE WATER ACCESS; NO LAND ACCESS, BUT ACCESS BY BOAT FROM ANOTHER LAKE OR RIVER.

SECTION 1

SECTION MAP FOR —
Corner Lake
Long Lake (S3, T37N, R7E)
Alva Lake
Beaver Lake
Liege Lake
Timber Lake
 (S15, T37N, R7E)
Spruce Lake
 (S22, T37N, R7E)
Josie Lake
West Horsehead Lake
 (Little Horsehead Lake)
East Horsehead Lake
Boggy Lake
Buck Lake
 (S33, T38N, R7E)
O'Day Lake
Ruth Lake
Simmons Lake
Swamp Lake
Tyler Lake
Whitey Lake

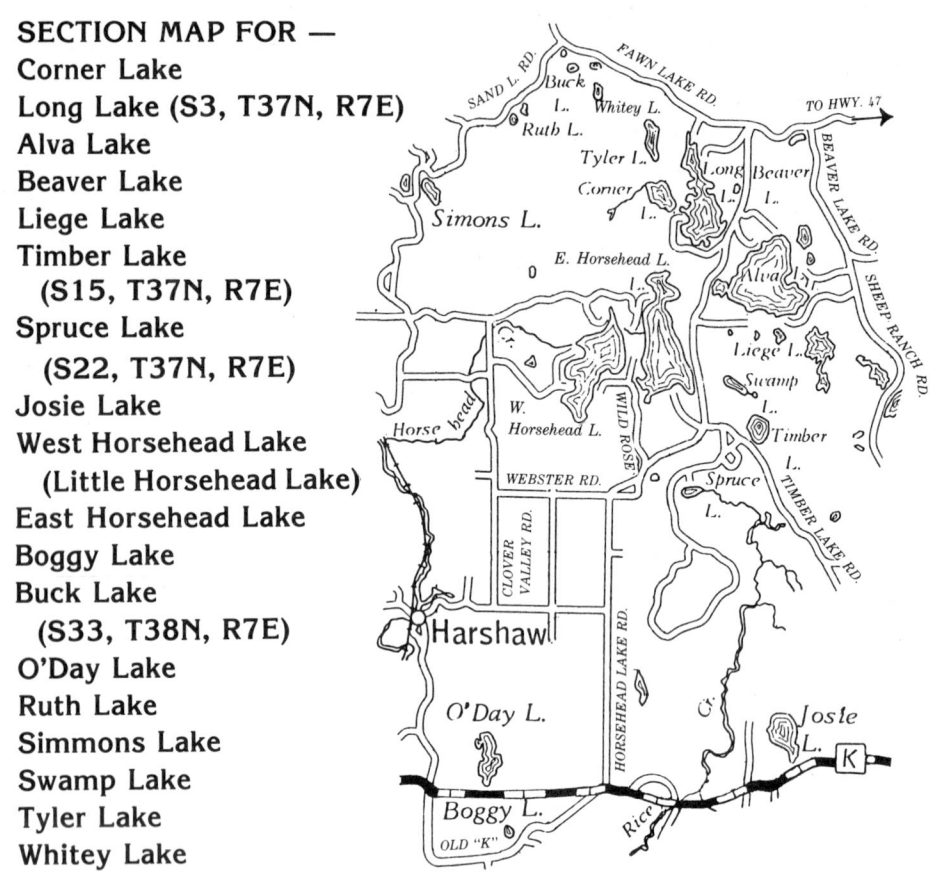

CORNER LAKE

LOCATION — In the northwest part of the area, just west of Long Lake.

ACCESS — Type IV (Public): To the east side of the lake; a difficult unmarked wilderness access over state-owned land. A portage from Long Lake is also possible, but not easy.

SPECIAL FEATURES — A very scenic wilderness setting.

LAKE CHARACTERISTICS
 Size and Depth - 28 acres and 65 feet.
 Water Source - Seepage lake: No inlet or outlet.
 Shoreline - Predominantly upland with an adjacent conifer bog on the north end. 1,000 feet is publicly-owned.
 Bottom - 35% gravel, 25% muck, 20% sand, 20% rubble.
 Water - Highly infertile with moderate clarity. The upper limit of the thermocline is at 16′.

Vegetation - Chiefly floating and emergent types around an extremely narrow littoral zone.

FISHERY
Species - Largemouth Bass, Perch, Bluegill.
Comment - No data is available on the largemouth bass population. However, the panfish are reported to be stunted.

LAKE MANAGEMENT
Lake Investigation Data - None.
Stocking - None.

CONCLUSION — Reports from a few ambitious local anglers provide the only fishing information available on Corner Lake. Don't expect more than a few average size panfish and perhaps a decent bass. Most anglers suggest that the results do not often merit the effort required to reach this lake.

LONG LAKE (S3, T37N, R7E)

LOCATION — In the northwest segment of the area, west of McNaughton and north of Alva Lake.

ACCESS — **Type I (Public):** To the north end of the lake; drive Fawn Lake Road west from Highway 47 for 0.7 mile to a "Y" intersection. Bear left, staying on Fawn Lake Road another 2.4 miles to South Doe Lane. Turn left onto South Doe Lane and proceed 0.2 mile to the landing. A paved ramp, turn-around, and parking for 3 rigs are provided. A loading pier is an added feature of this quality facility.

SPECIAL FEATURES — Good access facility to a highly scenic lake.

LAKE CHARACTERISTICS
Size and Depth - 113 acres and 58 feet.
Water Source - Seepage lake: No inlet or outlet.
Shoreline - Mostly upland with minor areas of adjoining bog. Almost one mile is in public ownership.
Bottom - 70% sand, 15% gravel, 10% rubble, 5% muck.
Water - Highly infertile and very clear.
Vegetation - Quite sparse. Limited growths of lily pads and bulrush are found along the narrow shoreline zone.

FISHERY
Species - Largemouth Bass, Smallmouth Bass, Northern Pike, Perch, Bluegill, Pumpkinseed, (Walleye), (Muskie).
Comment - Both walleye and muskie are limited in numbers. All panfish species are overly-abundant and stunted.
Forage - Golden shiner, bluntnose minnow, and juvenile panfish.

LONG LAKE (S3, T37N, R7E)

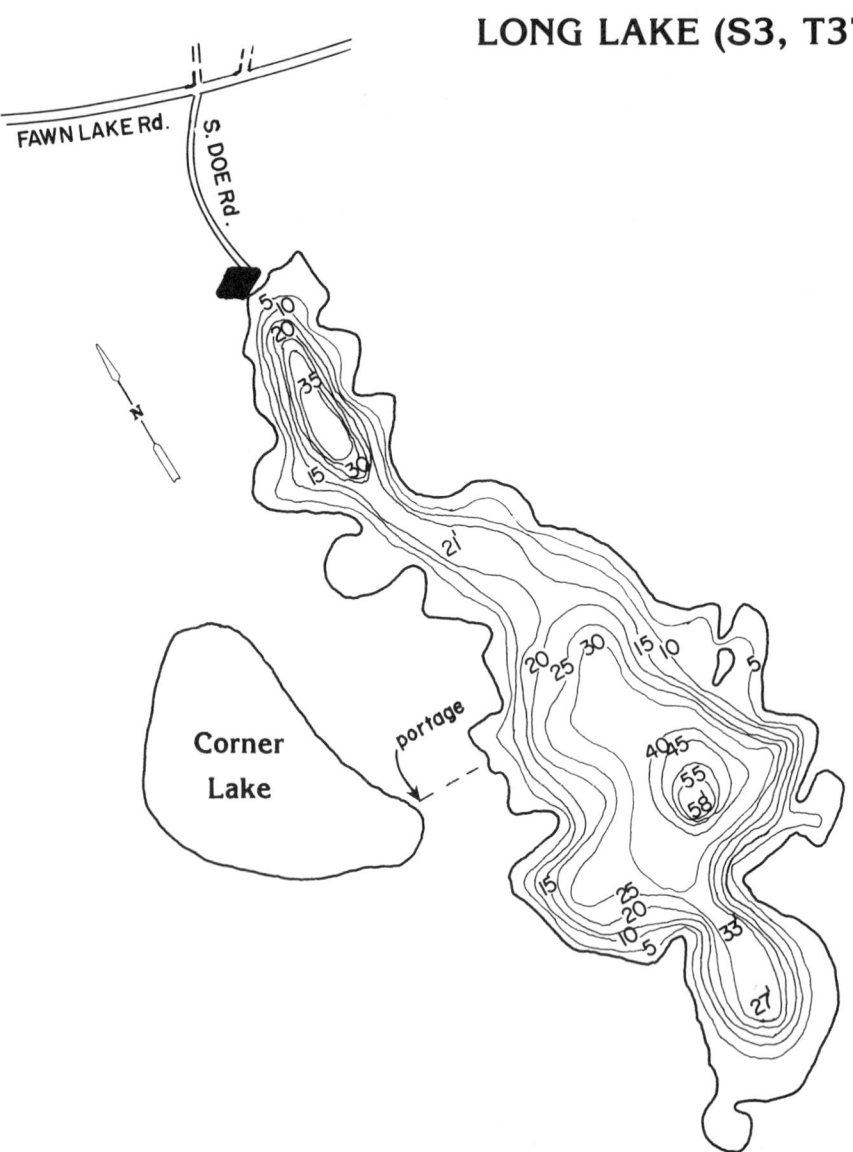

LAKE MANAGEMENT

Lake Investigation Data - A fall 1983 electrofishing survey was performed to assess survival of stocked walleye fingerling. Negligible fingerling survival was noted for the 1981-1983 plantings. The study also noted an abundant forage base, yet few large predatory fish. Largemouth bass longer than 10" were rare, as angler harvest has appeared to have severely cropped the larger fish.

Stocking -

YEAR	SPECIES	NUMBER	SIZE
1981	Walleye	6,600	3"
1982	Walleye	6,000	3"
1983	Walleye	6,000	2"

Stocking was discontinued because of poor fingerling survival.

FISHING TIPS — The elongated basin and fast dropping bottom create a very narrow shoreline zone with wood as the primary form of cover. Work the wood for largemouth using 4"-6" plastic worms. Purple, black, or blue will work best in this clear water. Crankbaits, such as Shad Raps, cast along the shore can also take fish.

The clear water will require fishing the early morning or evening hours. Bass anglers should use light, small diameter line. Clear or green lines are preferred over fluorescent colors. Also, scale down your tackle size and even consider trying some night fishing.

CONCLUSION — Long Lake is tough water to fish... its clarity, low fertility and narrow fast dropping shoreline zone pose a significant challenge to fishermen. A few quality size bass are available, but excessive angler harvest appears to be limiting this fishery. Catch and release is essential on this type of lake.

ALVA LAKE

LOCATION — In the extreme northwest portion of the book area, west of Highway 47 and north of Highway K.

ACCESS — **Type III (Public):** On the east side of the lake; take Fawn Lake Road west from Highway 47 for 1.8 miles to Beaver Lake Road. Turn left (south) and drive 1.4 miles to Alva Lake Road. Make a right onto Alva Lake Road and continue for another 0.6 mile to the access at the end of Alva Lake Road. Parking for this narrow undeveloped facility is quite limited. Please be respectful of the adjacent private properties since they are in extremely close proximity to this town-owned access site.

LAKE CHARACTERISTICS

Size and Depth - 200 acres and 44 feet.

Water Source - Seepage lake: No inlet or outlet.

Shoreline - Primarily wooded uplands with steep banks and moderate development. Entirely private except for 50' where a town-owned road (Alva Lake Road) ends at the lake.

Bottom - Mostly sand, with significant areas of gravel and rubble. Minor areas of muck are also present.

Water - Very clear and of low fertility.

Vegetation - Generally sparse, except for the shallow west side bay.

ALVA LAKE

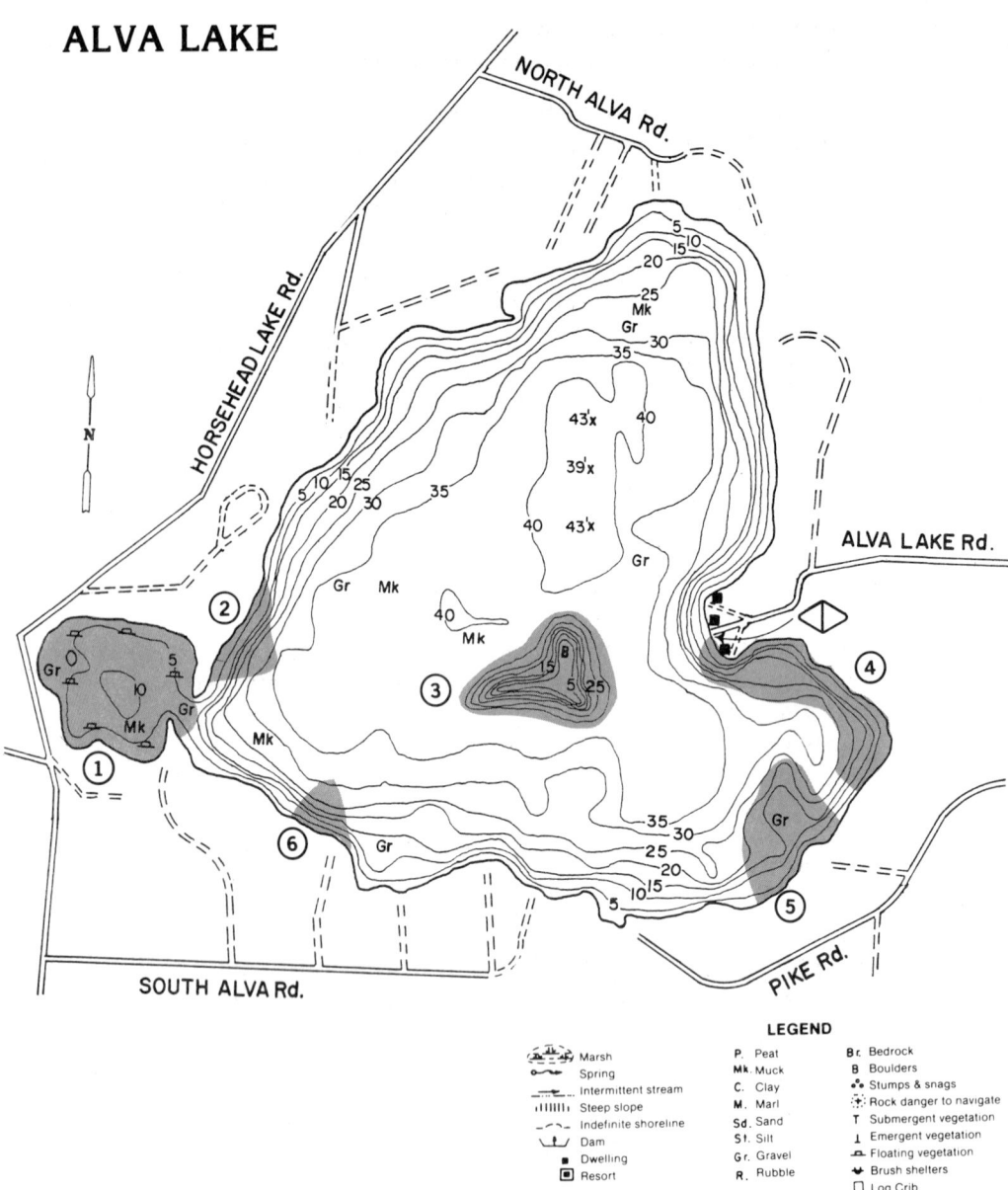

FISHERY
Species - Walleye, Largemouth Bass, Smallmouth Bass, Perch, Bluegill, Crappie, Rock Bass, Pumpkinseed, Bullhead, Sucker, (Muskie).

Comment - Walleye and smallmouth are the dominant gamefish species. Recent reports indicate that largemouth bass are increasing in numbers. An abundant white sucker population is present.

LAKE MANAGEMENT
Lake Investigation Data - None, due to the limited public access.

Stocking - None recently.

Treatment - 20 log cribs were installed in 1957.

LAKE SURVEY MAP — Fishing Areas Shaded

Area (1) The shallow bay on the west side will produce both largemouth and panfish. Work the shallow weeds around the perimeter. Also, try fishing the submerged wood.

Area (2) This stretch of irregular dropping shoreline will hold walleye and perhaps a smallmouth. A jig and minnow has been productive here. Remember to keep your jig in contact with the bottom.

Area (3) The exposed boulder marks this mid-lake rock bar. Walleye can be found here year-around. Fish the sides of the structure, trying different depths until you locate fish. Local anglers favor black, green, or blue jigs tipped with a large fathead. Ice fishermen should try 3"-4" suckers below a tip-up and jigging Rapalas or spoons.

Area (4) Smallmouth bass will relate to the fallen trees and logs along the shore. Small-sized plastics such as Twister Tails or 4" worms are a good choice.

Area (5) Spring walleye are available on this gravel bar. Jig and minnow combos are always effective. Slowly retrieved crankbaits are also worth a try.

Area (6) A large boulder on shore marks this fast dropping hole that often attracts early season walleye.

FISHING TIPS
— Except for the one mid-lake rock pile, shoreline structure and cover offers the most potential on Alva...fallen trees, logs, and the limited weed areas must be fished. The clear water dictates down-sized tackle and light line.

CONCLUSION
— Alva Lake offers a quality fishery that until recently has been fished primarily by lake front property owners. The access is far from perfect, but this lake merits your attention. Catch and release is essential to maintaining this fishery.

BEAVER LAKE

LOCATION — In the northeast part of the book area, just north of Alva Lake and west of Highway 47.

ACCESS — **Type III (Public):** On the north side of the lake; take Fawn Lake Road west from Highway 47 for 0.7 mile to a "Y" in the road. Stay to the left and follow Fawn Lake Road another 1.2 miles to the roadside access on the left. A short carry-in down a moderate gradient is required.

LAKE CHARACTERISTICS

Size and Depth - 8 acres and 17 feet.

Water Source - Seepage lake: No inlet or outlet.
Shoreline - 75% upland and 25% wetland. About 1/2 mile is publicly-owned.
Bottom - 80% muck, 20% sand and gravel.
Water - Clear and quite infertile.
Vegetation - Limited to floating and emergent types around the shoreline fringe.

FISHERY
Species - Largemouth Bass, Bluegill, (Crappie).
Comment - Crappie were introduced by an unknown private party and are stunted.

LAKE MANAGEMENT
Lake Investigation Data - None.
Stocking - None.

FISHING TIPS — Fallen trees and other shoreline cover will hold both bass and panfish. Also work around the bog on the southwest end for bass.

CONCLUSION — Beaver Lake has some ability to produce decent bluegill and perhaps a few nice bass, but don't anticipate too much from this small infertile 'pothole.'

LIEGE LAKE

LOCATION — In the northwest part of the area, west of Highway 47 and just south of Alva Lake.

ACCESS — **Type IV:** To the east side of the lake; drive Sheep Ranch Road north off Highway K for 2.2 miles to an unmarked logging road on the left. A series of rough, ill-defined roads lead to a difficult wilderness access. The use of a quadrangle map is suggested (McNaughton Quad). A four wheel drive vehicle with high ground clearance is also advised.

SPECIAL FEATURES — A navigable channel connects the north basin to the smaller southern basin.

LAKE CHARACTERISTICS
Size and Depth - 33 acres and 7 feet.
Water Source - Seepage lake: No inlet or outlet.
Shoreline - 55% upland and 45% wetland. One-half mile is publicly-owned.
Bottom - 70% muck, 25% sand, 5% gravel.
Water - Slightly acidic and infertile with moderate clarity. Winterkill has been seen in the past.
Vegetation - Dense growths of lily pads around the perimeter with moderately heavy quantities of submergent types.

FISHERY
Species - Northern Pike, Perch, Bluegill, (Largemouth Bass).
Comment - Expect dramatic fluctuations in the status of the fishery as periodic winterkill does occur. Perch are excessive in numbers and generally small in size.

LAKE MANAGEMENT
Lake Investigation Data - None.
Stocking - None.

FISHING TIPS — Work brightly colored spinnerbaits over the weeds for northern pike.

CONCLUSION — The winterkill situation greatly limits the fishing potential. Years of successive mild winters can result in decent fishing for those willing to exert the effort to get on the lake.

TIMBER LAKE (S15, T37N, R7E)

LOCATION — In the northwest section of the book area, north of Highway K and west of Highway 47.

ACCESS — **Type II (Public):** On the south shore of the lake; follow Horsehead Lake Road north from Highway K for 3.4 miles to the intersection with Timber Lake Road. Turn right onto Timber Lake Road and drive 1/2 mile to the unmarked landing on the left. This unimproved facility has a rough sand/gravel ramp and landing. Although four wheel drive vehicles with small trailers can use this access, carry-in is recommended.

LAKE CHARACTERISTICS
Size and Depth - 24 acres and 28 feet.
Water Source - Seepage lake: No inlet or outlet.
Shoreline - Predominantly bog with minor areas of uplands. A total of 1,300 feet is publicly-owned.
Bottom - 70% muck, 25% sand, 5% gravel.
Water - Light brown in color and infertile.
Vegetation - Primarily floating and emergent species. Heaviest growth is along the south end.

FISHERY
Species - Largemouth Bass, Bluegill, Perch.
Comment - Panfish dominate the lake's biomass. However, Timber Lake apparently supports moderate numbers of quality-sized bass.

LAKE MANAGEMENT
Lake Investigation Data - An old survey indicated that good panfish and largemouth bass populations were present. As seen below, the panfish species attained decent size.

FYKE NET SURVEY		
SPECIES	**NUMBER**	**SIZE RANGE**
Largemouth Bass	27	4"-18"
Bluegill	119	5½"-10½"
Perch	263	4½"-10½"

FISHING TIPS — Fallen trees, logs, and stumps provide the major source of cover on Timber Lake. The abundant shoreline wood should be worked for bass and panfish alike.

CONCLUSION — Timber Lake has the potential for a quality bass and perhaps some decent panfish. The relatively easy access into this remote 'pothole' should make it worth a try.

SPRUCE LAKE (S22, T37N, R7E)

LOCATION — In the northwest segment of the book area, due south of East Horsehead Lake.

ACCESS — **Type I (Public):** On the north side of the lake; drive 3.4 miles north from Highway K on Horsehead Lake Road to Timber Lake Road. Make a right onto Timber Lake Road and go 0.1 mile to Spruce Lake Road. Make another right and stay on Spruce Lake Road for 0.4 mile to a "Y" in the road. Bear left on this unmarked access road to the rough gravel/sand facility. Parking is available for 2 rigs. Four wheel drive vehicles are recommended.

LAKE CHARACTERISTICS

Size and Depth - 11 acres and 15 feet.

Water Source - Seepage lake: No inlet, although an intermittent outlet is found on the east side.

Shoreline - Entirely wetland and undeveloped. 100% county forest lands.

Bottom - 100% muck.

Water - Quite infertile with medium brown color and moderate clarity.

Vegetation - Dense growths of floating varieties around the shoreline zone.

FISHERY

Species - Largemouth Bass, Perch, Bluegill.

Comment - As is often the case in small pothole lakes of low fertility, stunted panfish are numerous.

LAKE MANAGEMENT

Lake Investigation Data - None.

Stocking - None.

CONCLUSION — Spruce Lake is a typical bog lake characterized by high infertility and stunted panfish. The few decent bass that may be present is all there is to attract your attention.

JOSIE LAKE

LOCATION — In the west central part of the book area, just north of Highway K and about 7 miles west of Rhinelander.

ACCESS — Currently, none public. Previous public access has been eliminated due to a change in land use policy at the adjoining agricultural facility.

SPECIAL FEATURES — The University of Wisconsin Foundation Seed Potato Farm completely surrounds the lake.

LAKE CHARACTERISTICS
Size and Depth - 46 acres and 15 feet.
Water Source - Seepage lake: No inlet or outlet.
Shoreline - Almost entirely upland, having only minor wetland areas.
Bottom - 65% sand, 15% gravel, 10% rubble, 10% boulders and muck.
Water - Slightly fertile and moderately clear.
Vegetation - Generally sparse.

FISHERY
Species - Largemouth Bass, Smallmouth Bass, Bluegill.

LAKE MANAGEMENT
Lake Investigation Data - None.
Stocking - None.

CONCLUSION - Josie Lake had a reputation of being a fine bass-panfish lake. The recent change in the access situation unfortunately removes this water from your list of fishing opportunities.

WEST HORSEHEAD LAKE
(LITTLE HORSEHEAD LAKE)

LOCATION — In the northwest portion of the book area, immediately west of East Horsehead Lake.

ACCESS — **Type I (Public):** To the west side of the lake; from Highway K go north on Horsehead Lake Road for 2.5 miles to Webster Road. Turn left (west) and drive 1 mile to Clover Valley Road. Make a right onto Clover Valley Road and travel 1.2 miles north to the intersection with Little Horsehead Road. Turn right and drive 0.8 mile to the marked access road on the right...follow this a short distance to the landing. A gravel ramp landing and parking area are provided. The facility is best suited for smaller boats.

LAKE CHARACTERISTICS
Size and Depth - 145 acres and 26 feet.

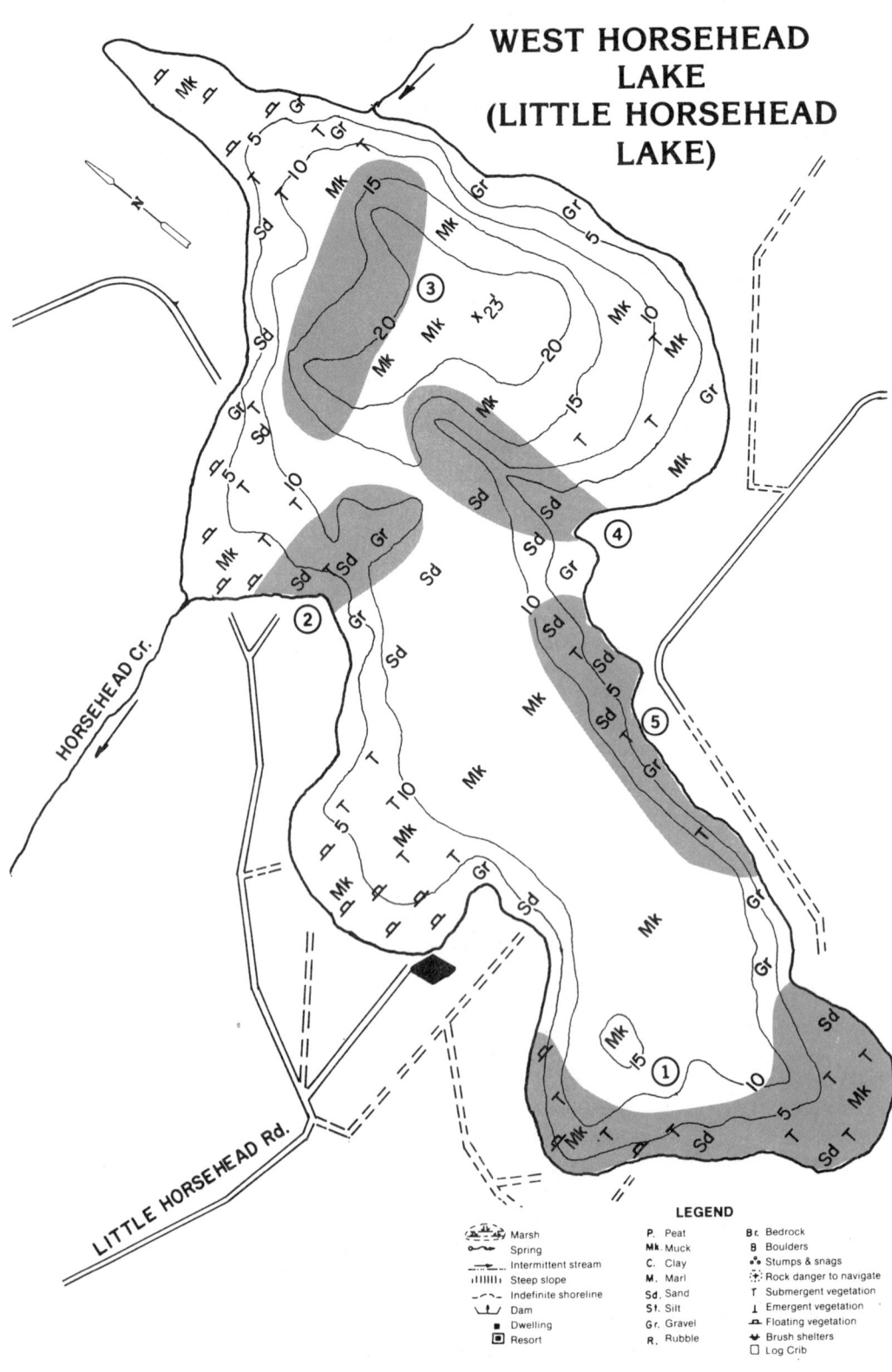

Water Source - Drainage lake: An inlet from East Horsehead Lake and an outlet to Horsehead Creek on the west side.
Shoreline - Only 50' in public ownership. 85% upland, 15% wetlands.
Bottom - 45% muck, 25% sand, 15% gravel, 10% rubble, 5% boulders.
Water - Slightly fertile and light brown in color.
Vegetation - Both emergent and submergent types are abundant.

FISHERY
Species
Primary - Northern Pike, Largemouth Bass, Bluegill.
Secondary - Muskie, Crappie.
Limited - Walleye, Perch.
Comment - The walleye population is comprised of a few large fish, little evidence of natural reproduction exists. Periodic stocking maintains the muskie population.

LAKE MANAGEMENT
Lake Investigation Data - None.
Stocking - Muskie were stocked throughout the 60's and 70's. Recently, 150 11" fingerling were planted in 1983.
Treatment - Chemical treatments have been used in the past to remove excessive panfish. Nuisance aquatic vegetation has also been chemically treated.

LAKE SURVEY MAP — Fishing Areas Shaded
Area (1) Cast along the weed edge on the southern end of the lake for pike and bass. A silver spoon and pork rind combo is a good choice for bass. Look for the turn-ins, turn-outs, and pockets to be the most productive weed areas. Also, if the wind is right, try drifting with a large shiner or sucker for pike.
Area (2) The sand/gravel point extending off the west side is one of the best spots on the lake. Muskie, northern, and bass can all be caught here. Be sure to fish both the top and gently sloping sides.
Area (3) Muskie fishermen should try drifting and casting along this stretch with crankbaits and bucktails.
Area (4) This sand bar is another spot worth a try for muskie. Work it thoroughly, but don't spend too much time here.
Area (5) Scattered weeds in this gravel-bottomed area will attract both northern pike and bass. Spinnerbaits will take both species.

FISHING TIPS —
The entire shoreline can be fished for bass, pike, and even muskie. Row or use an electric motor to work around the lake. Don't forget to fish back into the 'slop' for bass.

Ice fishing for pike and panfish is also popular. Tip-ups rigged with large shiners do the job for winter anglers.

CONCLUSION — West Horsehead is quite fertile compared to other lakes in the Rhinelander area and supports a good fishery.

Expect largemouth to provide the bulk of the gamefish action as bass appear to be increasing in numbers over the past few years. Don't overlook muskie - 20#-30# fish have been reported.

West Horsehead is an out-of-the-way lake worth fishing. At 145 acres it is small enough to learn quickly. Catch and release is critical to preserve quality fishing for the future.

EAST HORSEHEAD LAKE

LOCATION — In the extreme northwest section of the book area.

ACCESS — **Type I (Public):** On the west side of the lake; drive Horsehead Lake Road 2.5 miles north from Highway K to the intersection with Webster Road. Stay to the right and follow Horsehead Lake Road and additional 0.3 mile to Wild Rose Road. Turn left onto Wild Rose Road and drive 0.8 mile to Jimmy Lane. Make a right onto Jimmy Lane (at the "Slow" sign), proceed 0.4 mile to Bass Lane. Turn right, the access is located at the end of the road. A gravel ramp, concrete plank landing, and turn-around are provided.

RELATED SERVICES
Resorts - Yes, one.
Public Parks - None.
Campgrounds - None.
Bait Shops - Yes, at the resort.

LAKE CHARACTERISTICS
Size and Depth - 184 acres and 27 feet.
Water Source - Spring-fed with a small outlet stream that flows into West Horsehead Lake.
Shoreline - Mostly private except for the access. Mainly upland, with a small wetland area on the northeast corner.
Bottom - Chiefly sand with some gravel, rock, and muck.
Water - Light brown in color with moderate clarity and limited fertility.
Vegetation - Lily pad, pickerel weed, cabbage, and coontail are the common varieties.

FISHERY
Species
Primary - Walleye, Perch, Bluegill.
Secondary - Largemouth Bass, Smallmouth Bass, Pumpkinseed, Crappie, Bullhead.
Limited - Muskie, Northern Pike, Rock Bass.
Comment - All species are sustained by natural reproduction and/or the movement of fish through the outlet stream from West Horsehead Lake...particularly muskie and pike.

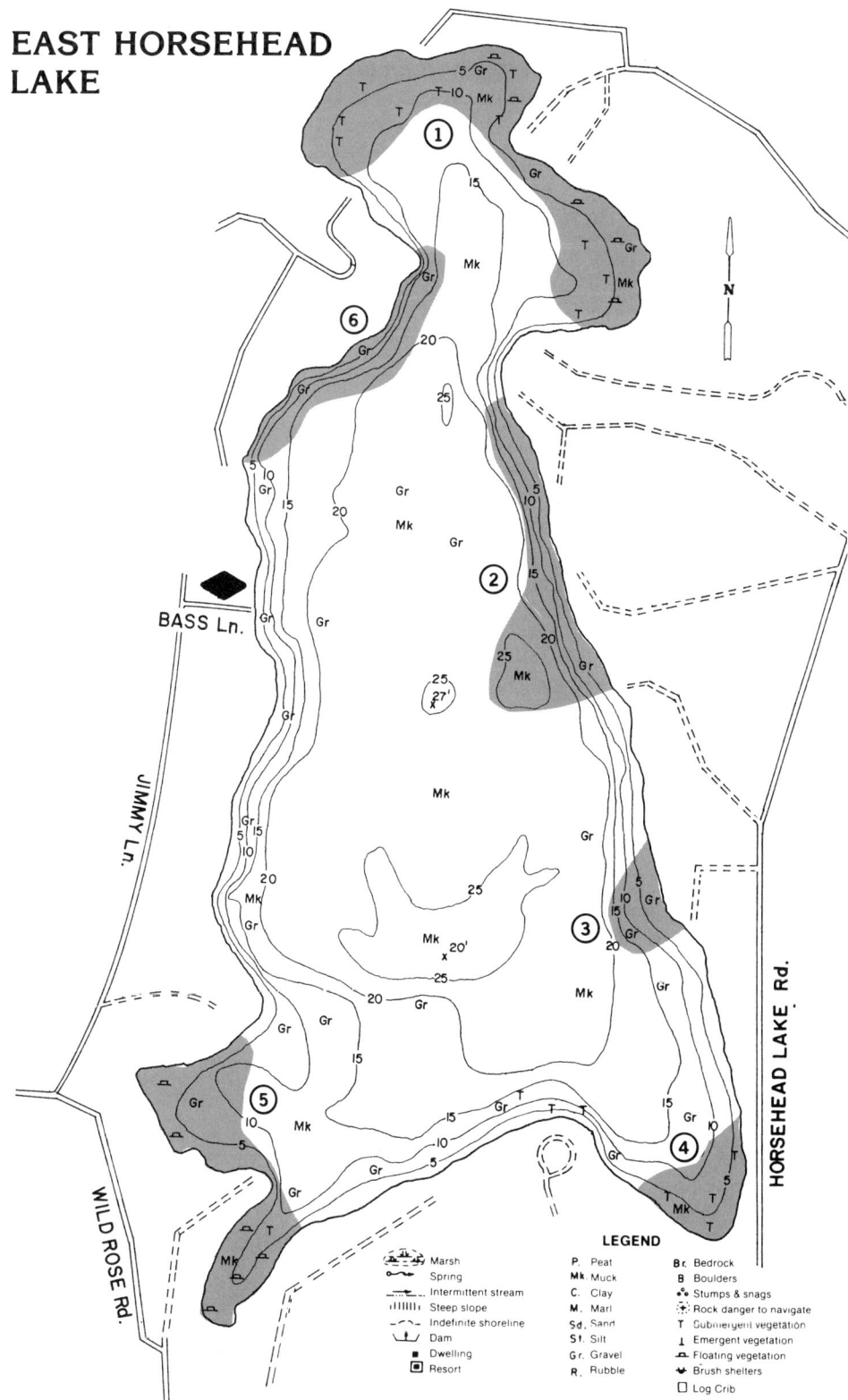

LAKE MANAGEMENT

Lake Investigation Data - Below are the results of a 1983 electrofishing survey. Gamefish populations, especially walleye, were evaluated.

SPECIES	NUMBER	SIZE RANGE
Walleye	203	4"-22"
Largemouth Bass	8	6"-12"
Smallmouth Bass	4	4"- 9"
Muskie	7	18"-31"
Northern Pike	1	18"

Walleye were reproducing quite well...as 160 of the 203 fish sampled were 4"-6" naturally produced fingerling.
Stocking - None since the late 1950's.

LAKE SURVEY MAP — Fishing Areas Shaded

Area (1) Cast for muskie along the weedline in the north bay... both bucktails and jerkbaits have produced here. Jigging spoons or jigging Rapalas are effective for walleye during the 'early ice' period.

Area (2) The steep dropping east shore can be fished for smallmouth and walleye. Try small crankbaits or plastics for smallies. Live bait presentations are preferred for walleye. Be sure to work the 25'+ hole for summer walleye.

Area (3) This small subtle gravel point can hold walleye during the winter months and early spring. Use a small jig tipped with a minnow for early season fish.

Area (4) Ice fishing for walleye is popular on this small bay. 'Early ice' is most productive.

Area (5) Muskie, largemouth, and smallmouth are all attracted to the two small bays in the southwest corner. Look for the smallies to move in during the evening...surface lures or crankbaits can be effective at this time.

Area (6) Work along the west shore for muskie...especially in the fall.

FISHING TIPS — Muskie fishermen working the shallow weedy areas should cast bucktails, jerkbaits, or shallow running crankbaits. Remember to use smaller size lures since East Horsehead's muskie are generally small...10-20 pounds.

For largemouth, jig n' eel, plastic worms, and spinnerbaits have all produced for local anglers. Key on the shoreline areas especially around docks or other cover. Large panfish are usually found off the deeper weed edges during summer...often suspended.

CONCLUSION — East Horsehead is a quality lake with a balanced fishery. Its small size and out-of-the-way location make it a good choice for those who are tired of large busy lakes.

-LAKES LIMITED IN ACCESS OR FISHERY IN SECTION 1-

BOGGY LAKE
BUCK LAKE (S33, T38N, R7E)
O'DAY LAKE
RUTH LAKE
SIMMONS LAKE
SWAMP LAKE
TYLER LAKE
WHITEY LAKE

LOCATION — In the northwest portion of the book area, all north of Highway K and west of Highway 47.

ACCESS — None public.

LAKE CHARACTERISTICS

Size and Depth - These lakes range in size from 3-39 acres and from 7'-39' in depth. Most have a maximum depth of about 15 feet.

Water Source - Seepage lakes: No inlets or outlets.

Shoreline - Almost exclusively bog or other wetlands, except for some uplands around O'Day and Tyler Lakes.

Bottom - Primarily muck, although limited areas of firm bottom materials are present.

Water - Ranging in color from clear to light brown. All are extremely infertile.

Vegetation - Generally lacking, although floating and emergent types are often present around the shore. Boggy and Simmons Lakes have moderate densities of vegetation.

FISHERY

Species - Largemouth Bass, Panfish.

Comment - With no means of public access, information on the fishery is either nonexistent or at best, rather old. Past records indicate that all have largemouth bass and panfish populations, except Swamp Lake which has had severe winterkill problems, and therefore a limited or nonexistent fish community.

Panfish species usually present are bluegill, pumpkinseed, and perch. All typically are stunted.

CONCLUSION — Without public access all eight of these lakes remain out of reach to the general public. However, you won't miss a thing, since their extreme infertility and poor fisheries make these lakes best left unfished.

SECTION 2

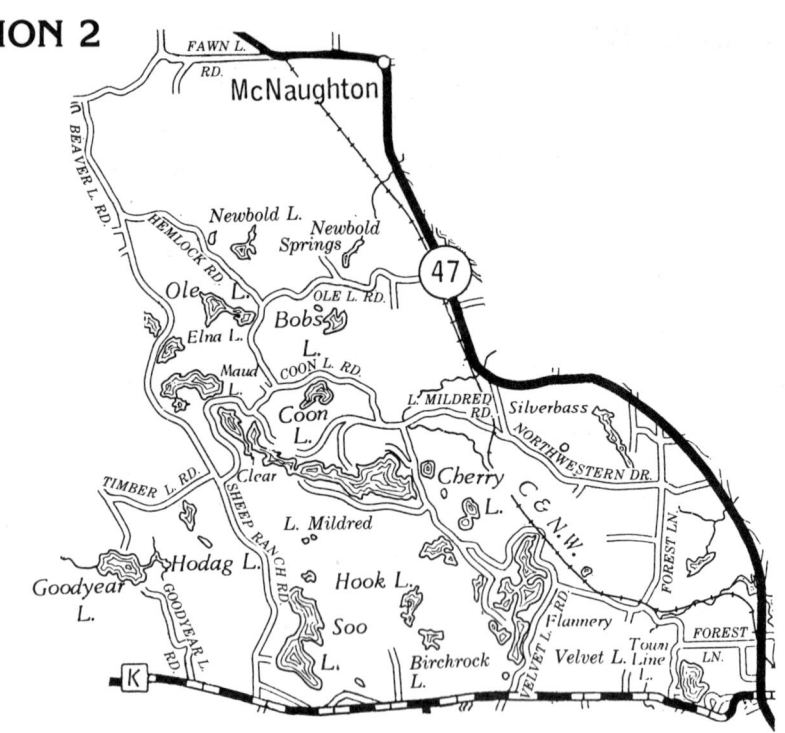

SECTION MAP FOR —

Elna Lake	Velvet Lake	Cherry Lake
Maud Lake	Townline Lake	Hook Lake
Clear Lake	Soo Lake	Newbold Lake
(S24, T37N, R7E)	Goodyear Lake	Newbold Springs
Lake Mildred	Hodag Lake	Ole Lake
Coon Lake	Birchrock Lake	Silverbass Lake
Flannery Lake	Bob's Lake	

ELNA LAKE

LOCATION — In the northwest part of the book area, approximately 6 miles northwest of Rhinelander.

ACCESS — **Type III (Public):** On the western side of the lake; drive 3.6 miles north on Sheep Ranch Road from Highway K. This roadside facility is on the east side of the road. A short easy carry-in must be made. Off-road parking is provided.

SPECIAL FEATURES — A good bass-panfish lake with scenic surroundings and little pressure.

LAKE CHARACTERISTICS
  Size and Depth - 22 acres and 14'.
  Water Source - Seepage lake: No inlet or outlet.

ELNA LAKE

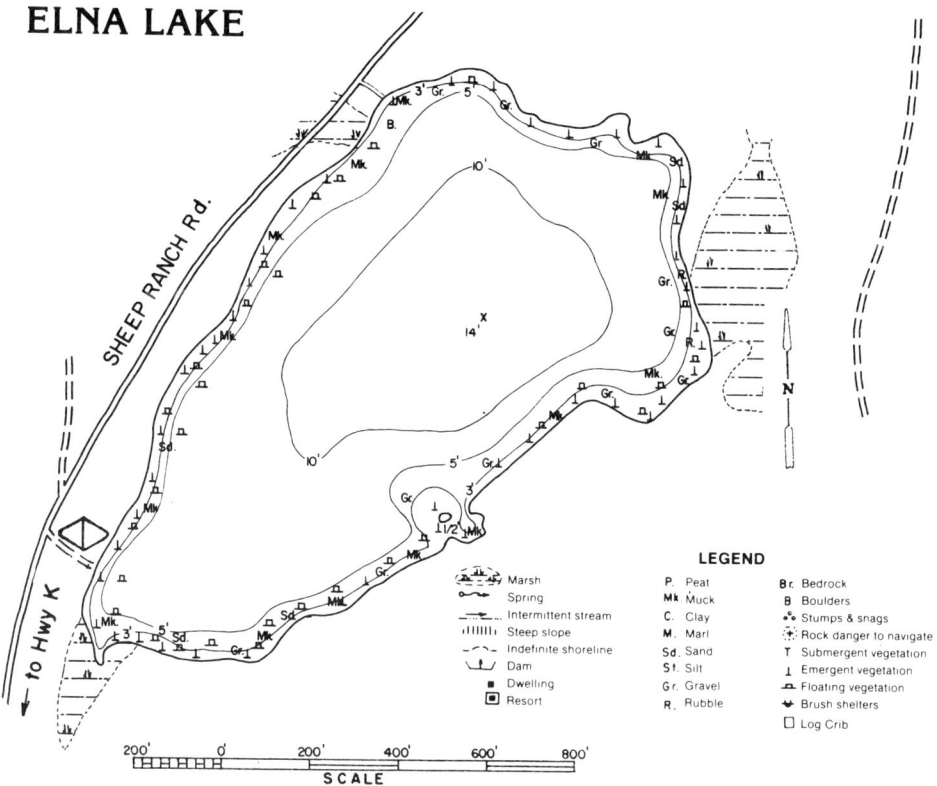

Shoreline - Mainly upland with a limited area of meadow/shrub wetland. 40% is publicly-owned.

Bottom - 45% sand, 20% muck, 15% gravel, 10% rubble, 10% boulders.

Water - Clear and very infertile.

Vegetation - Heavy around the shoreline. Mainly water lily, arrowhead, and water celery.

FISHERY

Species - Largemouth bass, Panfish, (Walleye).

Comment - One walleye appeared in a past survey, the origin of which is unknown... presumably introduced by a private party.

Forage - Fathead minnows.

LAKE MANAGEMENT

Lake Investigation Data - A survey was conducted in 1972 to assess the fishery. However, too few fish were captured to make any definitive conclusions.

Stocking - Largemouth bass and fathead minnows were stocked in the early 70's to reestablish a fishery after chemical treatment was completed.

Treatment - Chemical treatment was conducted in the late 60's to remove undesirable populations of stunted panfish and bullhead.

FISHING TIPS — Fish the weed edges and pockets for both bass and panfish. Small spinnerbaits such as Beetle Spins have been productive for bass.

Panfish can be taken on the usual fare; worms, nightcrawler pieces, etc. Don't forget to try a small ice fishing jig tipped with a waxie for spring and summer 'gills'. Also, bring along a fly rod for added fun!

CONCLUSION — Elna is a good 'small water' fishery. A few trophy size bass have been reported from this lake. The ease of access and quality fishing should put Elna on your list of lakes to fish.

MAUD LAKE

LOCATION — In the northwest segment of the area, to the west of Highway 47 and north of Highway K.

ACCESS — **Type IV:** To the south end of the lake; drive 2.2 miles north from Highway K on Sheep Ranch Road to Clear Lake Road. Turn right and follow Clear Lake Road 0.9 mile to Acorn Road. Make a left, the small unmarked access is 0.2 mile down on the right.

LAKE CHARACTERISTICS
Size and Depth - 65 acres and 6 feet deep.
Water Source - Seepage lake: No inlet or outlet.
Shoreline - 70% bog, 30% upland with a small section of adjoining county forest land.
Bottom - 80% muck, 15% sand, 5% gravel and rubble.
Water - Light brown and murky, quite infertile. Winterkill events have been documented in the past.
Vegetation - Moderate densities of submergent and floating types are present.

FISHERY
Species - Largemouth Bass, Bluegill, Perch.
Comment - Little is known about the fishery. However, when successive mild winters prevail a quality bass/panfish population has been reported.

LAKE MANAGEMENT
Lake Investigation Data - None.
Stocking - None.

CONCLUSION — Much about Maud remains unknown since the difficult access keeps most fishermen off. Some reports suggest that a good bass/bluegill fishery exists. However, the potential for winterkill may cause dramatic fluctuations in the fish community.

For those willing to work, Maud Lake should be fished at least once... it may be well worth the effort.

CLEAR LAKE (S24, T37N, R7E)

LOCATION — In the northwestern portion of the book area, immediately west of and connected to Lake Mildred.

ACCESS — **Type V:** A navigable channel from Lake Mildred on the east side.

SPECIAL FEATURES — The use of gas driven motors is prohibited on Clear Lake.

LAKE CHARACTERISTICS
   Size and Depth - 30 acres and 10 feet deep.
   Water Source - Seepage lake: No inlet or outlet.
   Shoreline - Mostly upland with minor wetland areas on the north end. Totally private.
   Bottom - 65% sand, 15% gravel, 10% muck, 10% rubble and boulders.
   Water - Highly infertile and moderately clear.
   Vegetation - Limited to floating and emergent varieties.

LAKE MANAGEMENT
   Lake Investigation Data - None.
   Stocking - None.

FISHING TIPS — The entire shoreline weed edge can be fished for bass...spinnerbaits buzzed over the weeds will attract shallow water fish. Floating minnow lures twitched over the deeper weed edge will also take active fish. A few northern are caught from Clear Lake - try the weedy north bay.

CONCLUSION — Clear Lake offers some decent bass and pike action in a quiet nonmotorized setting.

LAKE MILDRED

LOCATION — In the northwest part of the area, north of Highway K and west of Highway 47.

ACCESS — **Type I (Public):** To the east end of the lake; take Lake Mildred Road west from Highway 47 for about 1/2 mile to the intersection with Northwestern Drive. Stay to the right and follow Lake Mildred Road another 1.0 mile to the intersection with Coon Lake Road, turn left and continue on Lake Mildred Road 0.6 mile to the landing on the right side of the road. This recently developed state facility has a paved ramp and turn-around, concrete slab landing, and parking for five car/trailer rigs.

SPECIAL FEATURES — At normal water levels there is a small navigable channel to Clear Lake on the northwest end of the lake.

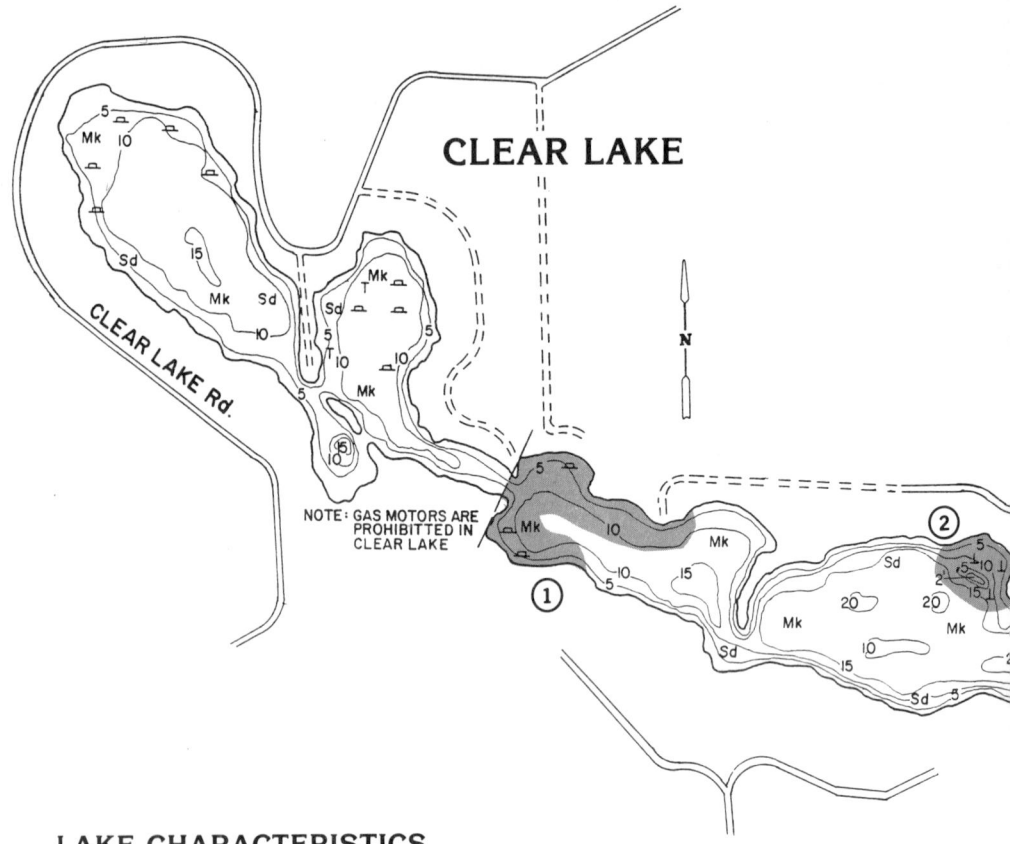

LAKE CHARACTERISTICS
Size and Depth - 190 acres and 45 feet.
Water Source - Seepage lake: No inlet or outlet.
Shoreline - Almost entirely upland and private except for the access.
Bottom - 65% sand, 15% rubble, 10% gravel, 10% muck.
Water - Very clear and infertile. The thermocline is established at a depth of 25'.
Vegetation - Generally sparse, pickerel weed and lily pads are found along the shoreline.

FISHERY
Species
Primary - Largemouth Bass, Smallmouth Bass, Bluegill.
Secondary - Northern Pike, Crappie, Perch.
Limited - Muskie, Walleye.
Comment - Gamefish numbers are rated as "modest" by the State. Bluegill and perch are slow growing.

LAKE MANAGEMENT
Lake Investigation Data - None recently, but a 1980 seine survey produced only a few young-of-the-year panfish.
Stocking - In 1980, 400 8" muskie were released.

LAKE SURVEY MAP — Fishing Areas Shaded

Area (1) Submerged wood and lily pads combine to attract crappie and bass to the region just east of the narrows leading to Clear Lake. Spring is best for crappie while largemouth can be taken all season long.

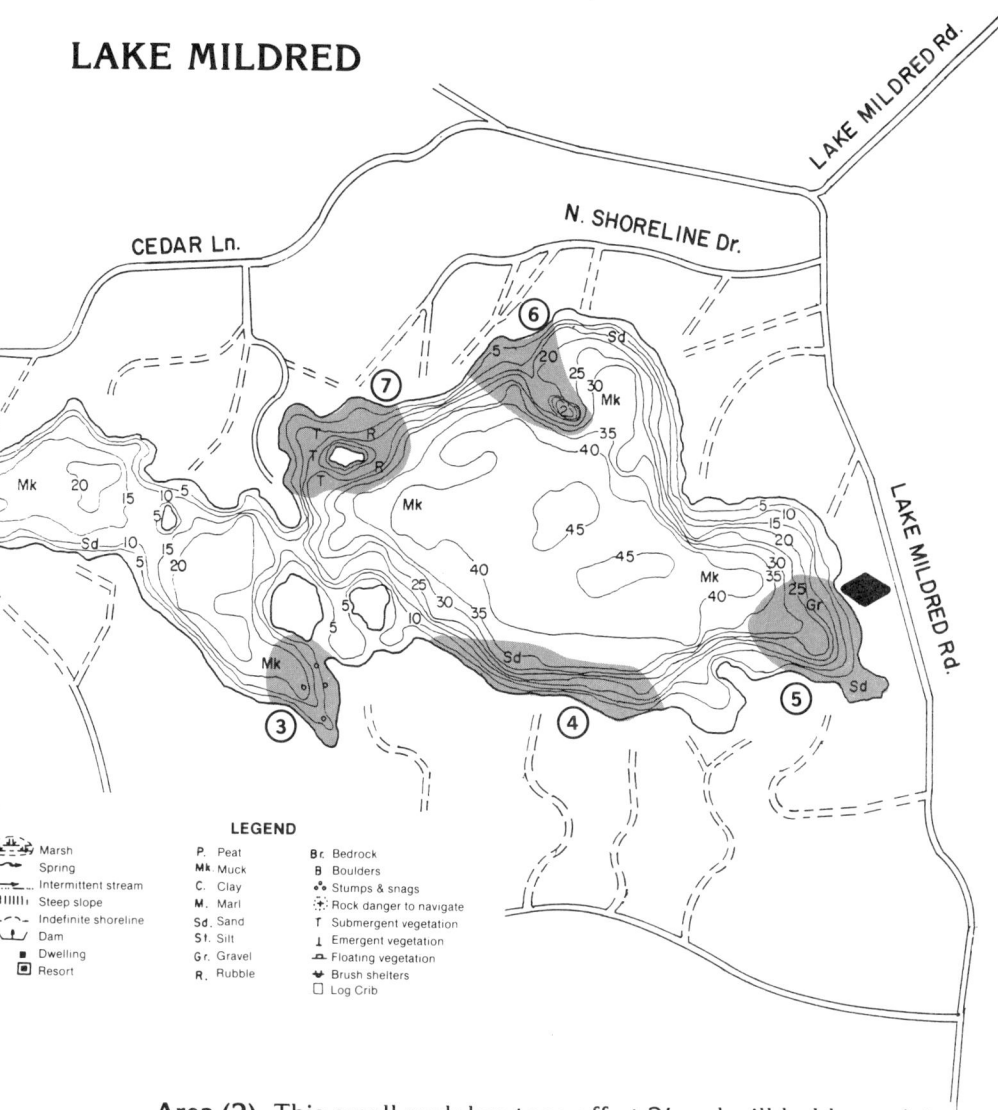

Area (2) This small rock bar tops off at 2' and will hold a variety of species. Work the top and shallower portions during early morning or evening...fish the deeper edges during the day. Muskie, bass, and northern are all a possibility here.

Area (3) The stumpy bay on the south side is another "Hot Spot" for muskie, northern, and bass. A Rapala twitched over the wood is an effective presentation...silver/black or silver/blue have been good producers.

Area (4) Row trolling suckers along the steep dropping south shore is a good bet for fall muskie. Large deep running crankbaits can take fish during summer.

Area (5) Ice fishermen set tip-ups here for northern pike. Large shiners or suckers are preferred baits. Crappie are also taken through the ice and again in early spring.

Area (6) Both muskie and bass will relate to the underwater point that extends off the north shore. Bucktails or crankbaits have been effective for muskie.

Area (7) Work around this island for smallmouth bass and an occasional walleye. Deep weeds and rock are the main attraction for gamefish.

FISHING TIPS — Light lines and down-sized tackle are a must for Mildred's extremely clear water. Best results are achieved by getting on the water early in the morning or during the evening hours. Night fishing is also productive.

Bass fishermen should try black, purple, or blue plastics. Surface baits after dark are also worth a try.

CONCLUSION — Mildred is a tough lake to fish. Its clarity, minimal cover, and fairly deep water combine to pose a significant challenge to fishermen. Although gamefish populations are not high in numbers, there are trophy fish available.

COON LAKE

LOCATION — In the northwestern section of the book area, due north of Lake Mildred and west of Highway 47.

ACCESS — None public.

LAKE CHARACTERISTICS

Size and Depth - 28 acres and 19 feet.
Water Source - Seepage lake: No inlet or outlet.
Shoreline - Chiefly upland and 100% private.
Bottom - Primarily firm material - sand, gravel, and rubble.
Water - Extremely infertile and rather clear.

FISHERY

Species - Largemouth Bass, Perch, Bluegill, Pumpkinseed.
Comment - Stunted panfish and a few quality bass are present.

LAKE MANAGEMENT

Lake Investigation Data - None.
Stocking - None.

CONCLUSION — The lack of public access proves inconsequential since the fishery is marginal at best.

FLANNERY LAKE

LOCATION — In the central portion of the area, west of Rhinelander and just north of Highway K.

ACCESS — **Type I (Public):** On the extreme north end of the lake; follow Velvet Lake Road north from Highway K for 1.2 miles to the Flannery Lake Road intersection. Turn left and proceed 0.8 mile, the landing will be on the left. Both a gravel ramp and turn-around are provided by the County. A loading pier and parking for 2-3 car/trailer units are also available.

SPECIAL FEATURES — Flannery Lake is connected to Velvet Lake via a navigable channel.

LAKE CHARACTERISTICS
Size and Depth - 112 acres and 33 feet.
Water Source - Seepage lake: No inlet or outlet.
Shoreline - Predominantly upland and private.
Bottom - 70% sand, 20% muck, 10% gravel and rubble.
Water - Very clear and highly infertile for a lake of this size.
Vegetation - Generally scarce and limited to lily pads. Growths of filamentous algae usually occur in late summer.

FISHERY
Species - Muskie, Northern Pike, Largemouth Bass, Smallmouth Bass, Perch, Bluegill, Crappie, Rock Bass, Pumpkinseed, Bullhead, Sucker.
Comment - The extreme infertility has resulted in stunted panfish populations and largemouth bass of poor condition. Movement of fish between Flannery and Velvet does occur.

LAKE MANAGEMENT
Lake Investigation Data - None.
Stocking - In 1980, 200 12" muskie were stocked. Another 100 were planted in 1982.

LAKE SURVEY MAP — Fishing Areas Shaded
Area (1) Try for muskie in the wood along the northwest shore. Largemouth bass may also be taken here.
Area (2) The mouth of the small bay can provide muskie action. Also, in the fall, work further out along the drop-off for late season fish.
Area (3) This deep water hole in the north basin attracts muskie in late summer. Drift and cast for these suspended fish.
Area (4) Muskie and northern pike will relate to the newly fallen trees along the north side of the point.
Area (5) Work these weeds along the west side for largemouth bass. Remember to fish both the inside and outside weedlines.

FLANNERY LAKE

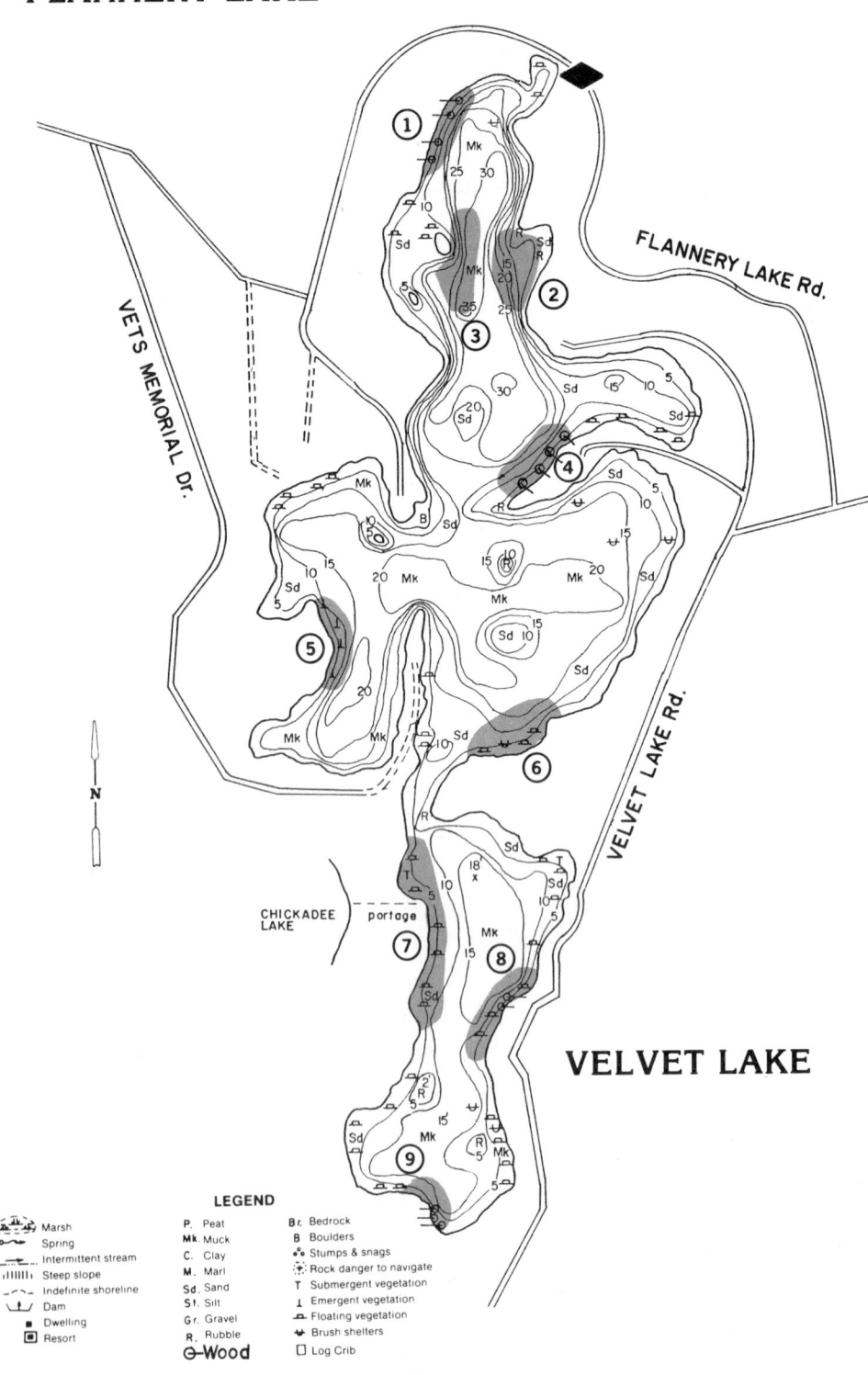

VELVET LAKE

LEGEND

- Marsh
- Spring
- Intermittent stream
- Steep slope
- Indefinite shoreline
- Dam
- Dwelling
- Resort

- P. Peat
- Mk. Muck
- C. Clay
- M. Marl
- Sd. Sand
- St. Silt
- Gr. Gravel
- R. Rubble
- Wood

- Br. Bedrock
- B. Boulders
- Stumps & snags
- Rock danger to navigate
- T Submergent vegetation
- Emergent vegetation
- Floating vegetation
- Brush shelters
- Log Crib

Area (6) Brush and weeds along the southern end combine to provide cover for largemouth bass.

FISHING TIPS — The north basin tends to be most productive for muskie and northern pike. Black lures are preferred by anglers on Flannery. With the extreme lack of weed cover, areas of submerged wood become the major fish holding spots.

CONCLUSION — In the past, Flannery had a reputation as a good bass-panfish lake. Unfortunately, excessive angler harvest has caused the fishery to deteriorate to its current status. Stunted panfish, a dwindling bass population, and poor condition muskie characterize the present fishery. The chance of catching a muskie or northern are perhaps the only remaining attraction for fishermen.

Obviously, catch and release is essential to maintaining any degree of quality fishing.

VELVET LAKE

LOCATION — In the central part of the book area, just north of Highway K and west of Highway 47.

ACCESS — Type V: On the north end from Flannery Lake.

LAKE CHARACTERISTICS
Size and Depth - 35 acres and 16 feet.
Water Source - Seepage lake: No inlet or outlet.
Shoreline - Primarily upland. Entirely private with moderate development on the east side.
Bottom - 65% muck, 25% sand, 10% gravel.
Water - Quite clear and highly infertile.
Vegetation - Very sparse and restricted to lily pads around the perimeter.

FISHERY
Species - Muskie, Northern Pike, Largemouth Bass, Smallmouth Bass, Perch, Bluegill, Crappie, Pumpkinseed, Bullhead, Sucker.
Comment - The panfish populations are considered stunted. Muskie are long and lean (poor condition) due to a limited supply of desirable forage.

LAKE MANAGEMENT
Lake Investigation Data - None.
Stocking - See Flannery Lake report.

LAKE SURVEY MAP - Fishing Areas Shaded
Area (7) Look for largemouth bass and bluegill around the 'drowned wood' and scattered clumps of lily pads. Don't expect the bluegill to be exceptionally large.
Area (8) Muskie and bass are attracted to this area of sub-

merged logs and branches on the east side. Work the outermost cover for muskie... moving closer toward shore for bass.

Area (9) Wood along the south side provides afternoon shade for bass. Evening is also productive. A few panfish can be expected too.

FISHING TIPS — Look for the east side of Velvet Lake to produce the best results. The extremely clear water makes periods of low light the prime time - try early morning or evening. As in the case in Flannery, wood is the main form of cover that fish will relate to. Concentrate your efforts accordingly.

CONCLUSION — In the tradition of so many lakes that have been over-exploited, Velvet has little left to offer. Expect small bass and stunted panfish. The only plus are the fragile populations of muskie and northern pike. Again, catch and release is a must.

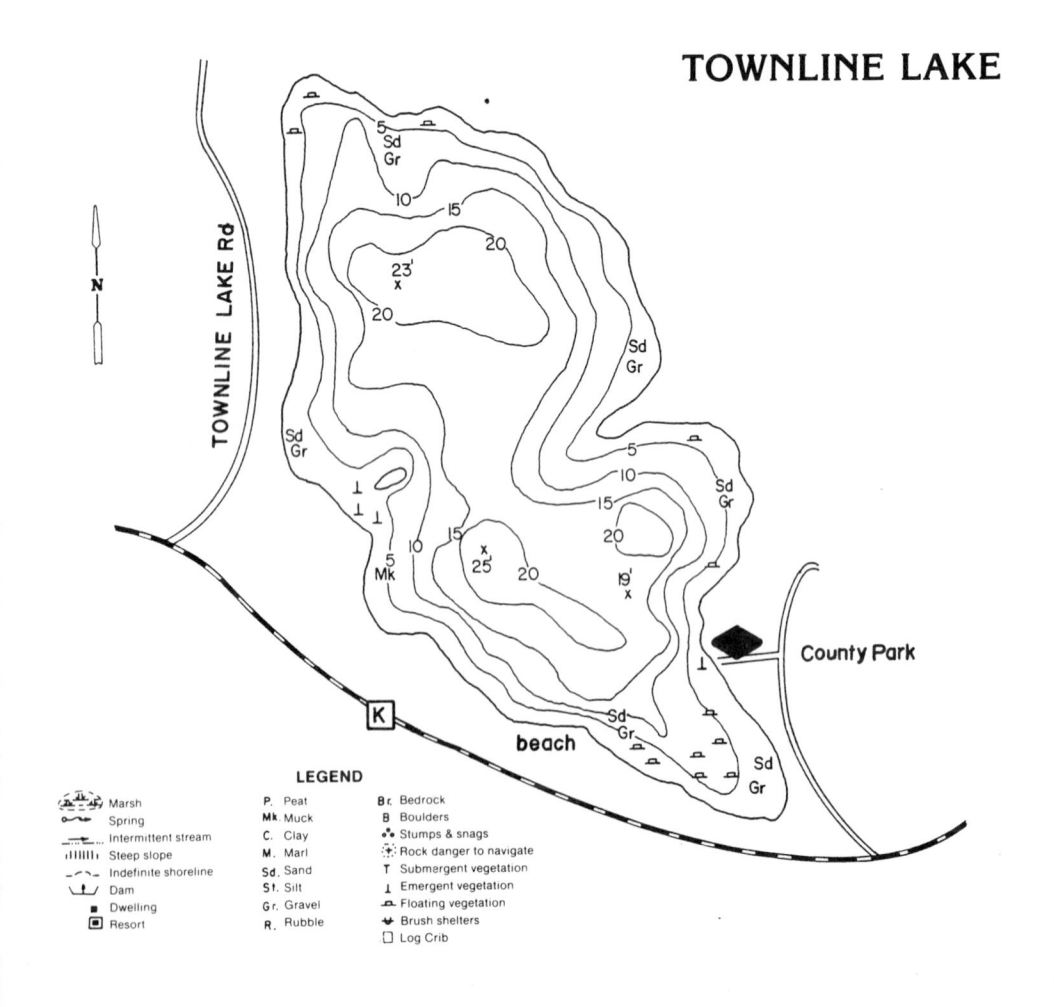

TOWNLINE LAKE

LEGEND

Marsh	P. Peat	Br. Bedrock
Spring	Mk. Muck	B Boulders
Intermittent stream	C. Clay	Stumps & snags
Steep slope	M. Marl	Rock danger to navigate
Indefinite shoreline	Sd. Sand	T Submergent vegetation
Dam	St. Silt	Emergent vegetation
Dwelling	Gr. Gravel	Floating vegetation
Resort	R. Rubble	Brush shelters
		Log Crib

TOWNLINE LAKE

LOCATION — In the central part of the book area, immediately west of Rhinelander on the north side of Highway K.

ACCESS — **Type I (Public):** On the southeast side of the lake within the county park; take Highway K 0.4 mile west from Highway 47. Turn right at the Town Line County Park entrance. The blacktop access is on the left. Two large rocks in the ramp make this a difficult access that is best for canoes or small boats. A pier and parking area are also present.

RELATED SERVICES
  Boat Rentals - None.
  Public Parks - Yes, a county park with picnic and swimming facilities.
  Campgrounds - None.

SPECIAL FEATURES — Townline Lake is a popular swimming and picnic site.

LAKE CHARACTERISTICS
  Size and Depth - 61 acres and 25 feet.
  Water Source - Seepage lake: No inlet or outlet.
  Shoreline - Predominantly upland and moderately developed.
  Bottom - 45% sand, 35% muck, 10% boulders, 10% rubble and gravel.
  Water - Very clear and quite infertile.
  Vegetation - Generally sparse, except for heavy growths of lily pads in the bays.

FISHERY
  Species - Largemouth Bass, Perch, Bluegill, Rock Bass, White Sucker.
  Comment - Extremely high numbers of stunted panfish are present. A few quality-sized largemouth are also available.

LAKE MANAGEMENT
  Lake Investigation Data - None.
  Stocking - None, since rainbow trout were planted in the 60's.

FISHING TIPS — The clear water dictates the use of light lines and smaller lures. Bass anglers should try twitching balsa minnows over the weeds and wood. As usual, plastic worms are also effective.

CONCLUSION — Townline Lake has a better reputation as a swimming lake than as a fishing lake. However, it does produce an occasional bass in the 5#-6# class.

SOO LAKE

LOCATION — In the west central part of the book area, west of Rhinelander and just north of Highway K.

ACCESS — None public.

LAKE CHARACTERISTICS
  Size and Depth - 135 acres and 13 feet.
  Water Source - Seepage lake: No inlet or outlet.
  Shoreline - Completely private. Mostly upland, having only limited areas of coniferous bog.
  Bottom - 35% sand, 30% muck, 25% gravel, 10% rubble and boulders.
  Water - Highly infertile and clear.
  Vegetation - Quite limited.

FISHERY
  Species - Muskie, Walleye, Largemouth Bass, Perch, Bluegill, Pumpkinseed, Bullhead, Sucker.
  Comment - Reports of quality gamefish populations are often heard from local anglers, but no studies have been conducted due to the access situation.

LAKE MANAGEMENT
  Lake Investigation Data - None.
  Stocking - None.

CONCLUSION — Soo Lake has a local reputation for producing some nice fish. However, the lake remains private and inaccessible to the general public.

GOODYEAR LAKE

LOCATION — In the western portion of the book area, north of Highway K and to the west of Highway 47.

ACCESS — **Type I (Public):** In the southeast corner of the lake; take Goodyear Lake Road north from County Highway K for 1.3 miles to the landing. Small rigs are suggested for this gravel facility. The parking area can accommodate 4-5 rigs.

SPECIAL FEATURES — A navigable access to Goodyear Springs is present which supports a modest brook trout fishery.

LAKE CHARACTERISTICS
  Size and Depth - 59 acres and 7 feet.
  Water Source - Drainage lake: An east side inlet from Goodyear Springs and the Goodyear Creek outlet on the west side.
  Shoreline - Primarily upland. Mostly private, with public ownership restricted to the south side access area.

Bottom - Mainly muck.
Water - Somewhat fertile and light brown in color. Winterkill has been known to occur in the past.
Vegetation - Very dense throughout the lake. Mainly pondweed and coontail. Lily pads are especially thick on the southeast side.

FISHERY
Species - Northern Pike, Largemouth Bass, Perch, Bluegill, (Muskie).
Comment - The northern pike and bass have the panfish population in relatively good balance - as a result nice size panfish are available.

LAKE MANAGEMENT
Lake Investigation Data - None.
Stocking - None recently. Muskie were planted periodically in the 60's and 70's.

FISHING TIPS — Goodyear must be fished early in the season as heavy weeds choke the lake by summer. Work spoons, spinnerbaits, and floating Rapalas over the weeds for pike and bass. For those interested in brook trout, Goodyear Springs can be reached by navigating the inlet with a canoe or pram.

CONCLUSION — One of the more popular and productive small lakes in the area, Goodyear provides good fishing in an out-of-the-way location.

HODAG LAKE

LOCATION — In the west segment of the area, north of Highway K and Goodyear Lake.

ACCESS — **Type I (Public):** To the west side of the lake; follow Sheep Ranch Road north off Highway K for 2.3 miles to Timber Lake Road. Turn left and drive 0.5 mile to an unmarked access road on the left. Make another left and go a short distance to the landing. This unimproved facility is best suited for small boats and canoes.

LAKE CHARACTERISTICS
Size and Depth - 18 acres and 20 feet.
Water Source - Seepage lake: No inlet or outlet.
Shoreline - Mostly upland with 100' in public ownership.
Bottom - 75% muck, 10% sand, 10% gravel, 5% rubble.
Water - Quite infertile and moderately clear.
Vegetation - Generally sparse.

FISHERY
Species - Northern Pike, Largemouth Bass, Perch, Rock Bass, Pumpkinseed, Bullhead, (Walleye).
Comment - Gamefish species appear to be in good condition due

to an abundant supply of forage. Conversely, panfish species are excessive in number and stunted in growth.

LAKE MANAGEMENT
   Lake Investigation Data - None.
   Stocking - None.

FISHING TIPS — Beaver activity has produced a great deal of fallen trees and brush. Work this cover for bass and pike.

CONCLUSION — Hodag Lake is a good choice for bass and pike action. The bass are numerous but tend to be small (9"-14"). Good-sized pike are Hodag's main attraction.

-LAKES LIMITED IN ACCESS OR FISHERY IN SECTION 2-

BIRCHROCK LAKE   NEWBOLD LAKE
BOB'S LAKE   NEWBOLD SPRINGS
CHERRY LAKE   OLE LAKE
HOOK LAKE   SILVERBASS LAKE

LOCATION — In the northwest part of the book area, all north of Highway K and west of Highway 47.

ACCESS — None public, except for Newbold Lake which is surrounded by county forest land but has no developed access.

LAKE CHARACTERISTICS
   Size and Depth - As a group these lakes range from 8 to 42 acres in size and 7'-19' in depth.
   Water Source - Seepage lakes: No inlets or outlets, except for Newbold Springs which is spring-fed and has a small outlet.
   Shoreline - Completely private. Largely upland, except for Newbold Springs, which is surrounded by bog.
   Bottom - Predominantly muck, with minor areas of firm material.
   Water - Highly infertile and generally clear.
   Vegetation - Limited to mostly floating and emergent forms around the perimeter. Lily pads, pickerel weed, and bulrush are common.

FISHERY
   Species - Largemouth Bass, Bluegill, Pumpkinseed.
   Comment - The private status of these lakes has minimized any information on their fisheries. Most have largemouth bass, bluegill, and pumpkinseed. Silverbass Lake also has smallmouth bass. Brook trout can be found in Newbold Springs.

CONCLUSION — These small inaccessible lakes are not a factor in the fishing opportunities available in the area. They are typical of many Northern Wisconsin 'pothole' lakes having high infertility, stunted panfish, and difficult or impossible access.

SECTION 3

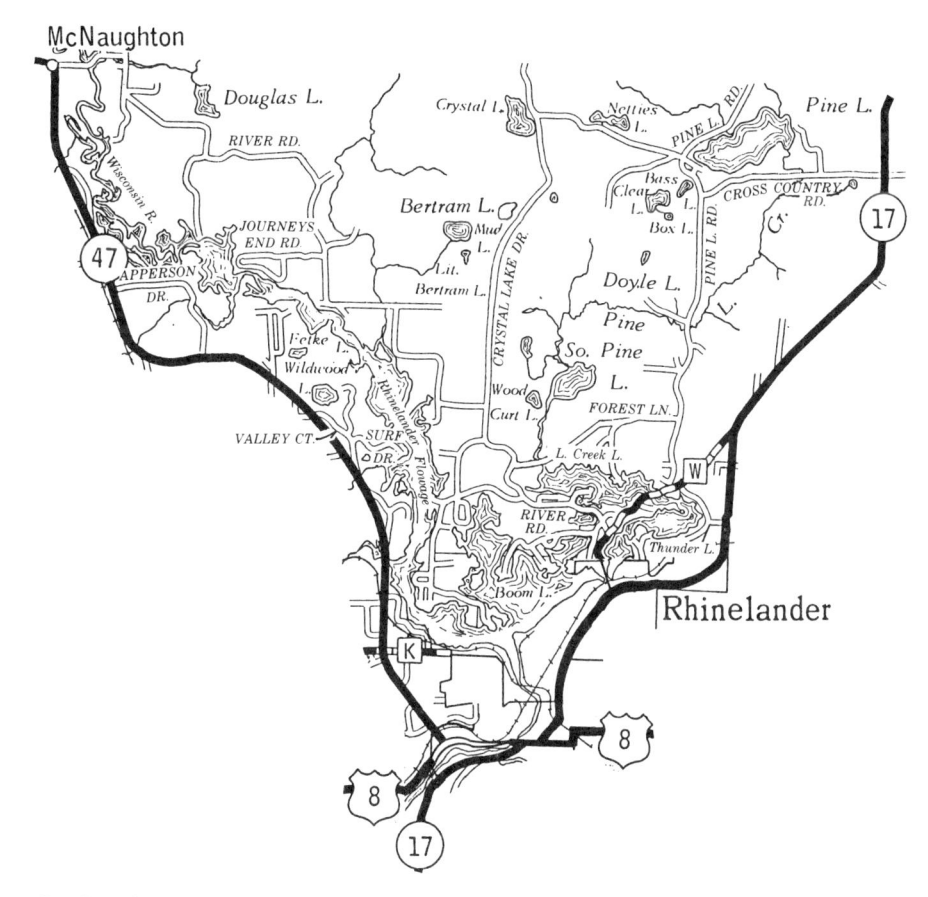

SECTION MAP FOR —
Wildwood Lake
Rhinelander Flowage
Boom Lake
Thunder Lake
Lake Creek Lake
South Pine Lake
Pine Lake
Netties Lake (Sylvan Lake)
Crystal Lake

Douglas Lake
Bass Lake (S8, T37N, R9E)
Bertram Lake
Box Lake
Clear Lake (S8, T37N, R9E)
Doyle Lake
Fetke Lake
Little Bertram Lake
Mud Lake (S7, T37N, R9E)
Wood Curt Lake

WILDWOOD LAKE

LOCATION — In the central part of the book area, north of Rhinelander and east of Highway 47.

ACCESS — Type IV (Public): To the north side of the lake; take Valley Court north off Highway 47 for 0.3 mile to Wildwood Drive (the middle road of a 3-way intersection). Continue on Wildwood Drive for 0.4 mile to Warner Lane. Make a left and go about 0.3 mile to the end of the road. Part of this undefined difficult access runs through a wetland and was rated as "not usable" by the State. (See Rhinelander Flowage Map for approximate location.)

SPECIAL FEATURES — A small lake with an interesting and diverse fishery.

LAKE CHARACTERISTICS

Size and Depth - 28 acres and 12 feet.

Water Source - Seepage lake: No inlet or outlet.

Shoreline - 60% upland with a significant wetland adjoining the west side.

Bottom - 50% sand, 40% muck, 10% gravel and rubble.

Water - Very infertile and fairly clear.

Vegetation - Moderate growths of both submergent and emergent types.

FISHERY

Species - Northern Pike, Walleye, Largemouth Bass, Smallmouth Bass, Perch, Crappie, Pumpkinseed.

Forage - State investigations noted a "complete absence of minnows" during a recent survey. Therefore juvenile panfish comprise the forage base.

LAKE MANAGEMENT

Lake Investigation Data - A comprehensive lake survey was conducted in the early 80's. Fyke nets were used as the primary sampling gear and produced the following results.

SPECIES	NUMBER	SIZE RANGE
Walleye	7	18"-23"
Northern Pike	2	24"-39"
Smallmouth Bass	3	5"-10"
Largemouth Bass	10	Young-of-the-Year
Pumpkinseed	74	4"-7"
Bluegill	41	4"-9"
Crappie	41	7"-11"

Scale samples were taken to provide age and growth data for various fish species. All showed above average growth rates with walleye displaying exceptionally rapid growth. Walleye scale analysis showed that a 19" fish was four years old. This greatly exceeded the average for Northern Wisconsin of 13.6" for walleye at age four. Also, note the size of the northern pike - quality fish for a lake of this size.

Stocking - In the summer of 1982, 1,000 3" walleye were released. Stocking by private parties has also been reported.

FISHING TIPS — For spring and summer panfish, try using a small ice fishing jig (tear drop style), tipped with a wax worm or angle worm suspended below a small bobber. These baits remain effective all year.

Both gamefish and panfish will be found relating to the weeds or weed edges. Look for open pockets in the weeds and don't forget the inside weedline.

CONCLUSION — Wildwood is an interesting lake with a diversified fishery for its 28 acre size. The fishery appears to be in relatively good balance with only the perch being stunted. Catch and release of gamefish is urged to maintain this balance.

RHINELANDER FLOWAGE

LOCATION — In the central part of the book area, north of Rhinelander and east of Highway 47.

ACCESS — **A** Type I (Public): To the northeast side of the flowage; take River Road north from Highway W for 5.7 miles to Journeys End Road. Turn left and drive 1.2 miles to the access. A gravel turn-around and ramp lead to a concrete plank landing. Parking for 5-6 rigs is provided. This is the best of the east side landings and is well suited for most boats.

B Type I (Public): To the east side of the flowage; drive 5.0 miles north off Highway W on River Road to this unmarked facility. A gravel ramp with concrete slab landing is provided. Parking is limited to 2-3 rigs.

C Type I (Public): On the east shore of the flowage; go 3.8 miles north on River Road from Highway W to this unmarked roadside facility. This is a shallow gravel landing with off-road parking for 1-2 rigs. The landing leads to a shallow stump infested area and should only be used by small boats.

D Type III (Private): At the extreme southern end adjacent to the outlet dam; take Phillip Street west off Highway 17 (Stevens Street) for 6 blocks to the dam. This is actually a marked canoe portage to the river below, but small craft can be launched. Owned by Rhinelander Paper Company, this site is used more for shore fishing than as a carry-in boat access.

E Type II (Public): On the west side of the flowage; take Valley Court north off Highway 47 for 0.3 mile to a 3-way intersection. Turn right onto Surf Road (street sign may be missing) and continue 0.6 mile on this gravel road to the access on the left. This is a narrow gravel landing into shallow water. Small boats are suggested.

F Type I (Public): At the northwest end of the flowage; take the northernmost leg of the Apperson Drive loop east off Highway 47

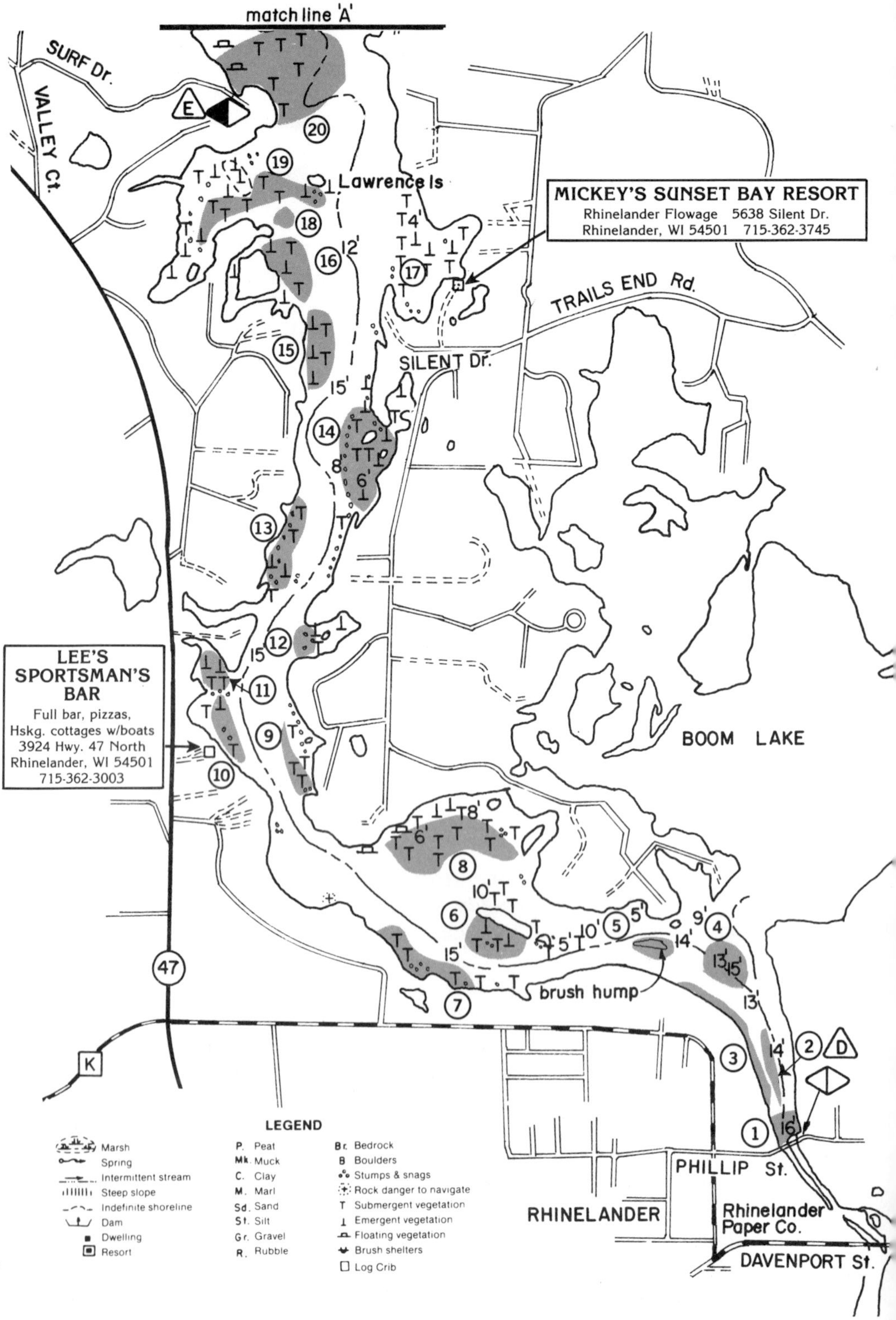
match line 'A'
SURF Dr.
VALLEY Ct.
E
Lawrence Is
MICKEY'S SUNSET BAY RESORT
Rhinelander Flowage 5638 Silent Dr.
Rhinelander, WI 54501 715-362-3745
TRAILS END Rd.
SILENT Dr.
LEE'S SPORTSMAN'S BAR
Full bar, pizzas,
Hskg. cottages w/boats
3924 Hwy. 47 North
Rhinelander, WI 54501
715-362-3003
BOOM LAKE
brush hump
47
K
D
PHILLIP St.
RHINELANDER
Rhinelander Paper Co.
DAVENPORT St.
LEGEND
Marsh
Spring
Intermittent stream
Steep slope
Indefinite shoreline
Dam
Dwelling
Resort
P. Peat
Mk. Muck
C. Clay
M. Marl
Sd. Sand
St. Silt
Gr. Gravel
R. Rubble
Br. Bedrock
B Boulders
Stumps & snags
Rock danger to navigate
T Submergent vegetation
Emergent vegetation
Floating vegetation
Brush shelters
Log Crib

RHINELANDER FLOWAGE

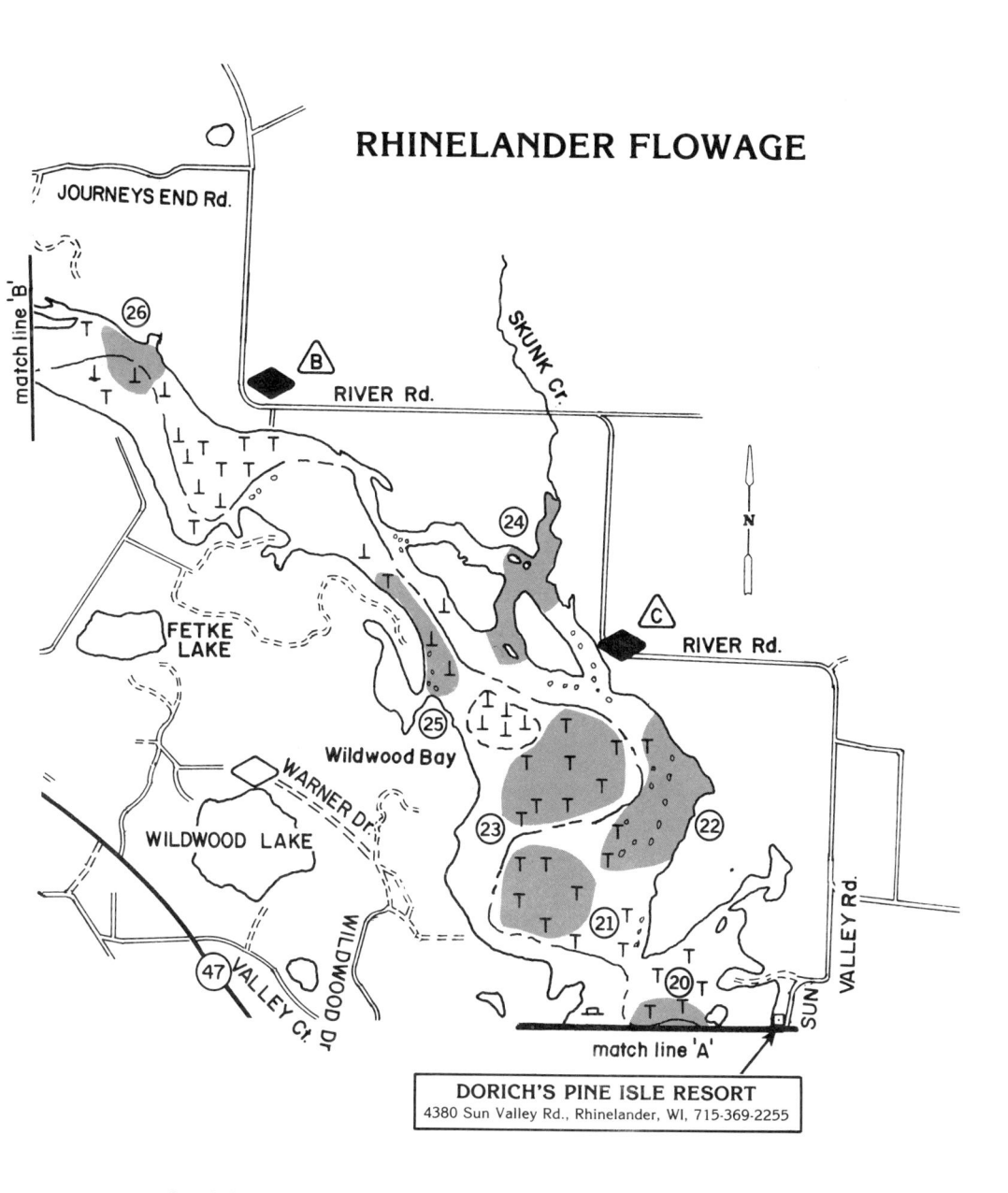

for 0.3 mile to the marked access road. Make a left and go another 0.2 mile to the landing. A gravel ramp, concrete slab landing, loading pier, and parking for 8-10 rigs are provided. This facility is jointly operated by the State, Rhinelander Paper Company, and the Town of Newbold.

Type V: A navigable access from Boom Lake to the southeast corner of the flowage.

NOTE: The boat launching facility at Hodag Park on Boom Lake is often used by anglers fishing the Rhinelander Flowage. See the Boom Lake report for details.

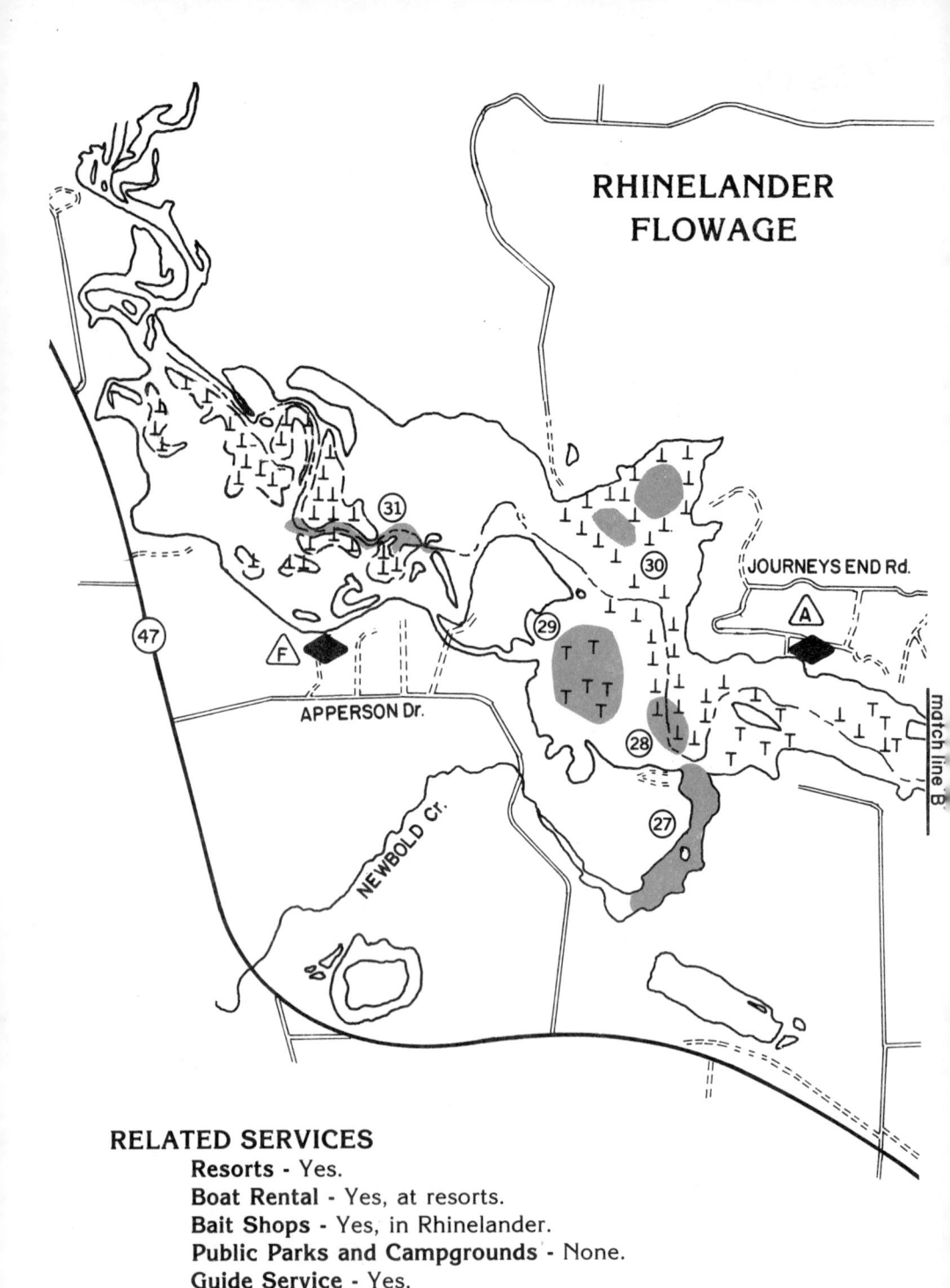

RELATED SERVICES
   Resorts - Yes.
   Boat Rental - Yes, at resorts.
   Bait Shops - Yes, in Rhinelander.
   Public Parks and Campgrounds - None.
   Guide Service - Yes.

SPECIAL FEATURES — Part of the Boom Lake-Wisconsin River impoundment complex. The Rhinelander Flowage is the premier fishery in the area covered in this book and is particularly well-known for its excellent muskie fishing.

LAKE CHARACTERISTICS
Size and Depth - 1,326 acres and 17 feet.
Water Source - Drainage lake: An impoundment of the Wisconsin River which enters on the north end. There are several other minor inlets. A 32' head dam maintains water levels by regulating the Wisconsin River outlet.
Shoreline - Chiefly upland with lesser areas of swamp and conifer bog. Mostly private and moderately developed.
Bottom - 75% sand, 23% muck, 2% gravel.
Water - Slightly fertile and brown in color.
Vegetation - Moderately heavy densities of submergent, floating, and emergent varieties. Common types are milfoil, cabbage, coontail, lily pads, bulrush, and pickerel weed. Wild rice is also common in the upper sections of the flowage.

FISHERY
Species
  Primary - Muskie, Northern Pike, Perch, Bluegill, Bullhead.
  Secondary - Walleye, Smallmouth Bass, Rock Bass, Crappie.
  Limited - Largemouth Bass, Pumpkinseed, Sucker.
Comment - As seen, the flowage supports a diverse fishery with most species displaying good growth rates.
Seasonal Migrations - Upstream movement of spawning walleye occurs...some going as far as the Rainbow Dam.
Forage - Various species of shiners, sucker, dace, bluntnose minnow, and juvenile panfish. Aquatic insects are also a significant food source.

LAKE MANAGEMENT
Lake Investigation Data - The State, in recent years, has not conducted any comprehensive fishery survey on the Rhinelander Flowage. However, the Northwoods Fishing Club of Rhinelander in cooperation with Muskies Inc. have a muskie tagging program in progress. Data on the harvest (catch) rate and movement of fish within the flowage system are being collected.

Stocking -

YEAR	SPECIES	NUMBER	SIZE
1981	Muskie	125	10"
1982	Muskie	2,300	12"
1984	Muskie	1,100	8"
1985	Muskie	2,500	10"

LAKE SURVEY MAP — Fishing Areas Shaded
Area (1) The outlet dam area has good depth and holds a mixed bag of fish species. Early in the summer crappie move in and suspend in loose schools. Walleye are caught fairly often.

Area (2) Look for this elongated ridge down the center of the outlet bay. It is adjacent to the original river channel and at times may hold walleye. Suspended summer crappie are also taken.

Area (3) Fish along this entire west shore. Concentrate on bluegill in the cover.

Area (4) There is a distinct drop-off from this elongated sand bar to the scour hole off the south end of the bar in the main channel. Work walleye and smallmouth bait down into the 17' depths.

Area (5) Directly out from the island is a small but pronounced brush hump. It is adjacent to the main river channel. Probe this structure for crappie and the occasional gamefish.

Area (6) South of the island, there is a small bar (4'-7' deep) with scattered weeds and two stumps on the point. The edge breaks into the main channel. Try for northern and muskie...also possibly for smallmouth bass.

Area (7) This 6' deep weed edge is next to the main channel. Scattered stumps also offer some cover. Fish this for both panfish and an occasional muskie.

Area (8) This bay consists of a 6'-8' stumpy 'flats' and patches of fairly dense weeds. Try casting for northern pike and muskie. Panfish also frequent this cover.

Area (9) This 4'-6' deep scattered stump field can be a consistent producer of northern pike. Work for an occasional muskie on the outside weed edge.

Area (10) Fish the back edge ($\pm$ 6') of weeds in this bay for largemouth bass and panfish, mostly bluegill and perch. The outside weedline provides good muskie habitat, dropping rather abruptly to the 15' deep river channel.

Area (11) Here is another shallow, weedy bay that should be checked for largemouth bass, bluegill or perch.

Area (12) The mouth of this bay marks the edge of a 6'-8' deep stump field. Shallow running bucktails and jerkbaits should produce muskie action.

Area (13) This shallow 4'-6' shoreline has stumps and weeds and produces good numbers of bluegill and perch. A few muskie are raised along the deep side.

Area (14) Stumps in the large bay east of the main channel provide decent habitat. The outside edge of the stumps and weeds should be worked for muskie, while the weedy interior will produce crappie, bluegill, and largemouth.

Area (15) Small northern pike are often found in this 6' deep weedbed. Look for heavy boating traffic to cut across the edge of these weeds.

Area (16) This 6' deep weed cover drops to 10' of water. Look for some excellent cabbage beds on the point. Work the weed point over to the front of the large bog for muskie. This is a very good spot. Fish adjacent to the deepest water as the season progresses and water temperatures rise.

Area (17) Sunset Bay has consistent 6' depths with plenty of weed cover and wood. The west edge drops to 10'. Look to this area as a regular producer of muskie.

Area (18) The 12' hole off the end of the long land point is a good summer walleye and crappie spot. It is also very good for walleye at 'first ice'.

Area (19) When fishing Muskie Bay try the weed edges along its mouth, together with the south and west sides of Lawrence Island. Muskie action can be good. Early in the season work the back, shallow side of the bay along with the west side of the "grass bed" for largemouth bass and northern pike. Most of this bay is 4'-5' deep, but there are also 2' humps. 'Early ice' attracts anglers for a mixed bag of action.

Area (20) The area west of Woods Island has good growths of cabbage and should be fished for muskie and walleye. Concentrate on the channel edge, but also try casting surface baits back into the weeds for muskie.

Area (21) Another good weedbed with a mixed variety including cabbage. Try here for muskie and northern pike.

Area (22) The stump field on the east side of Wildwood Bay is an excellent spot for muskie. In addition to the wood, submerged vegetation adds to the attraction. Smallmouth bass are also found around the stumps.

Area (23) To the west, a large weedbed offers good action for pike and muskie. Again, pay close attention to the weed edge near the channel.

Area (24) Panfish and perhaps a smallmouth bass can be found in the area where Skunk Creek enters the flowage. Fish the pockets and weed openings with traditional panfish offerings. In the evening try small minnows for crappie.

Area (25) Due west of Skunk Creek is a productive group of stumps. Muskie are the main attraction, but an occasional smallie is possible. Also check the stumps just north of the Skunk Creek inlet.

Area (26) Upstream from Access /B\ is a sharp bend with 12'-14' water. Walleye will hold in this deep water stretch as will muskie. Remember to fish the weed edge adjacent to the channel.

Area (27) The Newbold Creek (Eightmile Creek) inlet area should be fished for perch and northern pike. Look for pockets in the weeds to be most productive.

Area (28) A short distance upstream from Newbold Creek is another good outside bend that holds both walleye and muskie.

Area (29) To the north, another large weedbed can offer good action for northern pike. Panfish are also a good bet.

Area (30) Fish the openings in the emergent vegetation for pike, muskie, and perch. Muskie action can be expected throughout the season, while early spring and again in fall is best for pike and perch.

Area (31) Work the channel edge along this entire stretch for muskie.

FISHING TIPS — Being aware of seasonal changes in fish activity is the key to fishing success on the flowage. Local muskie anglers report that summer action doesn't really pick-up until mid-July and lasts through August. Fall muskie activity is also quite good.

Spring and fall are prime times for both northern pike and perch. Early summer can be productive for bluegill and crappie in the shallow weedy areas. Later, throughout summer, look for crappie in the channel regions during the day...moving back to the shallows to feed at night.

Don't forget the winter months...panfish are the main draw, especially crappie and perch during the 'late ice' period. Be careful on the ice since the current can create dramatic variations in ice thickness.

CONCLUSION — The Rhinelander Flowage - Wisconsin River complex is an excellent, but often overlooked, fishery. Muskie and panfish are now the primary attraction. A good walleye population exists, yet few anglers are able to take fish consistently.

The outlook for muskie is encouraging if state stocking and the highly emphasized catch and release effort continues.

BOOM LAKE

LOCATION — In the center of the book area, north of and adjacent to the City of Rhinelander.

ACCESS — ⚠️ **Type I (Public):** On the southeast side of the lake in Hodag Park; take Highway 17 (Stevens Street) to Phillip Street, turn west to Thayer Street, turn north to Rose Street and then west again to the landing at the end of the road. This excellent facility has several paved ramps, piers, and plenty of parking. This is the primary and recommended access.

⚠️ **Type II (Public):** On the west side of the lake to Moonlite Bay; take River Road west off Highway W for 1 mile. Stay to the left another 1.1 miles on Trails End Road to Moonlite Bay Road. This road dead ends in 0.2 mile at a beach type landing. There is a gravel ramp and a good drop-off. Parking is along the access road. The turn-around is inadequate for a large boat trailer.

⚠️ **Type II (Public):** Near the end of the main peninsula separating Boom Lake from the Wisconsin River; take River Road west off Highway W to the fork. Stay left on Trails End Road all the way to Riverview Road. Turn left to Nature Road and left again for 0.1 mile to the sharp curve and the gravel beach landing. The short approach road is unmarked and parking is along the road. This site is used sparingly.

Type V: Navigable access is possible from the Rhinelander Flowage to the west and Thunder Lake to the east.

RELATED SERVICES
Boat Rentals - Yes.
Bait Shops - Yes, several shops in Rhinelander.
Public Parks - Yes, Hodag Park on the east side. This includes a new public fishing pier and a swimming beach.
Campgrounds - None.
Resorts - Yes.
Guide Services - Yes.

SPECIAL FEATURES
— Boom Lake is part of the Wisconsin River-Rhinelander Flowage complex created by a dam in the City of Rhinelander. The Wisconsin River flows past the southwest end of the lake. The east side of Boom Lake was the site of early logging operations and several sawmills. Summer water traffic is heavy in the main basin of the lake.

LAKE CHARACTERISTICS
Size and Depth - 437 acres and 30' deep.
Water Source - Drainage lake: An impoundment of the Wisconsin River. Pine Lake Creek via Lake Creek and Thunder Lakes, is a minor inlet. The Rhinelander Paper Company dam maintains the water level.
Shoreline - Almost entirely upland and fairly well developed. There are a number of upland and bog islands, along with numerous bays and sheltered areas. Approximately 1/2 mile of shoreline is publicly-owned.
Bottom - Mostly sand and muck. The bays and backwaters are largely muck. The southeast side along the park has a diverse bottom of rock, sand, muck, logs, wire, and just about anything else that was once associated with sawmills and railroads.
Water - Moderately fertile and medium brown in color. Considering the proximity to the city, the water quality is very good.
Vegetation - The main basin of the lake does not have an abundance of weed cover. However, the shallower bays and smaller basins have moderate to dense vegetation. Primary weed types are elodea, coontail, milfoil, pondweed, duckweed, arrowhead, and lily pad.

FISHERY
Species
Primary - Muskie, Northern Pike, Crappie, Bluegill.
Secondary - Walleye, Largemouth Bass, Perch, Bullhead.
Limited - Smallmouth Bass, Rock Bass, Pumpkinseed.
Comment - The muskie population is rapidly improving, a result of continued stocking by the State. Both crappie and bluegill numbers remain very strong. Although smallmouth bass are reportedly few in number, some nice ones are caught on the east side of the main basin.

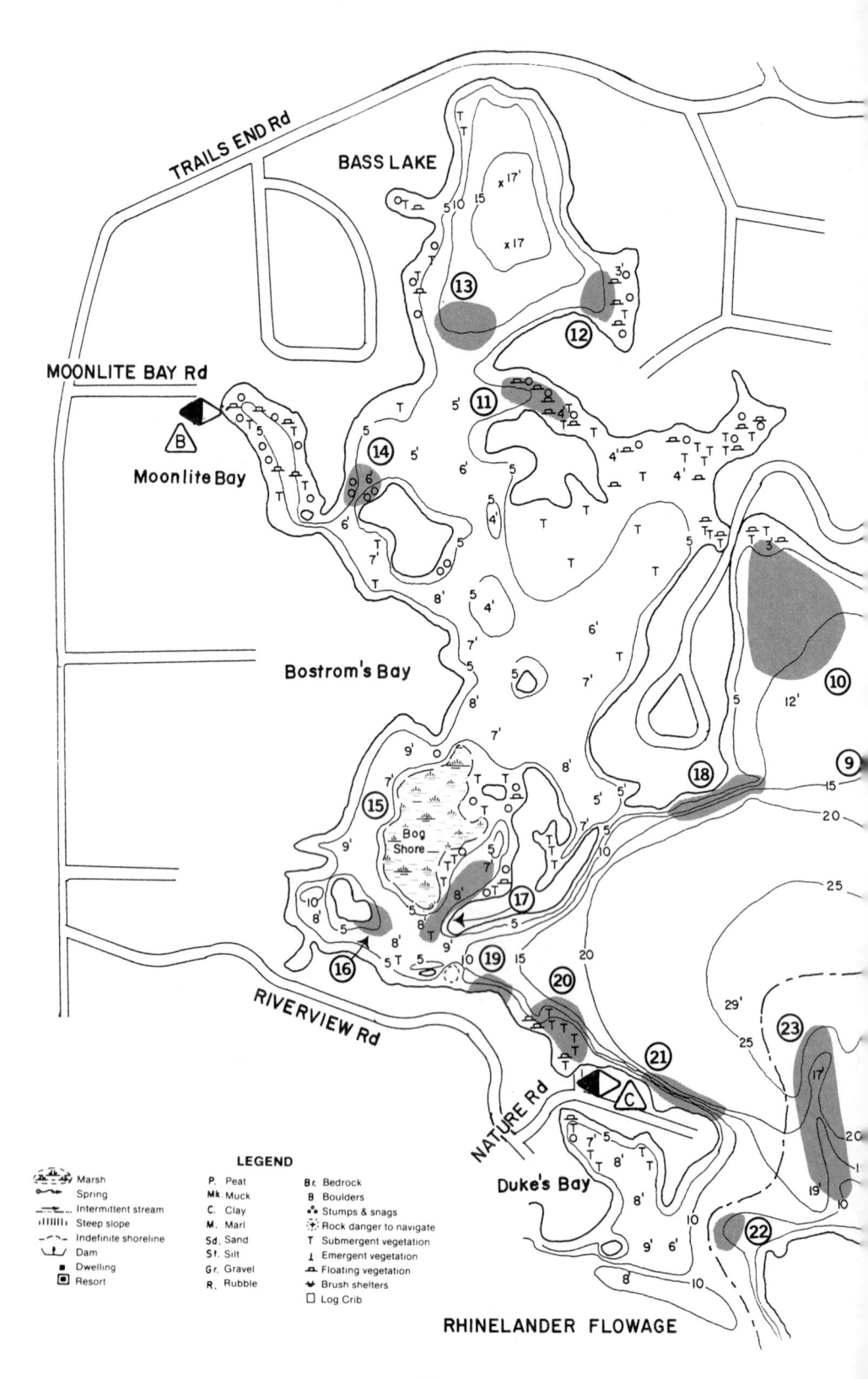

BOOM LAKE

Seasonal Migrations - Spawning movements are noted during the spring, especially for walleye up the Wisconsin River. The strength and distance of this migration is uncertain. Fishing pressure on this species has not been great enough to establish any pattern.

Forage - Various minnow species and young-of-the-year panfish.

LAKE MANAGEMENT

Lake Investigation Data - There has been very little recent lake study. In fact, only the current muskie stocking displays an intent to enhance the Boom Lake fishery. This level of management is probably a result of the good fertility and water quality, in addition to the influence of the Wisconsin River and Lake Creek. Both have considerable fish populations.

During the 60's, creel censuses indicated that large walleye were present but that smaller fish were lacking. It was believed that high numbers of panfish were feeding excessively on walleye fry and small fingerling.

Stocking - The State is currently supplementing the muskie population. This could eventually produce some of the finest muskie fishing in the state.

YEAR	SPECIES	NUMBER	SIZE
1979	Muskie	800	9"
1981	Muskie	1,250	8"-14"
1982	Muskie	760	9"
1984	Muskie	400	8"
1986	Muskie	300	8"
1987	Muskie	400	8"

Treatment - There are occasional weed control efforts in limited areas of the lake.

LAKE SURVEY MAP — Fishing Areas Shaded

Area (1) This is the old creek channel from Lake Creek with a large bar on the south side that extends from shore. Work off the edge of this bar for muskie, northern, and also crappie. Occasionly, walleye are taken. Make a few casts in the small, weedy bay to the north.

Area (2) This steep, rounded shoreline point is the location of the Rhinelander Country Club. The bottom is rocky and doesn't start leveling off until about 13'. Fish this during the fall for muskie.

Area (3) The north side of the island in Peggy Slough is a good spot to try for bluegill. This is also a popular area for winter panfish.

Area (4) The shallow end of Peggy Slough is very weedy. Try for northern along the weed edge and largemouth bass in the slop. Northern pike usually provide good action but may be small in size.

Area (5) The area between the bog island and the upland islands to the south is known for yielding spawning crappie. During winter the island area is ice fished for northern and some walleye. Start in 10'-12' of water.

Area (6) Southwest of the narrows to Peggy Slough, in the main lake basin, there is an elongated ridge running parallel to the shoreline. Work this structure, the "slot" in between, and the shore drop-off for muskie and an occasional walleye.

Area (7) This underwater point is well out from shore and is adjacent to the old creek channel. It might be the old railroad grade. This structure is not often fished and could hold excellent summer fish populations... especially walleye.

Area (8) The west end of the island drops off quickly. Try the break for muskie and spend some time for walleye. The north side of this island is shallow, stumpy, and weedy. Work in here early in the season.

Area (9) This is an area of deep water structure that consists of a sand bar projecting towards the center of the lake at the 13'-18' level. This relief is not well known or fished. Work it for walleye and sometimes muskie. During summer check it for suspended crappie.

Area (10) The bay east of Manor Road Island has a gradually sloping bottom with scattered weed cover. Northern pike, bass, and crappie are caught here throughout most of the summer. A few muskie are also being taken.

Area (11) In the large Bostrom's Bay, west of Manor Road Island, there is a channel between the island and the north shoreline. This channel is 4'-5' deep with heavy weed cover to the outside. Work it for largemouth bass and bluegill. Northern are also caught.

Area (12) & (13) Both of these areas are popular winter bluegill and crappie spots.

Area (14) This is another channel between an island and the shoreline. It is narrow but reaches a depth of 6'. There are logs and stumps along the shore that hold bass and bluegill.

Area (15) The alley between the bog and mainland gets worked with regularity for muskie. It also produces northern and panfish. The depth is slightly greater near the narrows (9'-10').

Area (16) Crappie spawn at the east end of this smaller island. It's shallow, but has good weed and brush cover. Look for a grouping of fishing boats around this tip when the crappie are hitting.

Area (17) This passage between the islands is really more of a bay since the north end is quite shallow. Weed cover is abundant. Cast into this area for muskie or northern, especially in the spring. Later, fish the snags and heavy cover for largemouth and panfish.

Area (18) Work the steep shoreline along the south side of Manor Road Island for a muskie as well as northern. In particular, fish the gravel point on the east side.

Area (19) This stretch of shore leading into the draw of the narrows also yields muskie.

Area (20) This weedy "L" shaped bar extends out from the bay and angles to the west. Much of this bar is only 3' deep, although there is 7' of water at the tip. Work the weeds for largemouth and bluegill. Fish the edges for northern and an occasional muskie. Always check out the inside pocket of the "L"; the water is deeper.

Area (21) The lake's steepest shoreline drop-off should be checked for suspended crappie or walleye.

Area (22) There are rock piles located well out from the point near the old creek channel. Once you locate them, it is a good spot to mark and consistently try.

Area (23) This defined ridge ends in a point well out into the lake. It is a prominent bottom structure. Work its entire length for walleye. Muskie may also relate to it. One problem with fishing in this area is the boat traffic. During the summer, it is wise to work this early or late in the day.

Area (24) Well out from the landing at Hodag Park is an interesting underwater point and adjacent inside turn. This structure is part of an old railroad berm that extended from the shoreline.

Area (25) This rock pile has a small 5'-7' diameter top and is about 100' off the landing and slightly to the north. Its sides drop off abruptly. Because of its closeness to the docks, it is seldom fished. Look for bluegill, crappie, and occasionally a cruising muskie. Brush is located on this hump.

Area (26) The shoreline along Hodag Park is very irregular with many points and inside turns. The bottom ranges from hard sand and rock to muck. Also, wire, logs, and other debris are present from the sawmill era. It is a good spot to lose a lot of terminal tackle but also a good area to catch most any species of fish. One problem is the heavy activity along the shore. Try here during winter for most species.

Area (27) At this location the shoreline drops off very sharply with the 16' depth being reached only a short distance from shore. This has been a favorite bullhead spot.

FISHING TIPS — Boom Lake has many different characteristics. The main basin is relatively deep with bottom structure being the key to fishing. The back bays are mostly shallow with plenty of weeds, stumps, and some bog areas. After the weeds die off in fall, concentrate along hard bottom areas. Try copper or nickel bladed bucktails and spinners along with orange, yellow, and fluorescent lures.

CONCLUSION — Northern pike, crappie, and bluegill have been the main species for years. Now muskie are joining this group. A few knowledgeable fishermen are scoring very well. Walleye are present but not exploited effectively as of yet. Again, only a few fishermen seem to be successful.

THUNDER LAKE

LOCATION — In the central portion of the area, due north of Rhinelander.

ACCESS — **Type III (Public):** At the south end of the lake; on the east side of Highway W just north of the bridge between Boom Lake and Thunder Lake. Off-road parking for 1-2 vehicles is provided.
Type V: A navigable access to the southwest corner of the lake via a short channel from Boom Lake.
Type V: A navigable access from Lake Creek Lake to the north end of the lake.

RELATED SERVICES
Boat Rentals - Yes, on nearby Boom Lake.
Bait Shops - Yes, in Rhinelander.
Resorts - Yes, on Boom Lake.
Public Parks - Yes, Hodag Park on Boom Lake.
Campgrounds - None.
Guide Services - Yes.

SPECIAL FEATURES — Part of the Boom Lake - Rhinelander Flowage complex. It is known locally as the "Dark Water."

LAKE CHARACTERISTICS
Size and Depth - 172 acres and 12 feet.
Water Source - Drainage lake: Water levels are influenced and maintained by the Rhinelander Paper Company dam.
Shoreline - 80% upland. 100% private and highly developed.
Bottom - 50% sand, 30% gravel, 20% muck.
Water - Slightly fertile and brown in color.
Vegetation - Primarily lily pads in addition to some scattered areas of cabbage.

FISHERY
Species
Primary - Muskie, Northern Pike, Crappie, Bluegill.
Secondary - Walleye, Largemouth Bass, Perch, Bullhead.
Limited - Smallmouth Bass, Rock Bass, Pumpkinseed.

LAKE MANAGEMENT
Lake Investigation Data - None.
Stocking - None since 1975 when 175 10" muskie were planted.

LAKE SURVEY MAP — Fishing Areas Shaded
Area (1) This bay on the east side should be fished for both muskie and bass. Be sure to work close to shore for bass, especially around any wood or weed cover.
Area (2) Another good spot for muskie...work the cabbage around the island. Also, the bay to the south should be checked for both largemouth and crappie.

LAKE CREEK LAKE

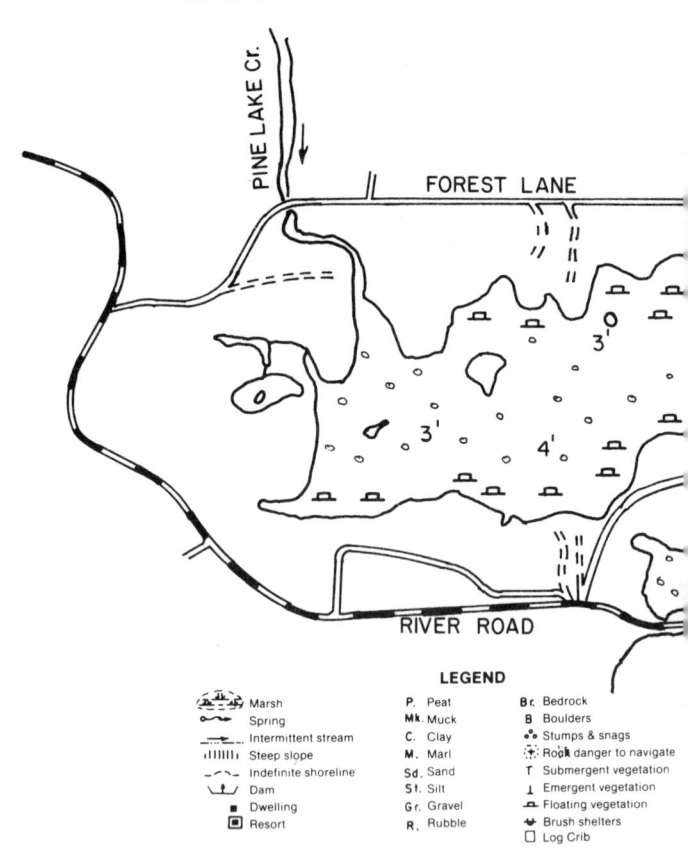

LEGEND

Marsh	P. Peat	Br. Bedrock
Spring	Mk. Muck	B. Boulders
Intermittent stream	C. Clay	Stumps & snags
Steep slope	M. Marl	Rock danger to navigate
Indefinite shoreline	Sd. Sand	T. Submergent vegetation
Dam	St. Silt	Emergent vegetation
Dwelling	Gr. Gravel	Floating vegetation
Resort	R. Rubble	Brush shelters
		Log Crib

Area (3) This small brush pile will hold crappie in spring. Try a small minnow fished below a bobber.

Area (4) The stumps and weeds along this entire stretch will attract muskie and largemouth bass. Try bucktails or jerkbaits for muskie.

FISHING TIPS — Fish the shoreline areas for muskie, bass, and northern pike. Look for areas that offer the most cover... logs, stumps, or weeds.

Panfish, mainly crappie, can provide some good action... remember to keep your hooks, bobbers, and jigs small. Bright lure presentations are a plus because of the dark water color.

CONCLUSION — Stumps and lily pads provide plenty of cover for both gamefish and panfish. Look for crappie to offer the best panfishing, especially in early spring.

Muskie anglers should give this water some attention if action is slow on Boom Lake.

THUNDER LAKE

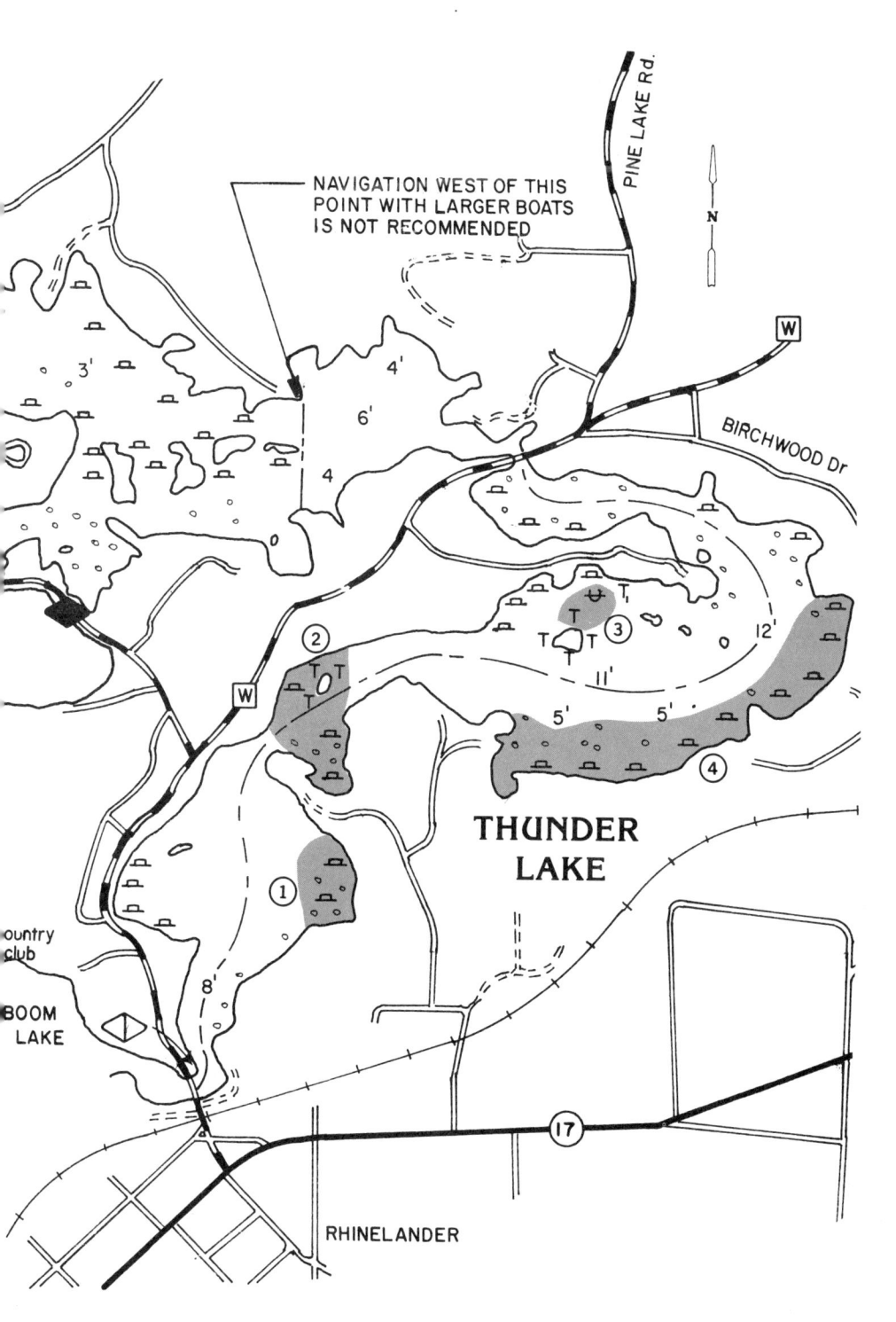

LAKE CREEK LAKE

LOCATION — In the central part of the book area, just north of the City of Rhinelander.

ACCESS — **Type I (Public):** On the south side of the lake; take River Road west off Highway W for 0.3 mile to the roadside landing on the right. This unimproved gravel facility has parking for 1-2 rigs.
Type V: A navigable access from Thunder and Boom Lakes.

SPECIAL FEATURES — Part of the Rhinelander Flowage - Boom Lake impoundment complex. Water levels are maintained by the Rhinelander Paper Company dam.

LAKE CHARACTERISTICS
  Size and Depth - 172 acres and 12 feet.
  Water Source - Drainage lake: Pine Lake Creek enters on the northwest side. An outlet channel to Thunder Lake is on the east end.
  Shoreline - 65% upland and mostly private with moderate development.
  Bottom - 55% sand, 35% muck, 10% gravel and rubble.
  Water - Slightly fertile and brown in color.
  Vegetation - Primarily lily pads.

FISHERY
  Species - Muskie, Northern Pike, Walleye, Largemouth Bass, Smallmouth Bass, Perch, Bluegill, Crappie, Rock Bass, Pumpkinseed, Bullhead.
  Comment - Crappie and bluegill are the most abundant panfish.

LAKE MANAGEMENT
  Lake Investigation Data - None.
  Stocking - None recently. 300 muskie were planted in 1973.

FISHING TIPS — Small boats and a set of oars are suggested for this shallow stumpy water. Panfish are the main attraction and are caught with the usual live bait offerings. A fly rod and a small popper can also be effective.

CONCLUSION — Bluegill can be caught throughout the year in addition to an occasional muskie. With such a large part of the lake non-navigable by most boats, little fishing activity occurs.

SOUTH PINE LAKE

LOCATION — In the central segment of the area, north of Rhinelander and west of Highway 17.

ACCESS — **Type V:** A navigable access to the southwest end of the lake via the Pine Lake Creek outlet. A canoe or small boat can be put in at the Forest Lane bridge crossing. The creek may be difficult to navigate due to beaver activity.

LAKE CHARACTERISTICS
Size and Depth - 77 acres and 7' deep.
Water Source - Drainage lake: Pine Lake Creek flows through the lake. It enters on the north side and forms the outlet in the southwest corner.
Shoreline - Mainly wetlands. Entirely private, but only with minor development.
Bottom - 60% muck, 25% sand, 15% gravel and rubble.
Vegetation - Heavy densities of both floating and submergent types.

FISHERY
Species - Muskie, Northern Pike, Walleye, Largemouth Bass, Perch, Bluegill, Crappie, Pumpkinseed, Bullhead.
Comment - Muskie and walleye numbers are quite rare compared to previous years. Numerous small pike are now the dominant gamefish.
Seasonal Migrations - Walleye have been known to move up the Pine Lake Creek inlet during the spawning period.

LAKE MANAGEMENT
Lake Investigation Data - None.
Stocking - None.

FISHING TIPS — Fish this lake early in the season before the weeds get too thick. In summer, heavy vegetation hampers both navigation and fishing.

CONCLUSION — South Pine currently offers little to attract anglers... stunted panfish, small northern pike, dense weeds, and a difficult access. Spend your time accordingly.

PINE LAKE

LOCATION — In the north central portion of the area, north of Rhinelander and just west of Highway 17.

ACCESS — **Type V:** Navigable access to the southeast side of the lake via the Pine Lake Creek outlet. Small craft may be put in at a Type III access downstream at the Cross Country Road bridge crossing.

RELATED SERVICES
Boat Rentals - None.
Resorts - Yes, one.
Campgrounds - Yes, a private facility on the east side.

PINE LAKE

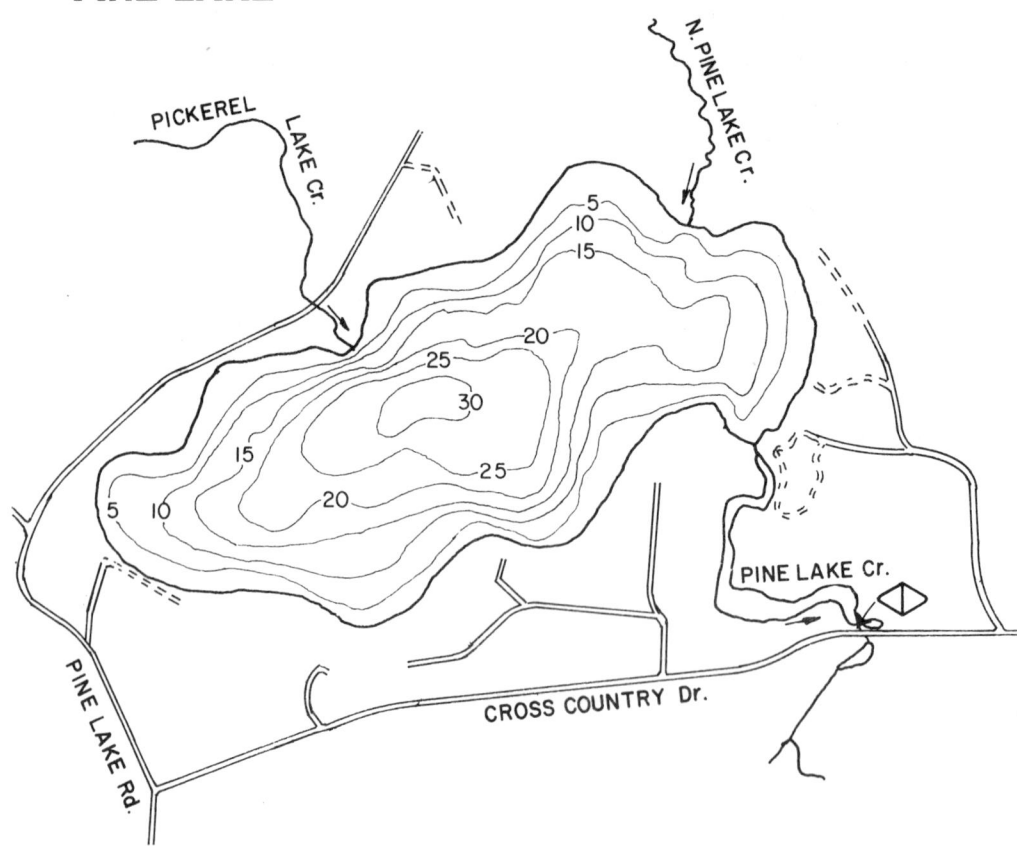

SPECIAL FEATURES — A fairly large lake with little development and no direct access.

LAKE CHARACTERISTICS
Size and Depth - 240 acres and 32 feet.
Water Source - Drainage lake: Two north side inlets - North Pine Lake Creek and Pickerel Lake Creek and a south side outlet to Pine Lake Creek.
Shoreline - 100% private. Mainly upland with some bog type wetlands.
Bottom - 75% sand, 10% gravel, 10% muck, 5% rock.
Water - Medium brown in color and of limited fertility.
Vegetation - Mainly lily pads and bulrush around the shoreline area. Submergent types are limited to depths of less than 5' due to the stained water.

FISHERY
Species - Muskie, Northern Pike, Walleye, Largemouth Bass, Smallmouth Bass, Perch, Bluegill, Pumpkinseed, Bullhead.
Comment - The walleye population is characterized by numerous small fish. Northern pike have a similar status.

Seasonal Migration - Some movement of spawning fish up the inlets occurs annually.

LAKE MANAGEMENT
Lake Investigation Data - None, due to the lack of adequate public access.
Stocking - None recorded.

FISHING TIPS — Distinct structure is virtually nonexistent; therefore subtle features will often hold fish. Also, work the weedlines for northern pike and walleye. The dark water permits active fish to remain quite shallow.

Brightly colored lures will be effective. . . try fluorescent orange or chartreuse for jigs, crankbaits, and spinnerbaits.

CONCLUSION — Without a direct public access both State investigation data and reports from local fishermen are quite rare. However, old reports told of good fishing years ago - little is currently known.

Although the access may require some extra effort, Pine remains an intriguing lake. With its good size and depth, modest fertility, and minimal fishing pressure, some good results should still be possible.

NETTIES LAKE (SYLVAN LAKE)

LOCATION — In the north central part of the area, north of the City of Rhinelander and west of Highway 17.

ACCESS — None public.

LAKE CHARACTERISTICS
Size and Depth - 23 acres and 10 feet.
Water Source - Seepage lake: No inlet or outlet.
Shoreline - Primarily coniferous bog and totally private.
Bottom - 75% muck, 20% sand, 5% gravel and rubble.
Water - Highly infertile and moderately clear. Winterkill is a problem.
Vegetation - Mainly limited to floating types around the shoreline.

FISHERY
Species - Perch, Bluegill, Pumpkinseed, (Largemouth Bass).
Comment - Problems associated with stunted panfish and winterkill continue to plague this lake.

LAKE MANAGEMENT
Lake Investigation Data - None.
Stocking - None, since largemouth bass were planted in the 1950's.

CONCLUSION — As is typical of many small bog lakes. Netties remains of limited fishing value other than its scenic quality.

CRYSTAL LAKE

LOCATION — In the extreme northern segment of the book area, 5 miles due north of Rhinelander and mid-way between Highways 47 and 17.

ACCESS — None public.

SPECIAL FEATURES — Camp Tesomas Boy Scout Camp surrounds Crystal Lake.

LAKE CHARACTERISTICS
- **Size and Depth** - 55 acres and 43 feet.
- **Water Source** - Seepage lake: No inlet or outlet.
- **Shoreline** - Upland and entirely private.
- **Bottom** - 65% sand, 25% gravel, 10% rubble.
- **Water** - Very clear and extremely infertile.
- **Vegetation** - Quite sparse.

FISHERY
- **Species** - Largemouth Bass, Bluegill, Rock Bass.

LAKE MANAGEMENT
- **Lake Investigation Data** - None.
- **Stocking** - None.
- **Treatment** - Two log cribs were installed in 1966.

CONCLUSION — The lack of both public access and fertility should greatly diminish any fishing interest.

DOUGLAS LAKE

LOCATION — In the north central part of the book area, north of Rhinelander and east of Highway 47 and McNaughton.

ACCESS — None public.

LAKE CHARACTERISTICS
- **Size and Depth** - 36 acres and 7 feet.
- **Water Source** - Drainage lake: An inlet on the east side from McCabe Creek. This stream also outlets on the north end to the Wisconsin River.
- **Shoreline** - Mainly wetland and 100% private.
- **Bottom** - 99% muck, 1% sand.
- **Water** - Highly infertile and dark brown in color.
- **Vegetation** - Limited to floating types around the perimeter.

FISHERY
- **Species** - Northern Pike, Largemouth Bass, Perch, Bullhead.
- **Comment** - Little is known of the fishery due to the access situation. Movement of fish up the outlet from the Wisconsin River may occur, although beaver activity may be a hindrance. Other species

may also be present as a result of migrations via the outlet stream.

LAKE MANAGEMENT
  Lake Investigation Data - None.
  Stocking - None.

CONCLUSION — Little is known of Douglas Lake other than what local fishing talk provides. Some anglers have reported good fishing in the past, especially for northern pike and perch.

-LAKES LIMITED IN ACCESS OR FISHERY IN SECTION 3-

BASS LAKE (S8, T37N, R9E)
BERTRAM LAKE
BOX LAKE
CLEAR LAKE (S8, T37N, R9E)
DOYLE LAKE
FETKE LAKE
LITTLE BERTRAM LAKE
MUD LAKE (S7, T37N, R9E)
WOOD CURT LAKE

LOCATION — In the north central part of the book area, all east of Highway 47, west of Highway 17, and north of Rhinelander.

ACCESS — None public, except for Doyle Lake which has a difficult wilderness type access.

LAKE CHARACTERISTICS
  Size and Depth - These lakes range in size from 3 to 33 acres and have maximum depths from 6' to 22'.
  Water Source - All but Bertram Lake are seepage lakes with no inlets or outlets. A small outlet flows from Bertram Lake.
  Shoreline - Bertram Lake and Fetke Lake are mostly upland. The remaining lakes are entirely surrounded by bog.
  Bottom - Predominantly muck.
  Water - Extremely infertile. Most are clear, but Box, Bertram, Doyle, and Wood Curt Lakes are brown in color.
  Vegetation - Mainly limited to lily pads around the shoreline zone. However, Bertram Lake and Clear Lake have significant growths of submergent varieties.

FISHERY
  Species - Largemouth Bass, Bluegill.
  Comment - In addition to bass and bluegill, Clear Lake contains northern pike and Fetke Lake is reported to have crappie.
    As expected, the access situation greatly limits information on these waters with some lakes completely lacking information on their fisheries.

CONCLUSION — Another group of small infertile lakes with poor to marginal fisheries that create little interest for fishermen.

SECTION 4

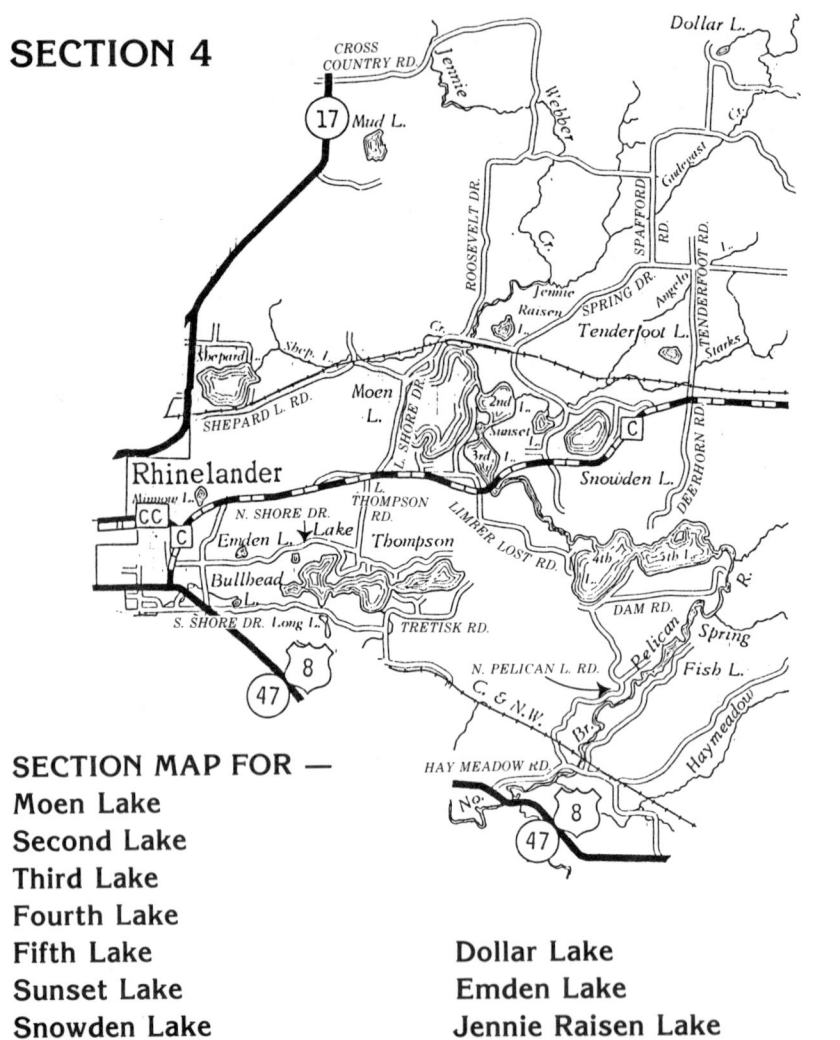

SECTION MAP FOR —
Moen Lake
Second Lake
Third Lake
Fourth Lake
Fifth Lake
Sunset Lake
Snowden Lake
Lake Thompson
Shepard Lake
Gudegast Creek
Bullhead Lake

Dollar Lake
Emden Lake
Jennie Raisen Lake
Long Lake (S11, T36N, R9E)
Minnow Lake
Mud Lake (S11, T37N, R9E)
Tenderfoot Lake

MOEN LAKE

LOCATION — In the east part of the book area, immediately north of Highway C and east of Rhinelander.

ACCESS — △ **Type I (Public):** On the west side of the lake; drive 0.9 mile north on Lake Shore Drive from Highway C to the marked access on the right. This county-owned facility has a blacktop approach to a concrete plank landing. Parking for 5-6 rigs is provided. This landing often suffers severe ice damage and can be rough.

Ⓑ Type III: At the southwest corner of the lake, take Lake Shore Drive 0.7 mile north off Highway C to this roadside facility. A short carry-in for small boats or canoes is required.

Type V: A navigable access from Second Lake and the rest of the Chain via a short channel on the east side.

RELATED SERVICES

Boat Rentals - Yes, at the resorts.
Bait Shops - Yes, in nearby Rhinelander.
Resorts - Yes, several.
Campgrounds - Yes, a private facility located on the west side.
Public Parks - None.
Guide Services - Yes.

SPECIAL FEATURES — Moen Lake is the largest of the five lakes on the Moen Chain. The other lakes of the Chain are Second, Third, Fourth, and Fifth Lake. Note: Be careful when navigating between lakes, as the channels are shallow and rocky in some places.

LAKE CHARACTERISTICS

Size and Depth - 460 acres and 11 feet.
Water Source - Drainage lake: Two inlets, Shepard Lake Creek and Gudegast Creek, enter on the north end. An outlet channel to Second Lake and the rest of the Chain is located on the east side.
Shoreline - Primarily upland with only limited areas of wetland. All in private ownership, except for the west side landing.
Bottom - 70% sand, 20% muck, 10% gravel and rubble.
Water - Dark brown in color and somewhat infertile.
Vegetation - Generally sparse, except for the shallow north end which has dense submergent growths near the inlets. Reeds, bulrushes, and lily pads are also present. The dark water limits weed growth to a depth of 5'.

FISHERY

Species
  Primary - Walleye, Crappie.
  Secondary - Muskie, Perch.
  Limited - Northern Pike, Smallmouth Bass, Largemouth Bass, Bluegill, Pumpkinseed, Rock Bass.
Comment - Although decent-sized fish are present, the walleye population is characterized by high numbers of small fish.
Seasonal Migrations - Some movement of spawning walleye up the inlet streams does occur. Also, there is a general movement of fish between the lakes of the Chain.
Forage - Mainly shiners and juvenile panfish. Forage fish appear to be in short supply.

LAKE MANAGEMENT

Lake Investigation Data - Despite the lake's size and heavy use, no comprehensive lake surveys have been conducted since the

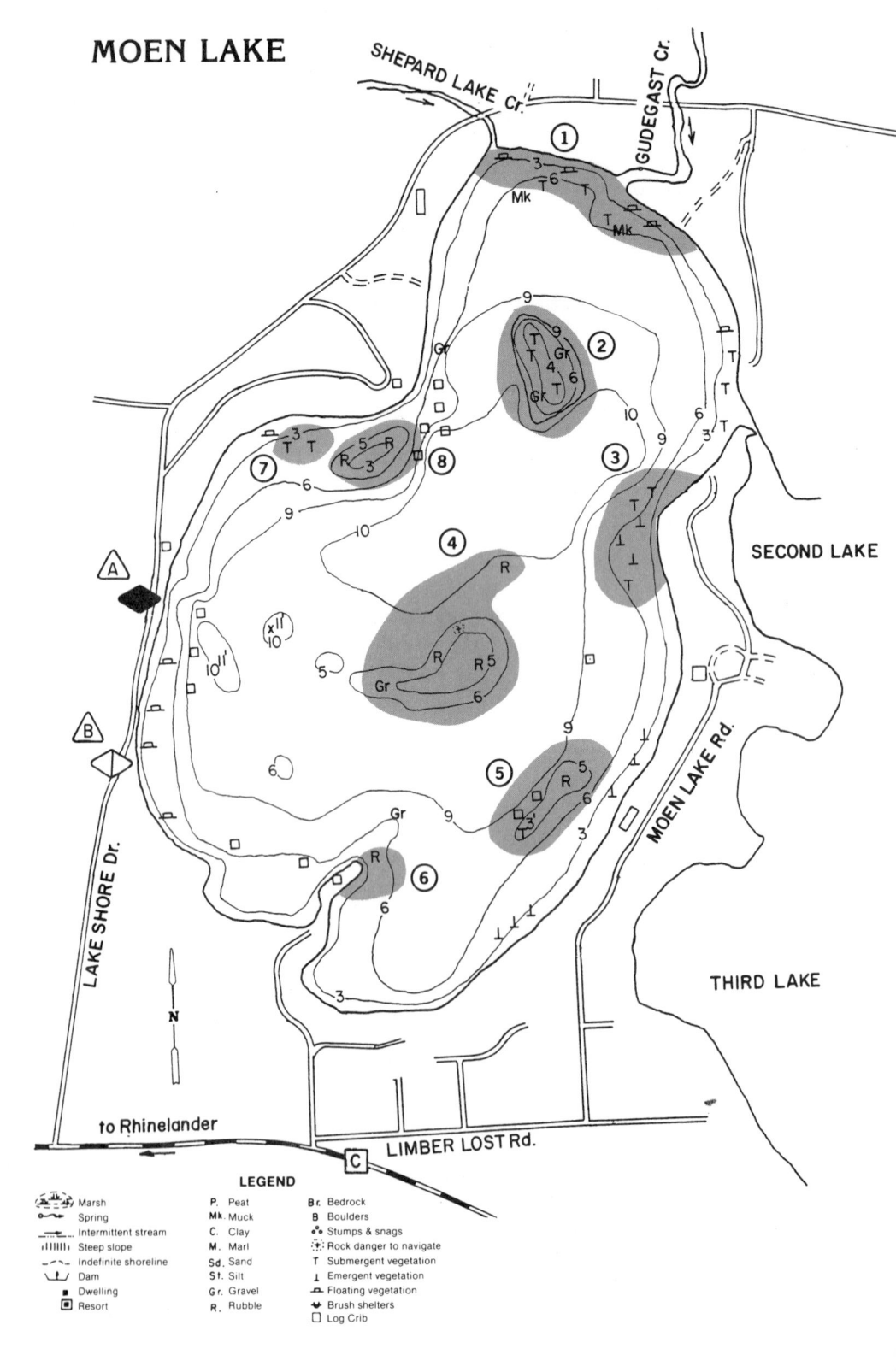

MOEN LAKE

LEGEND

- Marsh
- Spring
- Intermittent stream
- Steep slope
- Indefinite shoreline
- Dam
- Dwelling
- Resort

- **P.** Peat
- **Mk.** Muck
- **C.** Clay
- **M.** Marl
- **Sd.** Sand
- **St.** Silt
- **Gr.** Gravel
- **R.** Rubble

- **Br.** Bedrock
- **B.** Boulders
- Stumps & snags
- Rock danger to navigate
- **T** Submergent vegetation
- Emergent vegetation
- Floating vegetation
- Brush shelters
- Log Crib

early 60's. The State's management role has primarily involved stocking.

Stocking - A long history of muskie stocking exists... recent plantings are shown below.

YEAR	SPECIES	NUMBER	SIZE
1980	Muskie	470	12"
1981	Muskie	500	10"
1983	Walleye	23,000	Fingerling

Walleye have been stocked intermittently in the past.

Treatment - Twelve log cribs were installed in the mid-80's by the Moen's Lake Community Club (see map for location).

LAKE SURVEY MAP — Fishing Areas Shaded

Area (1) Inletting water and weeds will attract muskie throughout the season. The area around the mouth of Gudegast Creek is particularly good.

Area (2) This mid-lake weedbed can provide action for a variety of species. Look for panfish up in the weeds and walleye down on the sides.

Area (3) Work the break just out from the bulrush edge for crappie. Small minnows fished below a bobber are effective as are small tube jigs or Twisters. Cast for muskie with jerkbaits or bucktails.

Area (4) The edge of the large rocky flat is a "Hot Spot" for walleye. A jig and minnow will take early season fish. Shallow running crankbaits have produced fish after dark on top of the bar during summer.

Area (5) Look for crappie around this rock pile. Also try casting a jig and minnow for spring walleye.

Area (6) The east side of the point is a good spot for muskie all season long.

Area (7) Both muskie and northern pike can be found in the small weedbed off the west shore. Try spinnerbaits for pike and jerkbaits for muskie.

Area (8) This popular spring location is fished for walleye and crappie. Traditional jig n' minnow presentations should be used for walleye.

FISHING TIPS —
The dark brown water will call for brightly colored lures... fluorescent orange or chartreuse are good choices. Jigs rigged with yellow, white, or chartreuse Twister Tails have been effective for walleye. When jigging with live bait, minnows will be more productive than either leeches or crawlers.

Since distinct fish holding structure is minimal, walleye can often be found dispersed throughout the lake basin. Try drift fishing with jig combos or slip sinker/floating jigs for these scattered walleye.

Muskie anglers should work the numerous 'edge' areas along the bulrush beds, especially on the east side. Bucktails and light or natural colored jerkbaits are suggested.

CONCLUSION — Moen Lake is one of the better lakes in the area with muskie, walleye, and crappie being the main attractions. For best results fish it early in the season for walleye - summer can be slow.
Muskie anglers can expect good action throughout the season. Catch and release is urged.

SECOND LAKE

LOCATION — In the eastern segment of the area, east of, and connected to Moen Lake.

ACCESS — **Type V:** A navigable access from Moen Lake through a marked channel and one from Third Lake via a short channel.

RELATED SERVICES — See Moen Lake Report.

SPECIAL FEATURES — Part of the Moen Lake Chain.

LAKE CHARACTERISTICS
  Size and Depth - 111 acres and 11 feet.
  Water Source - Drainage lake: An inlet channel from Moen Lake on the west side, Starks Creek enters on the east side, and the outlet channel to Third Lake on the south side.
  Shoreline - Mostly bog, except for the west side. 100% privately-owned.
  Bottom - 55% muck, 30% sand, 10% gravel, 5% rock.
  Water - Infertile and dark brown in color.
  Vegetation - Moderate quantities of both floating and submergent varieties are present.

FISHERY
  Species - Muskie, Northern Pike, Walleye, Largemouth Bass, Smallmouth Bass, Crappie, Perch, Bluegill, Rock Bass, Pumpkinseed, Bullhead.
  Comment - Relative abundance similar to that of Moen Lake.
  Seasonal Migrations - Movement of fish between the lakes of the Chain occurs.

LAKE MANAGEMENT
  Lake Investigation Data - None.
  Stocking - None recently. 400 10" muskie were stocked in the mid-70's.

FISHING TIPS — Weeds, logs, and fallen trees comprise the essential fish holding cover within the bowl-shaped basin of Second Lake. The gravel area along the north shore offers the only spawning habitat for walleye... work this spot early in the season with jig and minnow combinations.
  Fish the entire shoreline for muskie using surface lures during summer. In fall, cast in and around the 'drowned wood' using large brightly colored crankbaits.

CONCLUSION — Second Lake is often overlooked when fishing the Chain. But be sure to give it a try... especially if action is slow or its too windy on the other lakes of the Chain.

THIRD LAKE

LOCATION — In the east central portion of the area, east of Rhinelander and north of and adjacent to Highway C.

ACCESS — **Ⓐ Type I (Private):** On the west side of the lake; take Limber Lost Road east from Highway C for 0.4 mile to Moen Lake Road. Turn left and follow Moen Lake Road another 0.4 mile to the resort/access facility located on the right. A metal grate landing with a loading pier is provided. Boat rental, gas, and oil are also available. Please get permission at the tavern before using this facility.
Ⓑ Type III (Public): On the south end of the lake at the Highway C bridge crossing. Shore fishing is also possible along the right-of-way.
Type V: A navigable access via the channel from Second Lake.
Type V: A navigable access to the south end of the lake from Fourth and Fifth Lakes via the North Branch of the Pelican River. Caution is recommended since portions of the river are shallow and rocky.

SPECIAL FEATURES — Third Lake is part of the Moen Chain.

LAKE CHARACTERISTICS
Size and Depth - 103 acres and 14 feet.
Water Source - Drainage lake: The channel from Second Lake enters on the north side and an outlet to the North Branch of the Pelican River is on the south end.
Shoreline - Predominantly upland and private.
Bottom - 45% sand, 35% muck, 20% gravel and rubble.
Water - Infertile and of medium brown color.
Vegetation - Moderate growths of both floating and submergent types... pondweeds and lily pads being the most common.

FISHERY
Species - Muskie, Northern Pike, Walleye, Largemouth Bass, Smallmouth Bass, Crappie, Perch, Bluegill, Rock Bass, Pumpkinseed, Bullhead.
Comment - See Moen Lake Report for species status.
Seasonal Migrations - A spring migration of walleye occurs from Fourth and Fifth Lakes up the North Branch of the Pelican River.

LAKE MANAGEMENT
Lake Investigation Data - None.
Stocking - None since 1977 when 300 8" muskie were released.
Treatment - Four fish cribs where installed by the Moen's Lake Community Club in the mid-80's.

THIRD LAKE

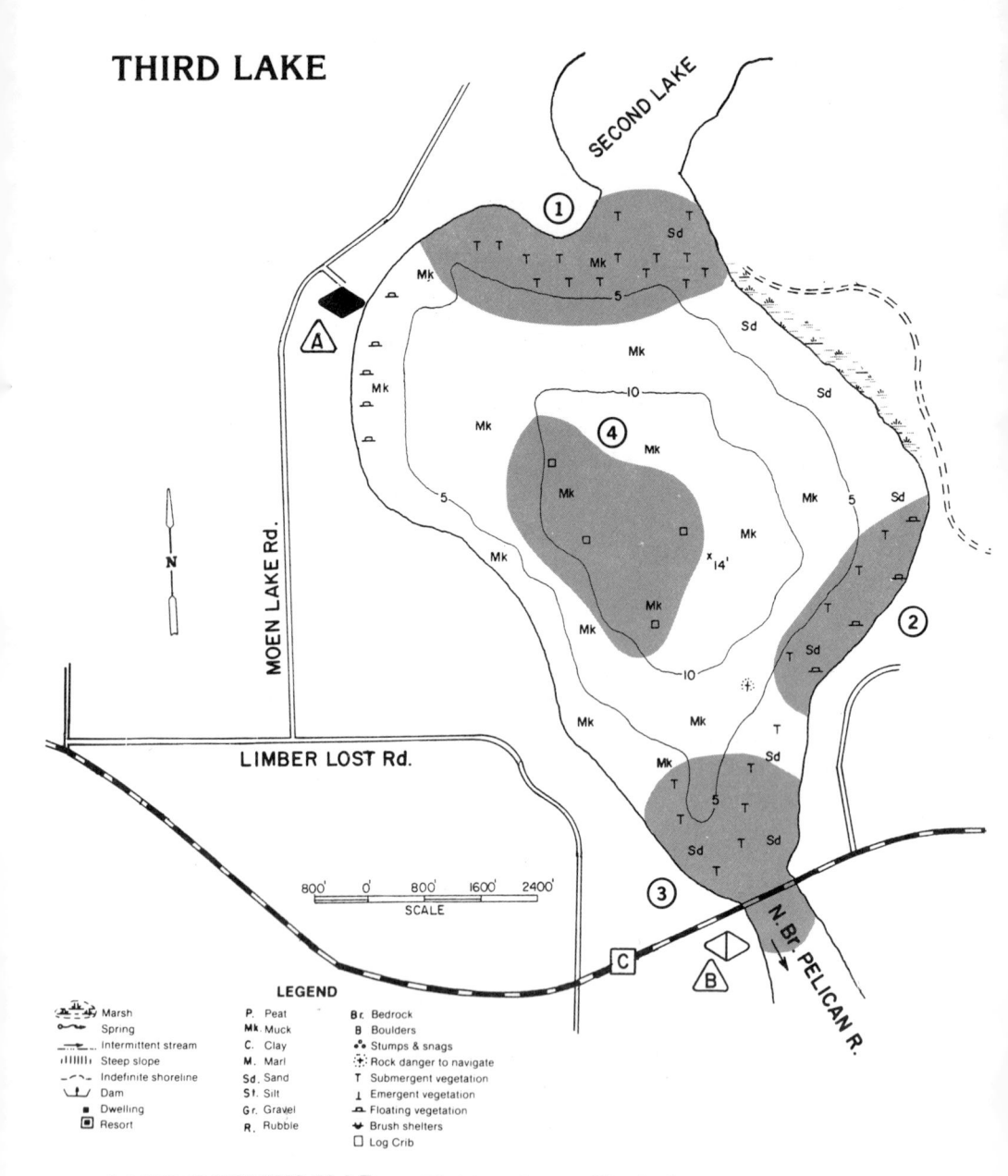

LAKE SURVEY MAP — Fishing Areas Shaded

    Area (1) The weedbed at the north end can be productive for panfish and muskie. Due to its proximity to the channel, fish it early or late in the day when boat traffic is down.

    Area (2) Work along the weed edge on the east side for muskie. Bucktails and jerkbaits are local favorites on the Chain.

    Area (3) This region near the Highway C bridge is most popular for early spring walleye. Shore fishing with jig and minnows or a slip bobber and minnow will take fish. Try here later in the season for panfish.

Area (4) Drift across the main basin for summer crappie with a small minnow or Twister Tail on a 1/16 oz. jig. Also, use your depthfinder to locate the four cribs - work these shelters for both panfish and walleye. This area is also an ice fishing "Hot Spot" for crappie during the winter months.

FISHING TIPS — Seasonal changes and trends must be considered in order to be successful on Third Lake. Fish early in the season and again in fall for walleye, summer and fall for muskie. Crappie can be active year-around.

Also, keep your lure selections bright. Fluorescent oranges and chartreuse are always good colors for jigs. Muskie bucktails with brass or copper blades are effective in the dark water.

CONCLUSION — Third Lake is another good lake on the Chain. It tends to be overlooked once the spring walleye run is over, but should be fished throughout the season...especially for muskie.

FOURTH AND FIFTH LAKES (NORTH PELICAN)

LOCATION — In the eastern portion of the book area, south of Highway C and east of Rhinelander.

ACCESS — **Type III:** To the extreme eastern end of the lake; take Haymeadow Road east off Highway 8 for 1.0 mile to North Pelican Lake Road. Turn left (north) and go 2.9 miles to the intersection with Dam Road. Stay to the right and follow Dam Road 1.8 miles to the carry-in access at the dam. Put in on the upstream side of the dam, the main part of the lake is a short distance up the channel.
Type V: A navigable access from Third Lake via the North Branch of the Pelican River.
Note: Navigate the river cautiously as there are many shallow rocky areas that can damage your motor.

RELATED SERVICES
Boat Rentals - Yes, nearby on Moen Lake and Third Lake.
Bait Shops - None.
Resorts - None.
Public Parks and Campgrounds - None.
Guide Services - Yes.

SPECIAL FEATURES — Part of the Moen Chain.

LAKE CHARACTERISTICS
Size and Depth - 498 total acres and 9 feet.
Water Source - Drainage lake: The North Branch of the Pelican River forms both the inlet and outlet. It enters on the north side of Fourth Lake and exits via a dammed outlet on the southeast corner of Fifth Lake.

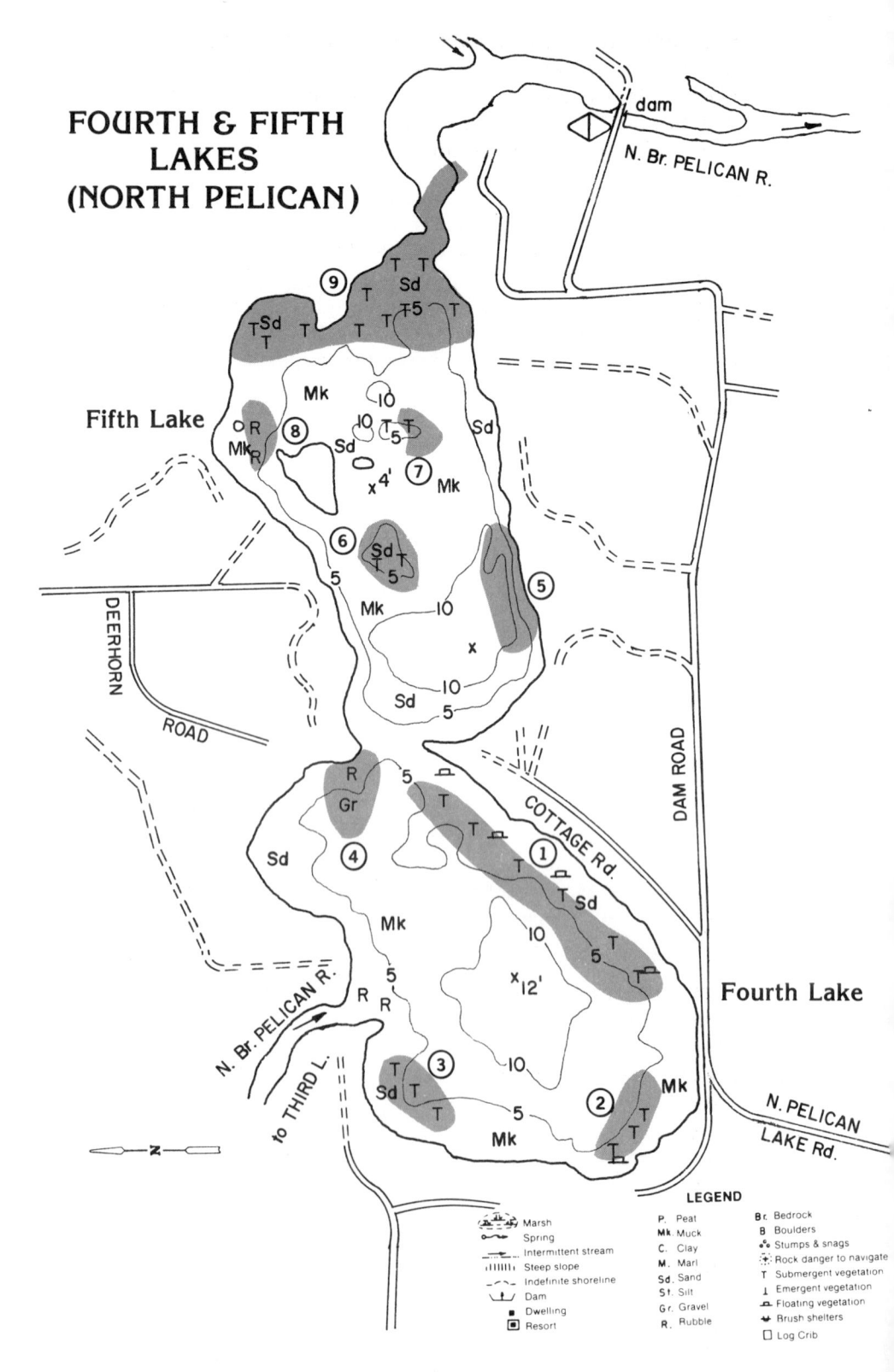

FOURTH & FIFTH LAKES (NORTH PELICAN)

Fifth Lake

Fourth Lake

LEGEND

- Marsh
- Spring
- Intermittent stream
- Steep slope
- Indefinite shoreline
- Dam
- Dwelling
- Resort

P. Peat
Mk. Muck
C. Clay
M. Marl
Sd. Sand
St. Silt
Gr. Gravel
R. Rubble

Br. Bedrock
B. Boulders
- Stumps & snags
- Rock danger to navigate
T Submergent vegetation
⊥ Emergent vegetation
- Floating vegetation
- Brush shelters
☐ Log Crib

Shoreline - 85% upland and almost entirely private.
Bottom - 65% sand, 20% rock, 10% gravel, 5% muck.
Water - Dark brown in color and infertile.
Vegetation - Moderate quantities of floating and submergent types. Generally limited to the shoreline zone or depths of less than 5'.

FISHERY
Species
Primary - Walleye, Crappie.
Secondary - Muskie, Perch.
Limited - Northern Pike, Smallmouth Bass, Largemouth Bass, Bluegill, Pumpkinseed, Rock Bass.

Comment - As in the rest of the Chain, crappie dominate the panfish community.

Seasonal Migrations - A spawning migration of walleye up the North Branch of the Pelican River occurs annually.

LAKE MANAGEMENT
Lake Investigation Data - None.

Stocking - The most recent was a 1977 planting of an unknown number of 6" muskie.

Treatment - Applications for chemical weed control have been made in the past.

LAKE SURVEY MAP - Fishing Areas Shaded

Area (1) The weed edge that runs along most of the south shore will hold both muskie and walleye. Cast bucktails parallel to the weedline for muskie.

Area (2) Early season walleye will relate to the drop-off just beyond the weedline at the west end of the lake. A fluorescent orange jig tipped with a minnow is a good choice.

Area (3) Immediately west of the Pelican River inlet is a good bed of cabbage. Muskie and panfish can be found here.

Area (4) This rocky bar extends off the point and has been a good producer of spring walleye. Work a redtail chub on a 1/16 oz. jig over the rocks and gravel.

Area (5) This zone off of the southern shore has the sharpest drop-off found in the lake and is another spot for spring and early summer walleye.

Area (6) Rising to about 5', this mid-lake sand flat has scattered patches of cabbage on top. Look for crappie in spring, while muskie may be found here all season long. Surface baits such as Hawg Wobblers should be worked over the weeds.

Area (7) Fish the drop-off adjacent to this cabbage bed for spring time crappie. A 1/16 oz. pink jig with a white Twister or a small minnow should do the job.

Area (8) A small rocky island holds spawning walleye . . . fish here early with a jig and minnow.

Area (9) The east end of Fifth Lake is shallow and quite weedy. Fish it early before the weeds get too thick. Once the weeds have developed move out along the edge. A variety of species can be taken here.

FISHING TIPS — The dark, highly stained water permits fish to remain active rather shallow - especially if weed cover is available. Don't overlook the shallows... even in summer.

Live bait selection is similar to that on Moen, with minnows being preferred year-around.

CONCLUSION — Fourth and Fifth Lakes receive the least amount of fishing pressure of any of the lakes on the Moen Chain... probably due to the limited direct public access and the rather long trip down river from Third Lake. Take the time to make the trip... the results can make it very worthwhile.

SUNSET LAKE

LOCATION — In the east segment of the book area, east of Moen Lake and north of Highway C.

ACCESS — Type V: A navigable access via Starks Creek from Second Lake of the Moen Chain. This creek passes through a culvert and is limited to small boats and canoes. Fluctuating water levels will also influence the use of this access.

LAKE CHARACTERISTICS
Size and Depth - 33 acres and 15 feet.
Water Source - Drainage lake: Starks Creek enters on the east side and outlets on the north end.
Shoreline - Mostly bog and privately-owned.
Bottom - Almost entirely muck with small areas of sand and gravel.
Water - Light brown in color and slightly fertile.
Vegetation - Moderate densities of submergent and floating varieties around the perimeter.

FISHERY
Species - Muskie, Northern Pike, Walleye, Largemouth Bass, Crappie, Perch, Bluegill, Pumpkinseed, Rock Bass, Bullhead.
Comment - Bluegill and crappie are the main panfish species. Some movement of fish to and from the Moen Chain occurs.

LAKE MANAGEMENT
Lake Investigation Data - None.
Stocking - None.
Treatment - None.

FISHING TIPS — Sunset is yet another small shallow lake where shoreline weeds and wood are the key to success. Work the edge for both panfish and gamefish.

Some nice bluegill can be taken in early summer. Look for muskie and bass to provide the gamefish action.

CONCLUSION — Without any direct public access fishing pressure on Sunset is limited to lake front property owners, or fishermen willing to navigate the stream. This can make for an enjoyable diversion from the Moen Chain.

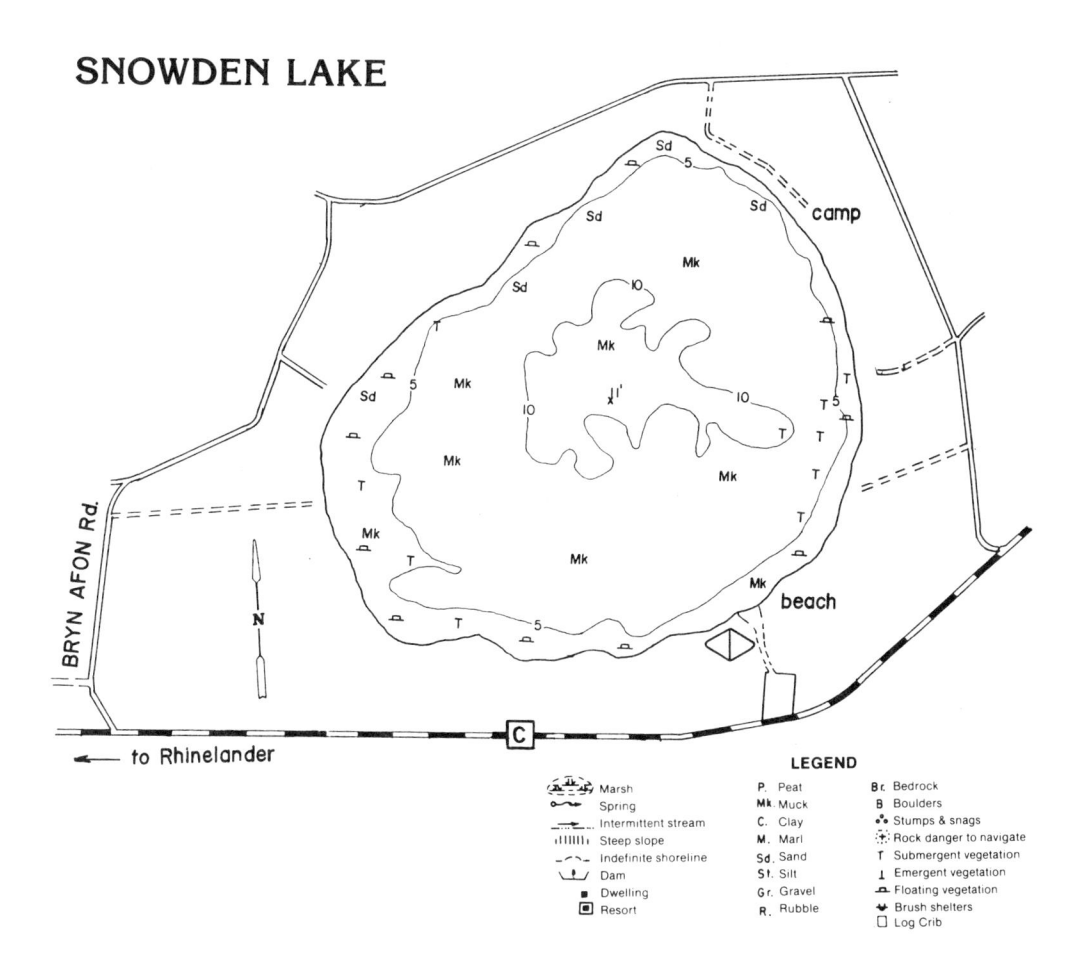

SNOWDEN LAKE

SNOWDEN LAKE

LOCATION — In the eastern portion of the area, north of Highway C and east of Moen Lake.

ACCESS — **Type III (Public):** On the south side of the lake; follow Highway C 0.7 mile east of the Highway C and Bryn Afon Road intersection to a small, unmarked gravel parking lot. A short trail leads to the beach/landing site.

SPECIAL FEATURES — A small town-owned swimming beach is provided.

LAKE CHARACTERISTICS
Size and Depth - 135 acres and 12 feet.
Water Source - Seepage lake: No inlet or outlet.
Shoreline - Predominantly upland with scattered areas of bog. Entirely private except for the access.
Bottom - 85% sand, 10% gravel, 5% muck.
Water - Somewhat clear and infertile. Winterkill has been known to occur in the past.
Vegetation - Heavy growths of floating and submergent types. Lily pads are common.

FISHERY
Species - Largemouth Bass, Smallmouth Bass, Perch, Bluegill, Crappie, Rock Bass, Pumpkinseed, Bullhead, (Muskie), (Walleye).
Comment - Largemouth bass are the dominant gamefish and bluegill the primary panfish species.

LAKE MANAGEMENT
Lake Investigation Data - None. However, state records indicate that periodic fish kills have occurred in spring during previous years. The exact cause of mortality was not determined.

FISHING TIPS — Working the shoreline weeds and wood is the best approach to fishing Snowden. Floating Rapalas or Beetle Spins will take bass. Try a small leech for bluegill. A fly rod can add to the fun when the 'gills' are active.

CONCLUSION — Some nice bass and a few decent panfish should make Snowden a lake to consider spending some time on.

LAKE THOMPSON

LOCATION — In the east central portion of the area, just east of the City of Rhinelander and north of Highway 8.

ACCESS — **Type I (Public):** To the north side of the lake; go east from Highway C on North Shore Drive for 2.4 miles to Lake Thompson Road. Turn right (south) staying on North Shore Drive another 0.5 mile to the town access on the right. There is a gravel approach to a concrete plank landing. Limited off-road parking can accommodate only 1-2 rigs.

RELATED SERVICES
Boat Rentals - Yes.
Bait Shops - Yes, in nearby Rhinelander.
Resorts - Yes, several.

Public Parks - None.
Campgrounds - Yes, a private facility on the south side.
Guide Services - Yes.

SPECIAL FEATURES — Lake Thompson is quite developed and has a high recreational use during summer.

LAKE CHARACTERISTICS

Size and Depth - 382 acres and 35 feet.

Water Source - Drainage lake: A small unnamed inlet enters on the northeast end and the Lake George Creek outlet is on the south side.

Shoreline - 99% private and quite developed. Mostly upland with some adjoining bog-type wetlands.

Bottom - 55% sand, 25% muck, 15% gravel, 5% rock.

Water - Light brown and moderately clear with limited fertility. Dissolved oxygen is inadequate below 17' during summer. The thermocline begins at 15'.

Vegetation - Floating, emergent, and submergent types are all found. Some of the common types are bulrush, cabbage, pickerel weed, and water lily.

FISHERY

Species

Primary - Walleye, Crappie, Bluegill, Perch.

Secondary - Muskie, Pumpkinseed, Rock Bass.

Limited - Northern Pike, Smallmouth Bass, Largemouth Bass.

Comment - Walleye growth rates are below the area average, while muskie growth rates are average for this part of the state.

Forage - Young-of-the-year bluegill, perch, and bluntnose minnows.

LAKE MANAGEMENT

Lake Investigation Data - Listed below are the results of a recent spring fyke net survey conducted to evaluate the fishery.

SPECIES	NUMBER	SIZE RANGE
Walleye	299	9"-22"
Muskie	25	25"-40"
Northern Pike	22	14"-34"
Crappie	335	6"-13"
Perch	183	5 1/2"-12"
Bluegill	59	4"-7"
Smallmouth Bass	2	8"-16"

A follow-up study later that fall assessed natural reproduction. Poor reproduction was evident for walleye, crappie, and muskie. However, good levels were seen for bluegill and perch.

Stocking -

YEAR	SPECIES	NUMBER	SIZE
1980	Muskie	980	10"
1981	Walleye	10,000	Fingerling
1983	Walleye	19,000	Fingerling
1984	Muskie	650	10"
1987	Walleye	19,000	3"

Treatment - A few fish shelters were installed in the early 60's.

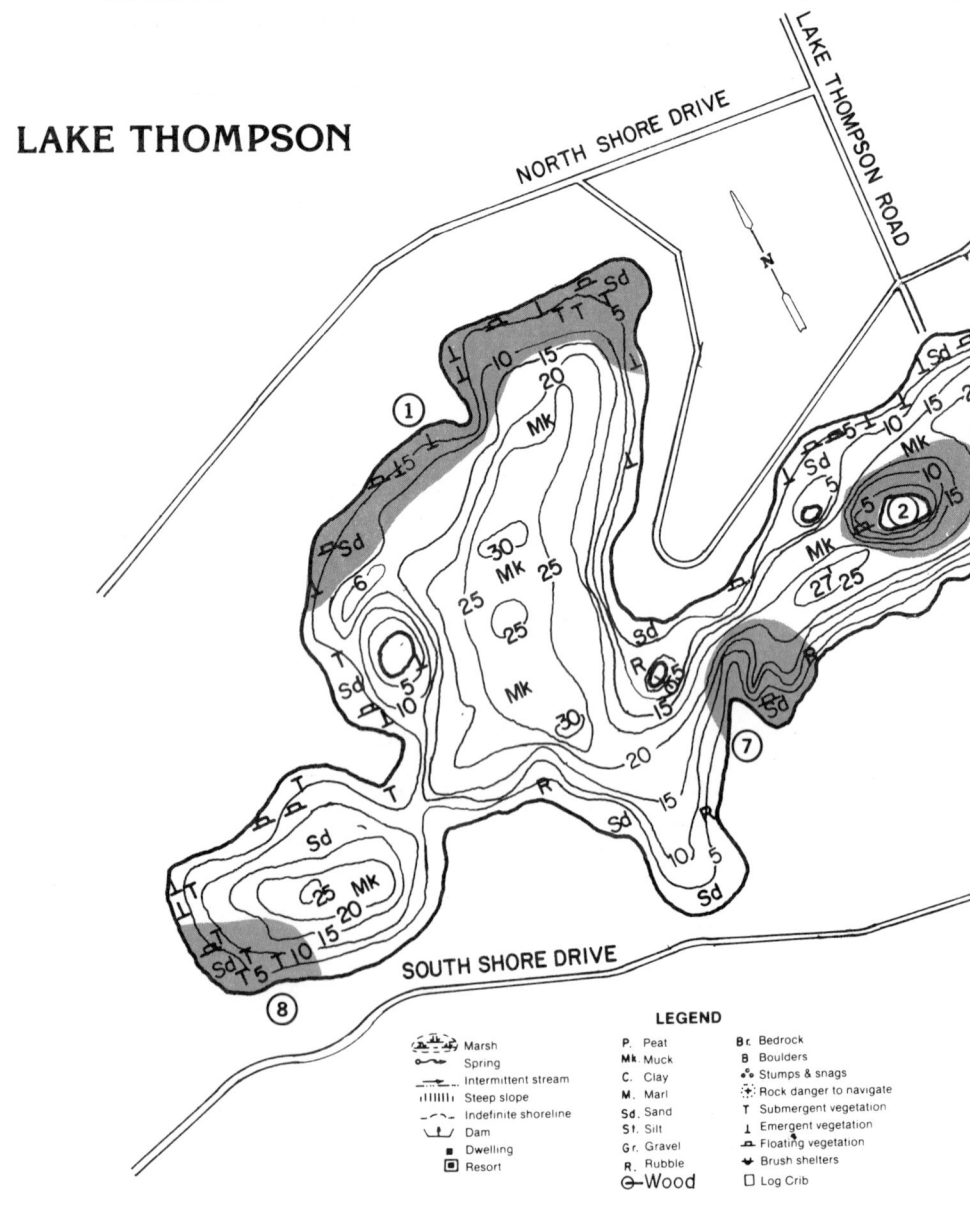

LAKE THOMPSON

LEGEND

- Marsh
- Spring
- Intermittent stream
- Steep slope
- Indefinite shoreline
- Dam
- Dwelling
- Resort

- P. Peat
- Mk. Muck
- C. Clay
- M. Marl
- Sd. Sand
- St. Silt
- Gr. Gravel
- R. Rubble
- Wood

- Br. Bedrock
- B. Boulders
- Stumps & snags
- Rock danger to navigate
- T Submergent vegetation
- Emergent vegetation
- Floating vegetation
- Brush shelters
- Log Crib

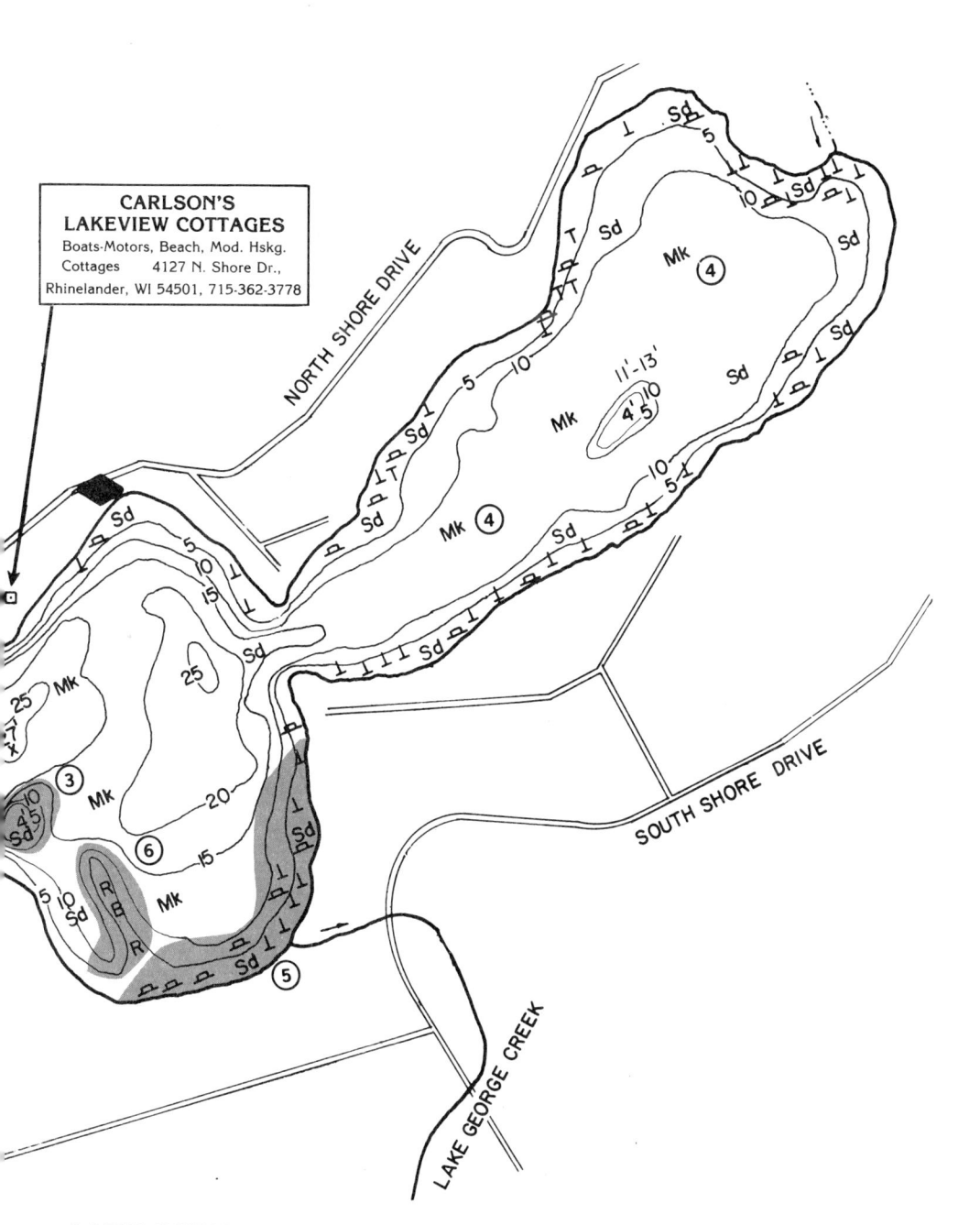

CARLSON'S LAKEVIEW COTTAGES
Boats-Motors, Beach, Mod. Hskg.
Cottages   4127 N. Shore Dr.,
Rhinelander, WI 54501, 715-362-3778

LAKE SURVEY MAP — Fishing Areas Shaded

    Area (1) This bay on the northwest end has cabbage extending out to about 5'. Try here for muskie in early summer and again in fall. Cast surface lures and jerkbaits over the shallower weeds... crankbaits and bucktails along the deeper edges.

    Area (2) Crappie and walleye relate to this island year-around. Fluorescent orange 1/16 oz. jigs tipped with a minnow will take early season walleye. After the weeds develop try a minnow or leech below a slip bobber. An occasional muskie is also possible.

Area (3) Try tossing bucktails and crankbaits around this offshore rock bar for muskie. Yellow/black and perch patterns are effective on this water.

Area (4) A number of species can be found around the weedy east end. Panfish are available all year. Use a slip bobber or small jig to take 'weed walleye'. Also drift and cast for muskie. Be sure to try around the underwater hump in the center.

Area (5) This stretch of the southern shore has good growths of cabbage. Both muskie and walleye can be found along the edge... especially where it turns in or out. Try crankbaits like Shad Raps or Shadlings for walleye.

Area (6) Muskie can be found relating to this rocky point. Jerkbaits and surface baits are productive.

Area (7) This point on the south side should be fished for crappie year-around. Small jigs and minnows or slip bobber rigs are suggested.

Area (8) The extreme southwest corner has a nice bed of cabbage that holds muskie.

FISHING TIPS — Extremely heavy use by boaters and water skiers demands that your fishing be done early or late in the day. Spring and fall are also recommended.

Muskie fishermen should work surface baits over the many shallow weedbeds. Globes and Flap-Tails have proven effective for some local anglers. Black or natural colored bucktails are also a good choice.

Walleye anglers must remain versatile... be prepared to use jigs, slip bobbers, and crankbaits, concentrating your efforts on the weedline areas.

CONCLUSION — Lake Thompson has a good blend of weeds and structure that make it one of the more interesting and popular lakes in the area. Crappie through the ice draw many anglers during winter, while open water fishermen will find muskie and walleye the main feature. Although heavy recreational use may hinder your efforts during summer, Lake Thompson definitely merits attention.

SHEPARD LAKE

LOCATION — In the central part of the book area, northeast of the City of Rhinelander and immediately east of Highway 17.

ACCESS — None public.

LAKE CHARACTERISTICS
Size and Depth - 179 acres and 18 feet.
Water Source - Drainage lake: Minor inlets from surrounding wetlands and an outlet on the east side to Shepard Lake Creek.
Shoreline - 50% upland, 50% wetland. Completely private.

Bottom - 60% sand, 20% rock, 10% gravel, 10% muck.
Water - Light brown in color and quite infertile.
Vegetation - Heavy concentrations have been a problem in the past.

FISHERY
Species - Muskie, Northern Pike, Walleye, Perch, Crappie, Bluegill, Pumpkinseed.

Comment - Stunted panfish are prevalent. The status of gamefish is essentially unknown due to the absence of public access, but are thought to be in poor standing in terms of both condition and numbers.

LAKE MANAGEMENT
Lake Investigation Data - None.
Stocking - None.

CONCLUSION
Shepard is yet another lake that at one time had a reputation as a decent recreational lake. But in addition to its extreme infertility and marginal fishery, the loss of its public access has greatly diminished any fishing interest.

GUDEGAST CREEK

LOCATION — In the very northeastern part of the book area, northeast of Moen Lake.

ACCESS — Public access is available at four town road bridge crossings; Section 9 Road, two crossings of Spafford Road, and Lakeshore Drive just upstream from Moen Lake.

SPECIAL FEATURES — Gudegast Creek is the only stocked trout stream in the book area.

STREAM CHARACTERISTICS
Size and Depth - 5.6 miles with an average depth of 2 1/2 feet. 4.1 of the 5.6 miles within the book area are considered trout waters.

Water Source - Originates as the outlet of Stella Lake. Hutchinson Creek, Lela Creek, and Jennie Weber Creek are the main tributaries.

Shoreline - About 50% of the adjacent lands are in agricultural use, while the other 50% is wooded.

Water - Slightly fertile and light brown in color.

FISHERY
Species - Brook Trout, Northern Pike, Crappie, Perch, Walleye, Burbot, Suckers.

Comment - The warmwater fish species are generally found downstream from the confluence of Jennie Weber Creek.

The stream has a Class I rating from the southernmost crossing of Spafford Road downstream to Jennie Weber Creek. Class

II status is assigned to the stretch between the two crossings of Spafford Road.

STREAM MANAGEMENT

Stream Investigation Data - None recently.
Stocking -

YEAR	SPECIES	NUMBER	SIZE
1983	Brook Trout	300	9"
1984	Brook Trout	300	Yearling
1985	Brook Trout	300	Yearling
1986	Brook Trout	300	Yearling
1987	Brook Trout	300	Yearling

Treatment - None.

CONCLUSION — If brook trout are your quarry and you like to fish small streams give this water a try.

-LAKES LIMITED IN ACCESS OR FISHERY IN SECTION 4 -

BULLHEAD LAKE
DOLLAR LAKE
EMDEN LAKE
JENNIE RAISEN LAKE
LONG LAKE (S11, T36N, R9E)
MINNOW LAKE
MUD LAKE (S11, T37N, R9E)
TENDERFOOT LAKE

LOCATION — In the eastern segment of the book area, all east of Highway 17 and north of Highway 8.

ACCESS — None public.

LAKE CHARACTERISTICS

Size and Depth - Five to fifty acres in size with a range of 11'-22' maximum depth.

Water Source - All but Bullhead Lake are seepage lakes: No inlets or outlets. Bullhead Lake is a drainage lake with a small outlet on the north side.

Shoreline - Mostly in private ownership. Largely bog type wetlands with only limited uplands. Bullhead and Long Lake are bordered by lands owned by local school districts, but remain difficult to reach.

Bottom - Nearly all muck, except for Jennie Raisen Lake which has significant areas of hard bottom.

Water - Very infertile and ranging from clear to dark brown in color.

Vegetation - Generally sparse and restricted to the shoreline zone.

FISHERY

Species - Largemouth Bass and Panfish comprise most of the fish communities.

Comment - The panfish in these lakes are often stunted as a result of the infertility. Bass, when present, are often slow-growing fish in poor condition. However, a few quality size bass may be present.

CONCLUSION — This group is characterized by a number of 'bog lakes' having stained acidic water of low fertility. With water chemistry such as this, the resultant fishery has little to offer anglers.

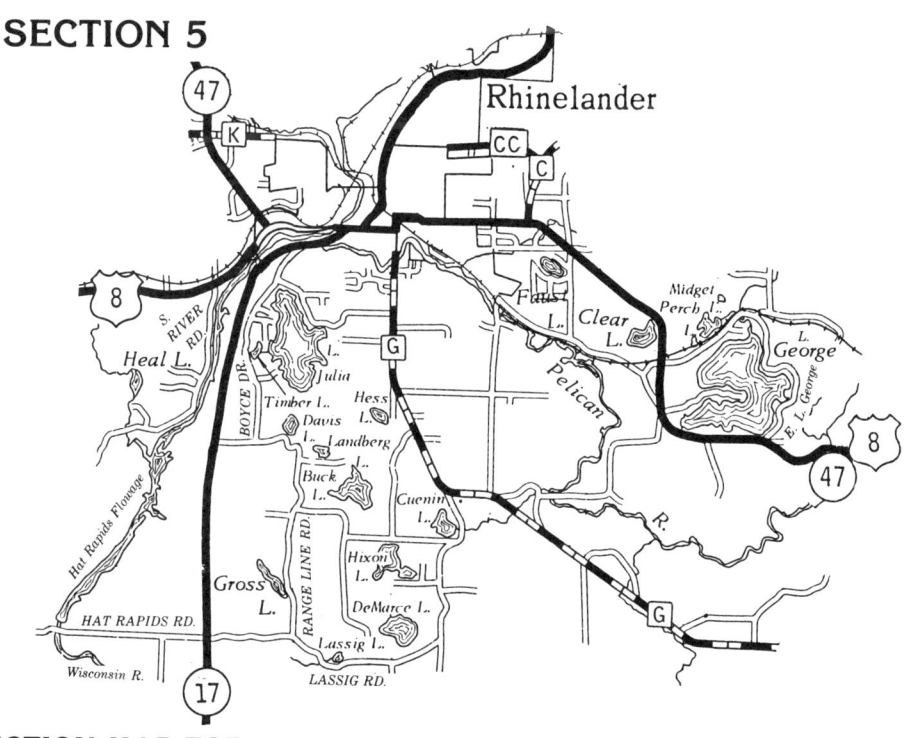

SECTION 5

SECTION MAP FOR —
Faust Lake (Foss Lake)
Clear Lake (S10, T36N, R9E)
Lake George
Cuenin Lake
Hixon Lake
Buck Lake (S19, T36N, R9E)
Lake Julia
Hat Rapids Flowage (Wisconsin R.)
Pelican River

Davis Lake
DeMarce Lake
Gross Lake
Heal Lake
Hess Lake
Landberg Lake
Midget Lake
Perch Lake (S10, T36N, R9E)
Timber Lake (S12, T36N, R8E)

FAUST LAKE (FOSS LAKE)

LOCATION — In the central part of the area, immediately east of Rhinelander and south of Highway 8.

ACCESS — Type III (Public): To the southern end of the lake; take Faust Lake Road south from Highway 8 for 0.3 mile to Barbara Street. Make a right and go 0.1 mile to a small clearing (just east of a row of pine trees). Off-road parking is available at this town-owned facility. A narrow overgrown trail leads to the water.

LAKE CHARACTERISTICS
Size and Depth - 23 acres and 22 feet.
Water Source - Seepage lake: No inlet or outlet.
Shoreline - Almost equal portions of wetlands and uplands with some development.
Bottom - 55% muck, 35% sand, 10% gravel.
Water - Quite infertile and light brown in color. Winterkill has been noted to occur.
Vegetation - Heavy growths have been a problem over the years. Floating varieties are quite abundant around the perimeter.

FISHERY
Species - Northern Pike, Largemouth Bass, Perch, Bluegill, Crappie, Pumpkinseed, (Walleye), (Muskie).
Comment - Panfish are reported to be stunted. Crappie have apparently been introduced by private parties. . . also walleye and muskie.

LAKE MANAGEMENT
Lake Investigation Data - None.
Stocking - None, officially recorded.
Treatment - Excessive numbers of stunted panfish were removed in the 60's.

CONCLUSION — Perhaps the condition of the access says more about this lake than anything. . . its virtually overgrown with brush from lack of use.

CLEAR LAKE (S10, T36N, R9E)

LOCATION — In the southeastern section of the area, three miles east of Rhinelander and just south of Highway 8.

ACCESS — None public.

RELATED SERVICES
Boat Rentals - None.
Resorts - Yes, one.
Public Parks - None.
Bait Shops - None.

LAKE CHARACTERISTICS
Size and Depth - 36 acres and 24 feet.
Water Source - Seepage lake: No inlet or outlet.

Shoreline - Entirely upland and completely private.
Bottom - 75% sand, 20% gravel, 5% rubble.
Water - Very clear with limited fertility.
Vegetation - Generally sparse.

FISHERY
Species - Northern Pike, Walleye, Largemouth Bass, Panfish, (Muskie).
Comment - Very little is known about the fishery due to the lack of public access.

LAKE MANAGEMENT
Lake Investigation Data - None.
Stocking - None.

CONCLUSION — Local fishing talk provides the only information on Clear Lake...some suggest that a good fishery exists. Without public access the lake essentially remains a mystery to the majority of anglers.

LAKE GEORGE

LOCATION — In the southeast portion of the book area, four miles east of Rhinelander and immediately north of Highway 8.

ACCESS — /A\ **Type I (Public):** On the east side of the lake; take Highway 8 east of Rhinelander about 4 miles to East Lake George Road. Turn north (left) and drive 1.0 mile to Nostalgia Lane. Make another left and proceed 0.2 mile to the landing. A paved ramp, concrete slab landing, loading pier, and parking for 8 rigs are provided. This is the recommended landing.
/B\ **Type I (Public):** On the east side of the lake, follow East Lake George Road north from Highway 8 for 0.7 mile to the roadside landing on the outlet channel. This shallow rocky channel leads to the lake and is only suitable for small boats and canoes. This access is not recommended.

RELATED SERVICES
Boat Rentals - Yes, at resorts.
Bait Shops - Yes, at resorts and in Rhinelander.
Resorts - Yes, several.
Public Parks - A small public beach is located on the east side.
Campgrounds - Yes, a private facility on the east side.
Guide Services - Yes.

SPECIAL FEATURES — Lake George is highly developed for its size yet still provides decent fishing opportunities.

LAKE CHARACTERISTICS
Size and Depth - 435 acres and 26 feet.

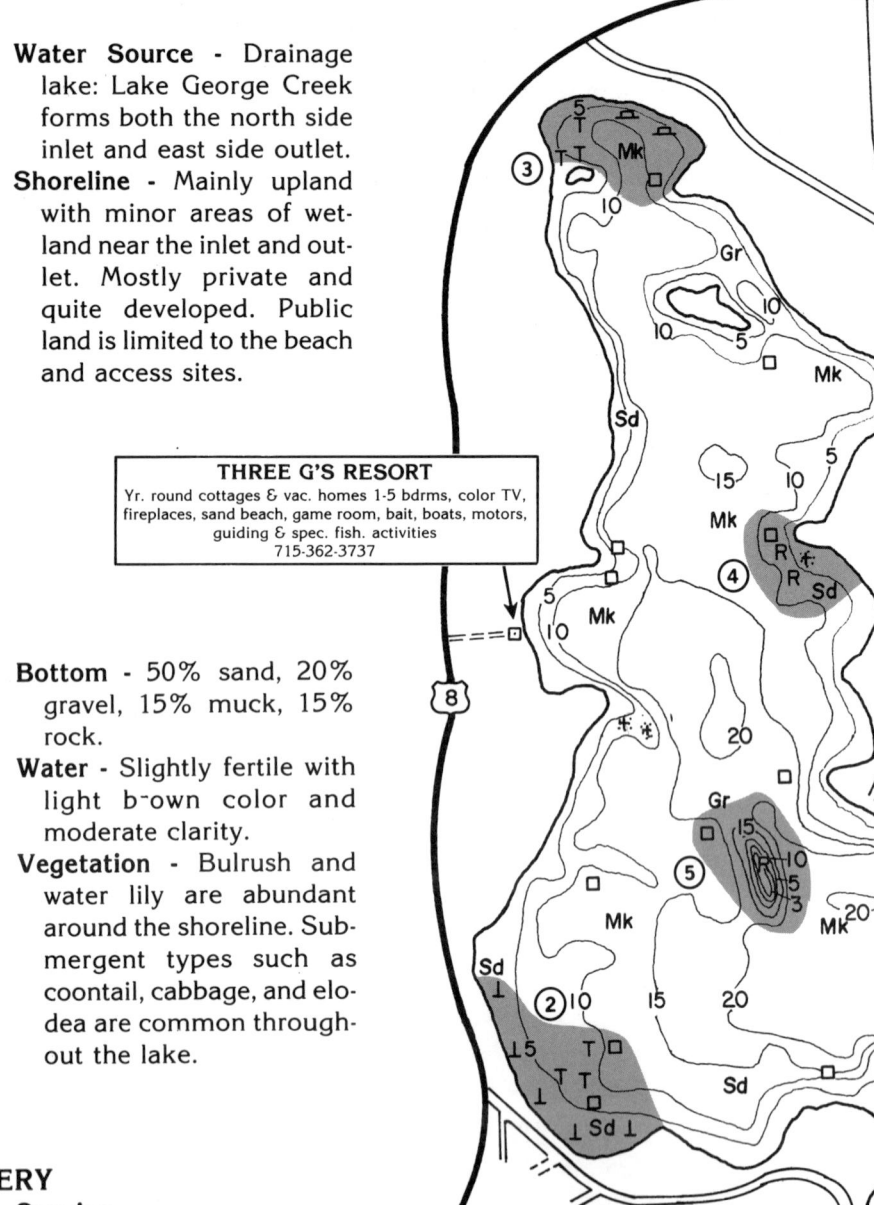

Water Source - Drainage lake: Lake George Creek forms both the north side inlet and east side outlet.

Shoreline - Mainly upland with minor areas of wetland near the inlet and outlet. Mostly private and quite developed. Public land is limited to the beach and access sites.

THREE G'S RESORT
Yr. round cottages & vac. homes 1-5 bdrms, color TV, fireplaces, sand beach, game room, bait, boats, motors, guiding & spec. fish. activities
715-362-3737

Bottom - 50% sand, 20% gravel, 15% muck, 15% rock.

Water - Slightly fertile with light brown color and moderate clarity.

Vegetation - Bulrush and water lily are abundant around the shoreline. Submergent types such as coontail, cabbage, and elodea are common throughout the lake.

FISHERY
Species
Primary - Walleye, Crappie.

Secondary - Muskie, Northern Pike, Perch, Bluegill, Pumpkinseed.

Limited - Largemouth Bass, Smallmouth Bass, Burbot.

Comment - Large populations of predator fish are suppressing panfish numbers. However, this has resulted in good panfish growth rates.

Forage - Bluntnose minnow, johnny darter, white sucker, golden shiner, young-of-the-year panfish.

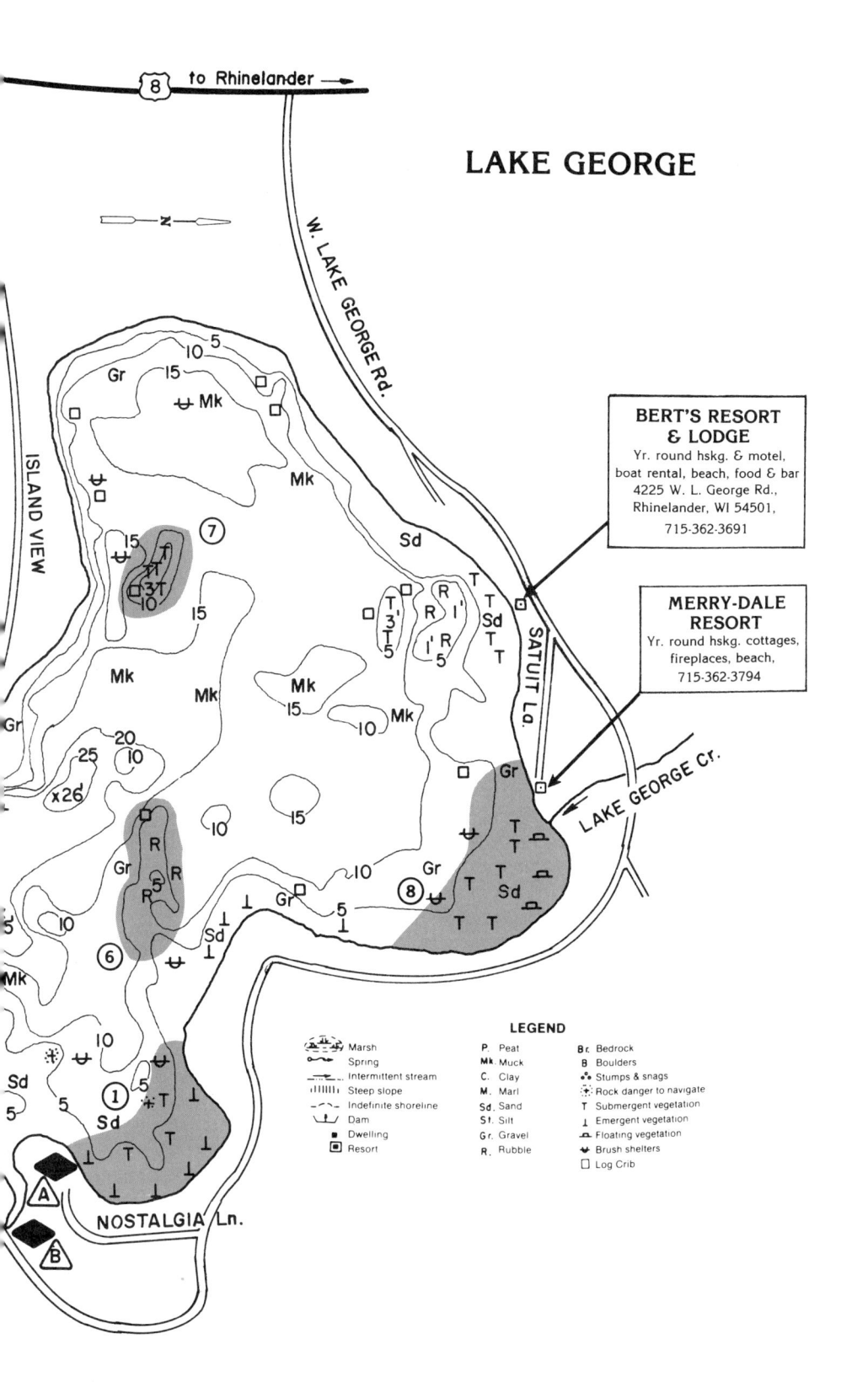

LAKE GEORGE

BERT'S RESORT & LODGE
Yr. round hskg. & motel, boat rental, beach, food & bar
4225 W. L. George Rd., Rhinelander, WI 54501,
715-362-3691

MERRY-DALE RESORT
Yr. round hskg. cottages, fireplaces, beach,
715-362-3794

LEGEND

Symbol	Meaning	Symbol	Meaning	Symbol	Meaning
	Marsh	P.	Peat	Br.	Bedrock
	Spring	Mk.	Muck	B.	Boulders
	Intermittent stream	C.	Clay		Stumps & snags
	Steep slope	M.	Marl		Rock danger to navigate
	Indefinite shoreline	Sd.	Sand	T	Submergent vegetation
	Dam	St.	Silt		Emergent vegetation
	Dwelling	Gr.	Gravel		Floating vegetation
	Resort	R.	Rubble		Brush shelters
					Log Crib

LAKE MANAGEMENT

Lake Investigation Data - An older comprehensive fyke net survey resulted in the following fish being captured.

SPECIES	NUMBER	SIZE RANGE
Walleye	261	5 1/2"-25"
Northern Pike	139	11 1/2"-30 1/2"
Muskie	9	11 1/2"-29 1/2"
Crappie	150	5"-13 1/2"
Perch	145	1"-10 1/2"
Bluegill	154	3"-10"
Pumpkinseed	56	3 1/2"- 7 1/2"
Rock Bass	47	4"- 9"

Note: the relative abundance of walleye and northern pike when compared to the panfish species... they are quite dominant. The bulk of the 261 walleye sampled ranged from 11"-15" and will comprise the majority of walleye action. A self-sustaining walleye population is present since no stocking of the species has occurred since the early 70's.

Stocking - In 1982, 800 12" muskie were planted. Another 900 12" muskie were released in 1987.

Treatment - 25 fish cribs were installed in 1985 by the Lake George Community Club. (Locations are indicated on the map.)

LAKE SURVEY MAP — Fishing Areas Shaded

Area (1) The shallow bay on the east end is rimmed with bulrush and has scattered patches of cabbage further out. Work the cabbage for northern pike using spinnerbaits or spoons. Panfish can also be taken throughout the year.

Area (2) Surface baits and jerkbaits are good choices for muskie along this east side weedbed. Early season largemouth are also possible. Try around the two cribs for panfish.

Area (3) The bay in the southwest corner is productive for northern pike, panfish, and an occasional largemouth. Brown bucktails with brass blades or red and white Daredevils are effective for pike.

Area (4) A fish crib is located in this rocky-bottomed area east of the small point. Cast crayfish-colored crankbaits for smallmouth bass. Summer muskie are often taken on jerkbaits or surface lures.

Area (5) This mid-lake rock bar is a prime "Hot Spot" for smallmouth and walleye. Crankbaits are productive, as are yellow, black, and chartreuse Twister Tails. Live bait anglers should try light weight slip sinker rigs or jig/live bait combos. Minnows are the best bet for early season walleye, with crawlers and leeches being preferred through summer. Switch back to minnows in the fall.

Area (6) Year-around walleye action highlights this rocky bar. Again, crankbaits are a good choice for walleye. Work the top of the bar for muskie with surface baits such as Hawg-Wobblers. Large crankbaits will also take muskie. Ice fishing for walleye is popular during the winter months.

Area (7) This small off-shore weedbed tops off at 5' and provides walleye, crappie, and muskie action. Early season walleye are taken on jig/minnow combos and slip bobbers. For summer crappie, fish close to the crib with minnows or small plastics, i.e. tube jigs and Twister Tails. Muskie fishermen should work surface baits over the weeds. As the deeper weedline develops, bucktails and crankbaits are effective along the edge.

Area (8) The inletting water of this north side bay warms up fast and provides early action for largemouth bass and northern pike. Spinnerbaits in chartreuse or orange are good for both species. Also try gold and black floating Rapalas. The bay is a good spot for panfish too.

FISHING TIPS — Fluorescent colored lures are best in the light brown water of Lake George. Chartreuse and orange remain good traditional selections for anything from crappie jigs to muskie bucktails.

When fishing the cribs, work your baits and lures close to these shelters, since fish will seldom stray very far.

Fish early or late in the season, or early or late in the day to avoid the heavy boat traffic and water activity.

CONCLUSION — Despite its heavy use, Lake George remains a productive fishing lake. It's a good choice for that first legal muskie or a panfishing trip for the family.

Catch and release of gamefish is urged to help preserve this heavily used but balanced fishery.

CUENIN LAKE

LOCATION — In the south central part of the book area, just west of Highway G and south of Rhinelander.

ACCESS — **Type III (Public):** On the east side of the lake; take Lassig Road south from Highway G for 1 mile to a right-of-way access at the culvert crossing. The area near the access point is a no parking zone, but roadside parking is available nearby. A short easy carry-in is required.

LAKE CHARACTERISTICS
  Size and Depth - 34 acres and 4 feet.
  Water Source - Spring-fed lake.
  Shoreline - Almost entirely wetland. 100% privately-owned except for the access.
  Bottom - 100% muck.

Water - Fertile and light brown in color. Winterkill continues to be a problem.

Vegetation - Moderate densities of both submergent and emergent species are found.

FISHERY
Species - Northern Pike, Bluegill, Pumpkinseed, Bullhead.

Comment - While the status of the northern pike population is unknown, panfish have been found to be stunted.

LAKE MANAGEMENT
Lake Investigation Data - None.
Stocking - None.

CONCLUSION — Stunted panfish and periodic winterkill pose serious limitations to quality fishing.

HIXON LAKE

LOCATION — In the south central portion of the area, about three miles south of Rhinelander and east of Highway 17.

ACCESS — **Type III (Public):** On the southeast side of the lake; go south on Lassig Road 1.2 miles from Highway G to Wilmar Lane. Turn right (west) and drive 0.2 mile to Buckhorn Lane. Make another right and proceed 0.2 mile to the unmarked access path. The access is located where the road first approaches the lake and leads to a shallow weedy area. A short carry-in is required and parking is limited to the roadside.

LAKE CHARACTERISTICS
Size and Depth - 50 acres and 28 feet.

Water Source - Seepage lake: No inlet, but a small outlet is found on the northeast side.

Shoreline - 95% upland. Completely private except for the narrow access zone.

Bottom - 65% sand, 25% muck, 10% gravel.

Water - Light brown, moderately clear, and slightly fertile.

Vegetation - Moderate growths of submergent, emergent, and floating varieties, with heaviest concentrations in the southeast basin.

FISHERY
Species - Largemouth Bass, Northern Pike, Walleye, Crappie, Bluegill, Perch.

Comment - Both bluegill and perch are considered stunted, but crappie display excellent growth. Walleye are limited in number but are of decent size.

LAKE MANAGEMENT
Lake Investigation Data - None.

HIXON LAKE Rd.

HIXON LAKE

BUCKHORN Ln.

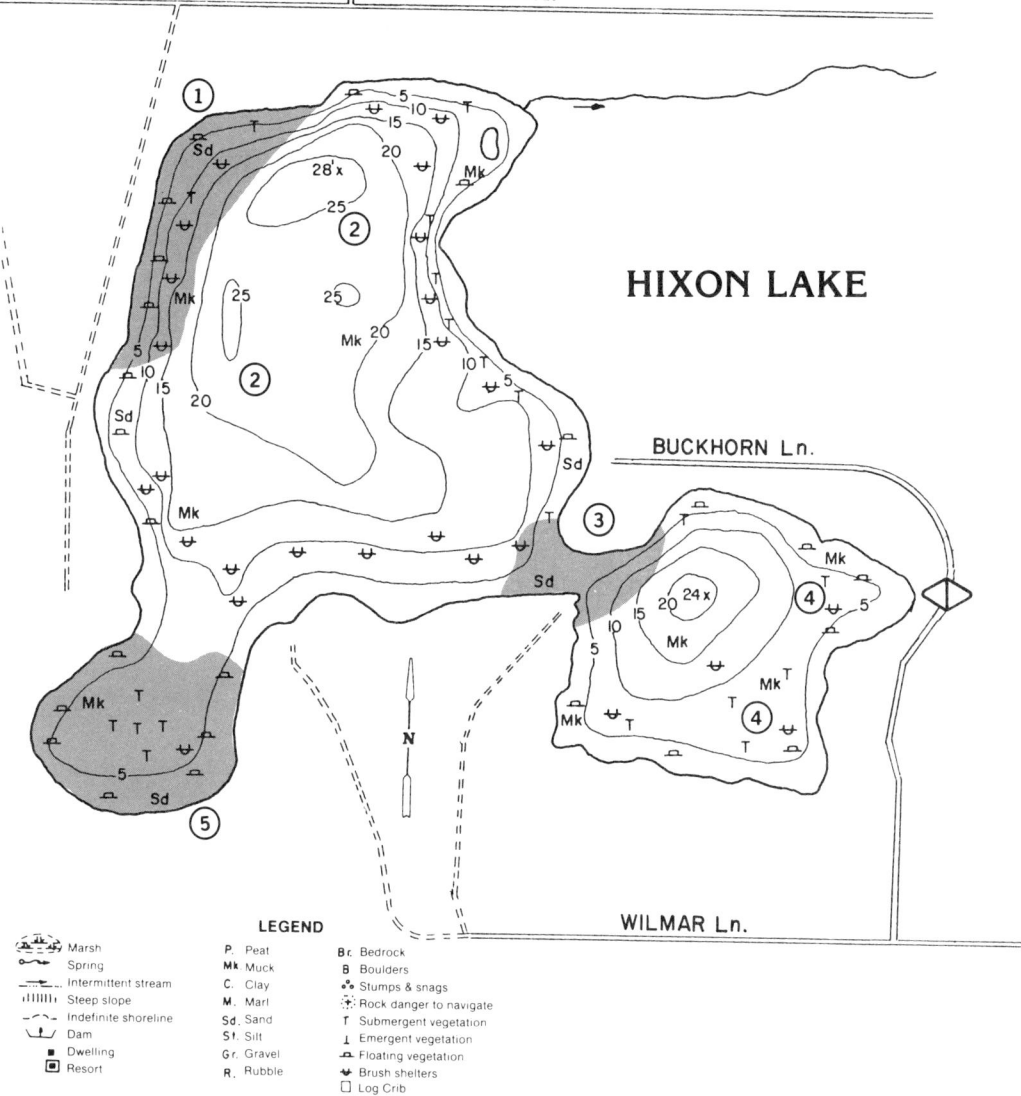

WILMAR Ln.

LEGEND

- Marsh
- Spring
- Intermittent stream
- Steep slope
- Indefinite shoreline
- Dam
- Dwelling
- Resort

- P. Peat
- Mk. Muck
- C. Clay
- M. Marl
- Sd. Sand
- St. Silt
- Gr. Gravel
- R. Rubble

- Br. Bedrock
- B. Boulders
- Stumps & snags
- Rock danger to navigate
- T Submergent vegetation
- Emergent vegetation
- Floating vegetation
- Brush shelters
- Log Crib

Stocking - None recorded.
Treatment - Chemical treatment of excessive weeds has occurred.

LAKE SURVEY MAP — Fishing Areas Shaded

Area (1) The northwest shore should be fished for northern pike. A sucker rigged below a large bobber and worked along the weed edge is a good bet.

Area (2) Drift the mid-lake zone of the west basin for suspended crappie from early summer to fall. Small minnows and Beetle Spin style spinnerbaits have been effective.

Area (3) The narrows between the east and west basin is a popular spot year-around. Both walleye and crappie relate to this area, especially during winter.

Area (4) Work the weedy east basin for largemouth bass. Try plastic worms, spinnerbaits, or surface baits during the evening hours. Live bait anglers may want to work a crawler over the weeds.

Area (5) Fish back into the slop for largemouth bass in this small weedy bay.

FISHING TIPS — Try this effective method when fishing for suspended crappie. Cast your lure or bait, then let it sink slowly, jigging or twitching it occasionally as it falls. By doing this as you drift, different depths over a large area can be efficiently covered.

CONCLUSION — Hixon is another small lake with an interesting fishery. Bass, crappie, and perhaps a few northern will provide most of the action. Ice fishing seems to offer the best opportunities for the few nice walleye in this decent little lake.

BUCK LAKE (S19, T36N, R9E)

LOCATION — In the central part of the book area, directly south of Rhinelander and east of Highway 17.

ACCESS — **Type III (Public):** To the Almon Recreation Area on the south side of the lake; drive south off Highway G on Lassig Road for 0.7 mile to Hixon Lake Road. Turn right and follow Hixon Lake Road 1.4 miles to this county-owned facility. A walkway leads down a steep grade to the water. Ample parking is provided.

RELATED SERVICES
   Boat Rentals - None.
   Resorts - None.
   Public Parks - Yes, with swimming and picnic facilities.
   Campgrounds - None.

SPECIAL FEATURES — Almon Recreation Area is a very popular year-around facility.

LAKE CHARACTERISTICS
   Size and Depth - 61 acres and 49 feet.
   Water Source - Seepage lake: No inlet or outlet.
   Shoreline - Completely upland.
   Bottom - 65% sand, 25% rubble, 10% gravel.
   Water - Extremely infertile and very clear.
   Vegetation - Quite limited.

FISHERY
   Species - Largemouth Bass, Smallmouth Bass, Bluegill, Pumpkinseed, Sucker.
   Comment - Extreme infertility has resulted in stunted panfish and slow growing bass.

LAKE MANAGEMENT
Lake Investigation Data - None.
Stocking - None.
Treatment - None.

CONCLUSION — A rare quality size bass may be the only item of interest to fishermen. Buck Lake is a good choice for a family outing...perhaps better suited for swimming than fishing.

LAKE JULIA

LOCATION — In the central part of the book area, immediately south of Rhinelander and east of Highway 17.

ACCESS — **Type II (Public):** To the west side of the lake; take Boyce Drive south from Highway 17 for 0.8 mile to Timber Lodge Road. Turn left and drive 0.6 mile to a "Y" in the road. Stay to the right (straight ahead) for a short distance to the access. A paved ramp, gravel landing, and roadside parking are present.
Note: The large adjacent parking lot is private and should not be used.

SPECIAL FEATURES — Nicolet Area Technical College is located on the southeast side of the lake.
Note: Use caution when navigating - there are many hazardous rock bars and boulders.

LAKE CHARACTERISTICS
Size and Depth - 238 acres and 19 feet.
Water Source - Seepage lake: No inlet or outlet.
Shoreline - Primarily in private ownership and considerably developed. Mostly upland with some wetland adjoining the south shore.
Bottom - 30% rubble, 25% sand, 20% gravel, 15% boulders, 10% muck.
Water - Infertile and moderately clear.
Vegetation - Moderate densities of lily pads, eelgrass, and coontail. Scattered areas of cabbage are also present.

FISHERY
Species
Primary - Largemouth Bass, Northern Pike, Perch, Bluegill.
Secondary - Muskie, Walleye, Pumpkinseed.
Limited - Smallmouth Bass, Rock Bass.
Comment - Numerous stunted panfish are present. Expect many "hammer handle" northern pike. Muskie, largemouth, and walleye are the main attraction.

LAKE MANAGEMENT
Lake Investigation Data - None.

LAKE JULIA

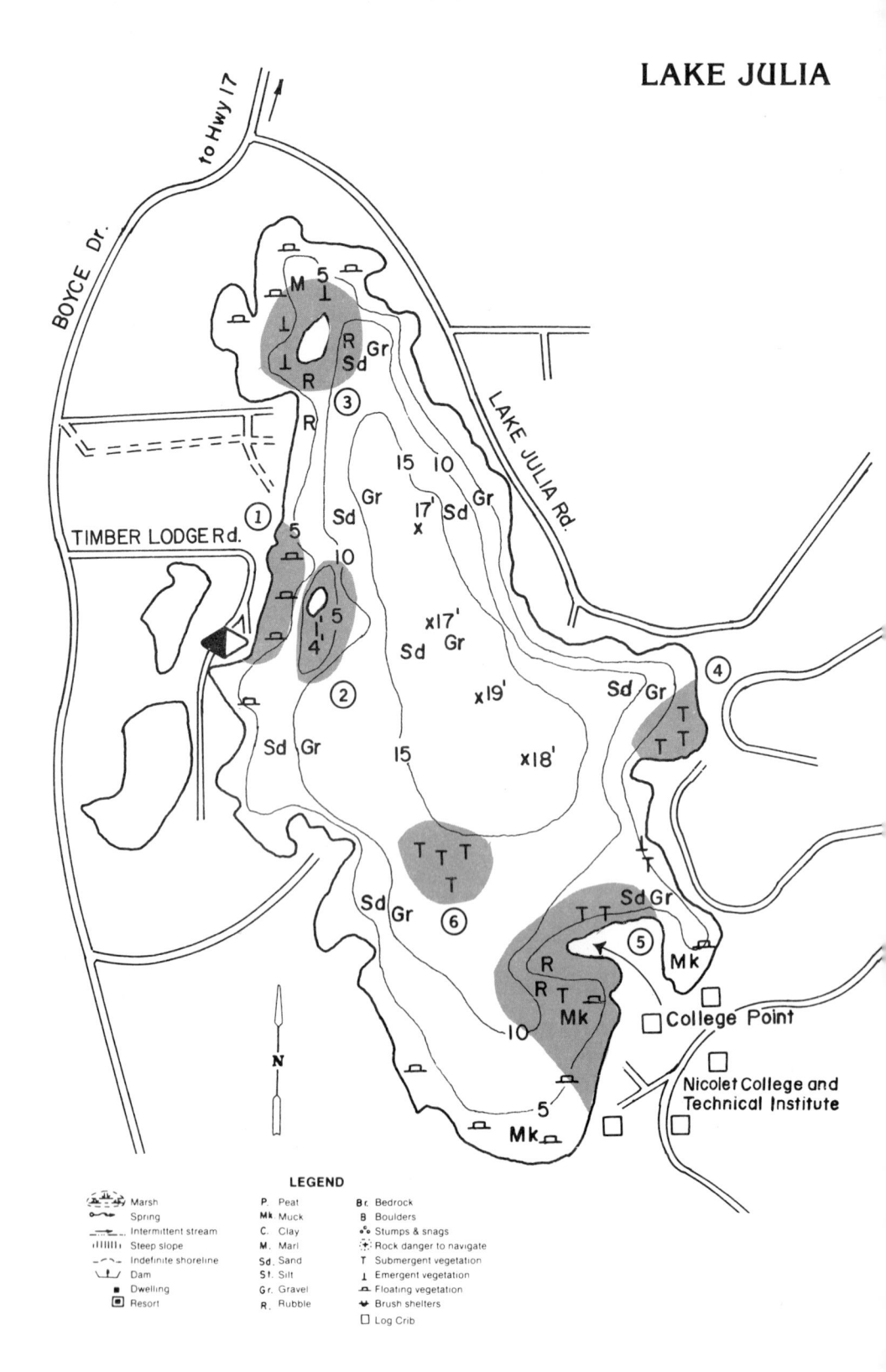

Stocking - In 1987, 12,000 walleye fingerling were planted. Prior to that, the most recent stocking was a 1976 release of 350 muskie.

LAKE SURVEY MAP — Fishing Areas Shaded

Area (1) A weedy bar extends off the south end of the island. A small jig tipped with a minnow will take walleye in spring and fall. The rocky north side of the island can also produce fish.

Area (2) This west side bed of eelgrass provides distinct edge habitat for muskie. Surface baits worked along the edge are productive.

Area (3) Scattered weeds and rock around the island will hold muskie and largemouth. Muskie are taken on shallow-running crankbaits. Plastic worms and spinnerbaits are advised for bass.

Area (4) Work the 'drowned wood' and docks along this shore for bass and muskie.

Area (5) College Point has a rocky bar extending off its tip and weeds on both the north and south sides. Try for muskie off the north side. Work spinnerbaits on the south side for largemouth. Spring walleye are available on the top of the bar using traditional jig and minnow presentations.

Area (6) This mid-lake weedbed is a "Hot Spot" for muskie. Weighted bucktails and crankbaits are preferred lure selections.

FISHING TIPS — Walleye anglers should remember to use as light a jig as depth and wind conditions will allow. Low light periods will be most productive... early morning, evening or cloudy days are the best bet. Surface lures are a good choice for bass during evening hours.

CONCLUSION — Lake Julia has good populations of gamefish and is considered by many to be one of the best largemouth lakes in the area. The walleye population is characterized by 13"-20" fish. Large fish are quite rare, but good walleye natural reproduction is occurring.

Lake Julia provides a good fishery that is often overlooked considering its close proximity to Rhinelander.

HAT RAPIDS FLOWAGE
(WISCONSIN RIVER)

LOCATION — In the central part of the book area, downstream from the Rhinelander Paper Company Dam to the Hat Rapids Dam.

ACCESS — Ⓐ **Type II (Public):** On the northwest side of the river; from the Wisconsin River bridge go west on Highway 8 a short distance taking the first road to the right. At the stop sign make a right onto Sutliff Avenue and drive 0.2 mile to Norway Street. Turn right, go 0.1 mile to where the road meets the river. A blacktop ramp leads

HAT RAPIDS FLOWAGE
(WISCONSIN R.)

to a gravel landing. Ample roadside parking is available nearby. This is the best landing for larger boats.

B Type III (Public): To the east side of the river at the DNR Ranger Station, go south on Highway 17 0.3 mile from the intersection of Highways 8 and 17. The ranger station is just north of the Pelican River bridge. There is an easy carry-in with adequate parking. Shore fishing at this site is popular.

C Type III (Private): At the extreme southern end of the flowage; take Hat Rapids Road west off Highway 17 for 0.9 mile to the Wisconsin Public Service Corporation dam/powerhouse facility. The access site is east of the powerhouse. Shore fishing is also popular here.

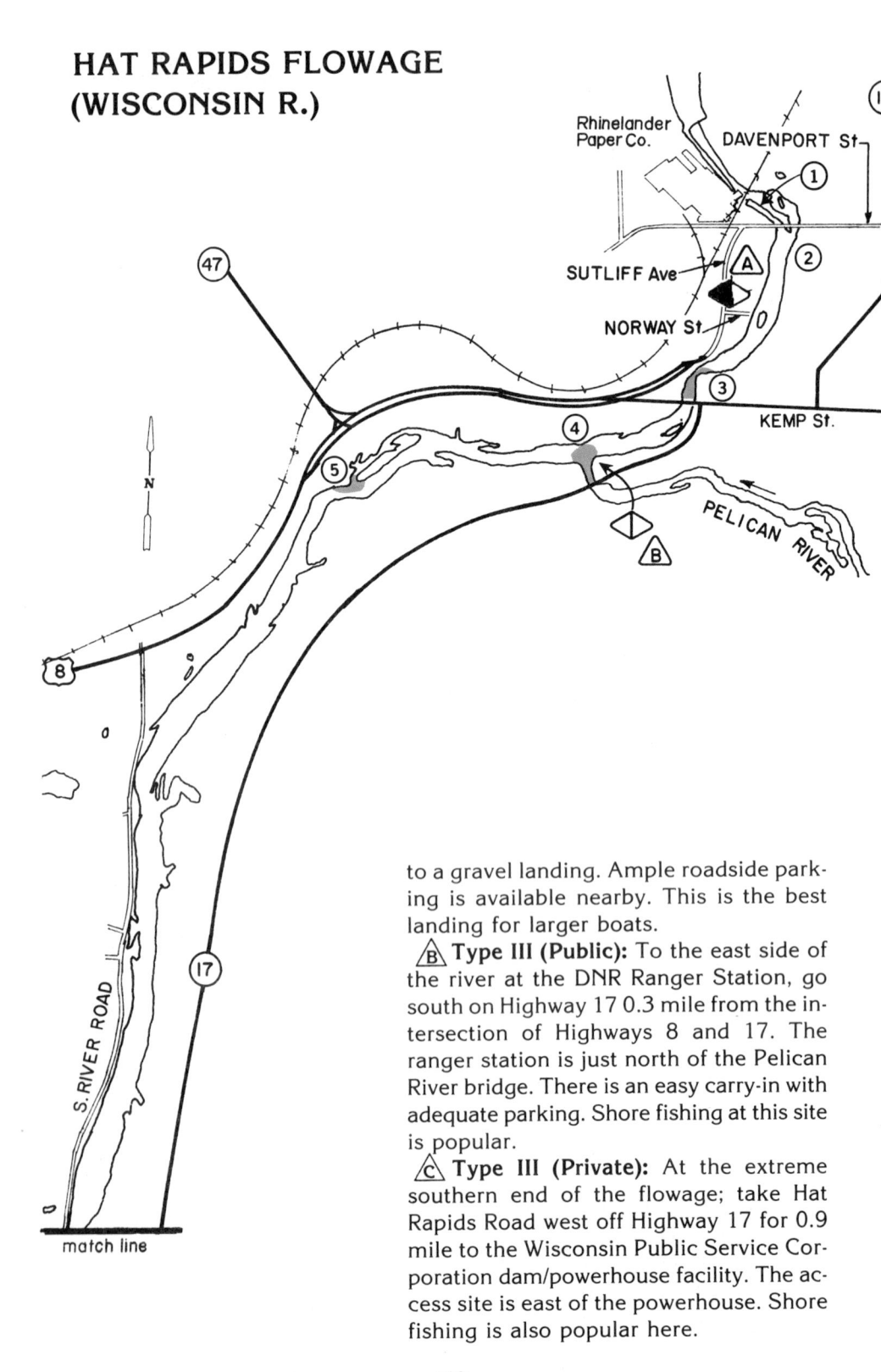

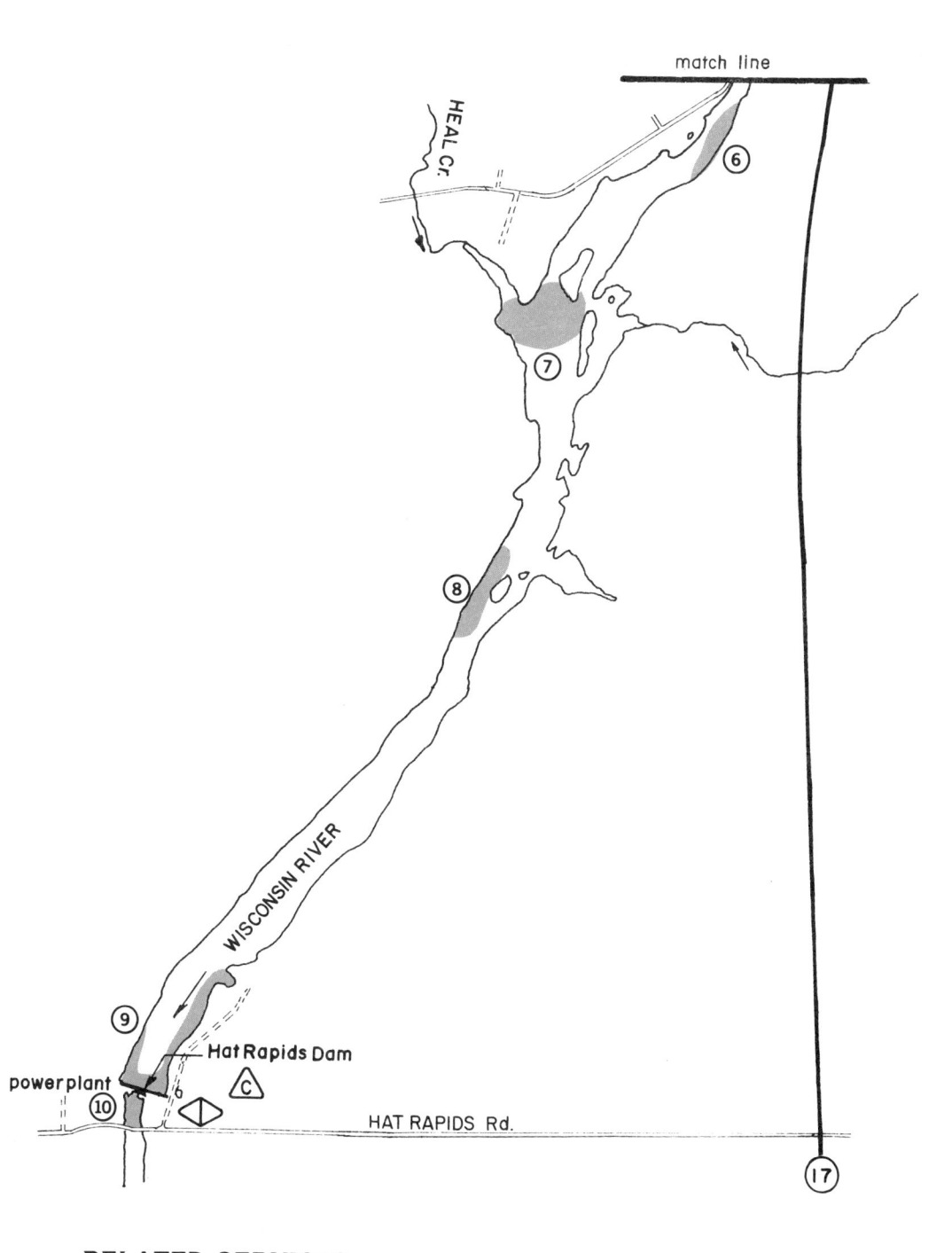

RELATED SERVICES
    Boat Rentals - None.
    Bait Shops - Yes, in Rhinelander.
    Resorts - None.
    Guide Services - Yes.

SPECIAL FEATURES — There is no closed season for gamefish except muskie downstream from the Rhinelander Paper Company Dam. This also includes the short stretch of the Pelican River upstream to the Highway 17 bridge.

LAKE CHARACTERISTICS
Size and Depth - 650 acres with depths reported in excess of 20 feet.
Water Source - Drainage lake: An impoundment of the Wisconsin River. The major tributary in this stretch is the Pelican River.
Shoreline - Mostly lowlands.
Bottom - Mainly sand, with significant areas of gravel and rubble. Areas of muck and silt are also present.
Water - Reasonably fertile, light brown in color, and slightly murky. Although poor water quality plagued the river for many years, increased regulation of municipal and industrial wastes has produced a vast improvement in water quality through the 70's and into the 80's.
Vegetation - Floating and emergent species along the shore areas in addition to scattered patches of submergent types.

FISHERY
Species
  Primary - Northern Pike, Walleye, Bullhead.
  Secondary - Smallmouth Bass, Crappie, Perch.
  Limited - Muskie, Bluegill.
Comment - Little is known of the muskie population, but is thought by some to be marginal. Bullhead are very abundant and can be a nuisance to anglers.

LAKE MANAGEMENT
Lake Investigation Data - None.
Stocking - None.
Treatment - None.

LAKE SURVEY MAP — Fishing Areas Shaded
Area (1) The water just below the Rhinelander Paper Company Dam should be fished with a jig and minnow for early season walleye. It is quite rocky so expect to lose some tackle.
Area (2) Immediately downstream from the Davenport Street bridge is a good spot for early spring perch.
Area (3) Work along the outside bend just upstream from the Highway 8 bridge for walleye.
Area (4) The area near the mouth of the Pelican River is one of the best spots on the entire flowage. Try here for walleye from mid-April to the 1st of June. Look for crappie action around the end of April. Shore anglers take pike all season long from the area near the ranger station.
Area (5) The large island downstream from the Pelican River should be fished for northern pike and crappie throughout the season.

Small Twister Tails or tube jigs are effective for crappie, while northern can be taken on spoons or spinners.

Area (6) Fallen trees along this outside bend will hold a number of species, but walleye and crappie are most common. Work the wood with a jig/minnow or jig/Twister Tail combination. Bring plenty of extras... you'll lose some tackle in the wood.

Area (7) The weed edge on the downstream side of the island is another "Hot Spot" for northern and crappie action. Move further downstream and cast the area around the mouth of Heal Creek for pike. Lily pads and submergent weeds provide the cover.

Area (8) The channel narrows about one mile upstream from the dam and has depths of 13'-15'. This is an excellent area for walleye. Jigs or slip sinker rigs are suggested.

Area (9) A small submerged hump is located upstream from the dam, about 100 yards out from the float line and between the 2nd and 3rd floats from the east. Try here for walleye and crappie. Also fish the shoreline weed edge around the lower flowage for northern pike.

Area (10) The tailwater area below the dam is a popular early season walleye spot. This area can continue to provide walleye action when the season closes elsewhere in the northwoods. Jig and minnows or floating jigs tipped with minnows are traditional Hat Rapids selections.

FISHING TIPS — Because of the many snags, be sure to use a little heavier line than usual... 8#-10# test is recommended. Look for walleye and smallmouth to relate to areas with current... concentrating on both current and structure breaks. Crappie and northern will prefer slack water zones that offer good cover. Weeds, stumps, and fallen trees should be fished.

CONCLUSION — The Hat Rapids Flowage now supports a 'reclaimed' fishery that was once a victim of severe water pollution. Anglers that fish it today report a diverse catch, without the foul taste that was present years ago.

It is because of this past reputation that the flowage remains underfished today. However, the current fishery has much to offer, so be sure to try this water.

THE PELICAN RIVER
(INCLUDING FISH LAKE ON THE NORTH BRANCH)

LOCATION — In the east and southeast portions of the book area.

ACCESS — Type III: Access to the river is possible at several road crossings and below the dam at the east end of Fifth Lake. Road crossings often used are Haymeadow Road, Highway 8, and River Bend Road.

Roadside parking is available at these bridge locations. The lower stretches of the Pelican River can be reached by using the DNR Ranger Station access. (See Hat Rapids Flowage Report.)

SPECIAL FEATURES — Includes Fish Lake, a shallow flooded lowland on the upper end of the North Branch.

STREAM CHARACTERISTICS

Size and Depth - A total of 22.1 miles including the 6.1 miles of the North Branch Pelican River. The river has an average depth of 3' and width of about 100'.

Water Source - The North Branch flows out of Third Lake of the Moen Chain, then through Fourth and Fifth Lake where a Wisconsin Valley Improvement Company dam regulates its flow. The Pelican River originates at the outlet of Pelican Lake with the North Branch being the major tributary... joining just south of Highway 8 about 5 miles southeast of Rhinelander.

Shoreline - Mostly upland and private.

Bottom - Predominantly sand and gravel. Five rapids are present in the River Bend Road area.

Water - Slightly fertile and light brown in color.

Vegetation - Scattered areas of submergent growths throughout, except for Fish Lake where dense quantities of floating and emergent varieties are found.

FISHERY

Species - Northern Pike, Walleye, Largemouth Bass, Smallmouth Bass, Perch, Bluegill, Crappie, Rock Bass, Pumpkinseed, Sucker, (Muskie).

Comment - Many nongame species are also present including darters, dace, sculpin, and shiners.

Seasonal Migrations - Spawning walleye will move up the Pelican River from the Hat Rapids Flowage. A spring sucker run also occurs.

STREAM MANAGEMENT

Stream Investigation Data - None recently.
Stocking - None.
Treatment - None.

FISHING TIPS — The Pelican River should be fished early in the season for best results. Look for walleye in the deep holes along the outside bends, especially in the lower reaches. Suckers can be taken with dip nets or hook and line during the spring run.

Try the dock behind the DNR garage on the north bank (near Highway 17) for spring walleye and crappie. Just downstream, the bank along the ranger station is good for crappie and northern throughout the season.

Remember, the continuous season for gamefish only applies to the small section of river downstream from the Highway 17 bridge.

CONCLUSION — The Pelican River, and its North Branch, are the only small rivers in the book area that provide a warmwater fishery. Canoe enthusiasts will find it an enjoyable float with plenty of 'holes' along the way. Again, early season is best not only for fishing but higher water levels make for easier navigation.

-LAKES LIMITED IN ACCESS OR FISHERY IN SECTION 5-

DAVIS LAKE	LANDBERG LAKE
DeMARCE LAKE	MIDGET LAKE
GROSS LAKE	PERCH LAKE (S10, T36N, R9E)
HEAL LAKE	TIMBER LAKE (S12, T36N, R8E)
HESS LAKE	

LOCATION — In the southeast part of the book area, generally south and east of Rhinelander.

ACCESS — None Public.

LAKE CHARACTERISTICS
   Size and Depth - A range of 4-49 acres in size and 6'-45' deep.
   Water Source - Mostly seepage lakes: No inlets or outlets. However, Midget Lake and DeMarce Lake are spring-fed while Heal Lake is a drainage lake.
   Shoreline - Entirely private. About half the lakes are surrounded by bog, the other half by significant areas of uplands.
   Bottom - Mostly muck, although DeMarce Lake, Davis Lake, and Hess Lake have large areas of hard bottom.
   Water - Highly infertile except for Midget Lake and DeMarce Lake which are rather fertile spring-fed lakes. Most lakes in this group are clear or light brown in color.
   Vegetation - Submergent, emergent, and floating types are present with great variation in density between lakes.

FISHERY — Generally largemouth bass and panfish. In addition, Heal Lake, DeMarce Lake, and Midget Lake also have northern pike.
   Comment - Very little data is available on these fisheries since they all lack public access.

CONCLUSION — Again, the public fishing opportunities are nonexistent on this group of small private lakes. Of the group, only DeMarce Lake and Midget Lake exhibit some interesting potential based on their unusually high fertility for lakes in this area.

SECTION 6

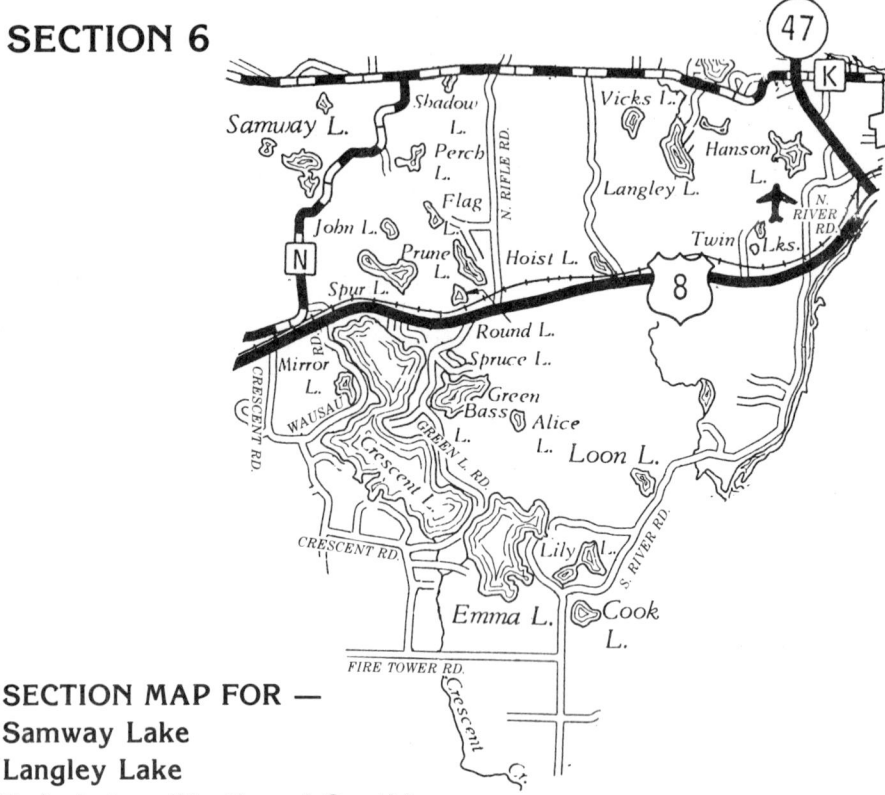

SECTION MAP FOR —
Samway Lake
Langley Lake
Twin Lakes (North and South)
Hanson Lake
Lily Lake (Lily Bass Lake)
Emma Lake
Crescent Lake
Green Bass Lake
Mirror Lake
Alice Lake
Cook Lake
Flag Lake
Hoist Lake
John Lake
Loon Lake
Perch Lake (S5, T36N, R8E)
Prune Lake
Round Lake
Shadow Lake
Spruce Lake (S16, T36N, R8E)
Spur Lake
Vicks Lake

SAMWAY LAKE

LOCATION — In the west central part of the book area, about 5 miles west of Rhinelander and just south of Highway K.

ACCESS — None public.

LAKE CHARACTERISTICS
  Size and Depth - 42 acres and 28 feet.
  Water Source - Seepage lake: No inlet, but an intermittent outlet may be present.

Shoreline - Completely upland and private.
Bottom - 70% silt and muck, 10% sand, 10% gravel, 10% rubble and boulders.
Water - Very clear and highly infertile.
Vegetation - Moderate densities of floating and submergent varieties.

FISHERY
Species - Largemouth Bass, Bluegill, Perch.
Comment - Little is known about the fishery although some reports of nice size bluegill have been noted.

LAKE MANAGEMENT
Lake Investigation Data - None
Stocking - None.

CONCLUSION — Samway has nothing to offer the fishing public. No access, high infertility, and a marginal fishery should dispel any interest.

LANGLEY LAKE

LOCATION — In the central portion of the area, south of Highway K and just west of Rhinelander.

ACCESS — **Type I (Public):** To the northeast corner of the lake; take the U.S. Forest Service Road south from Highway K at the Hugo Sauer Nursery sign. Drive this road for 0.4 mile past the laboratory buildings to the unmarked access on the right. The shallow gravel landing is best suited for smaller boats. Adequate parking is provided nearby.

SPECIAL FEATURES — The U.S. Forest Service's Experimental Station and Nursery adjoins the lake.

LAKE CHARACTERISTICS
Size and Depth - 48 acres and 9 feet.
Water Source - Seepage lake: No inlet or outlet.
Shoreline - Approximately 50% upland and 50% wetland. Mostly publicly-owned.
Bottom - 65% muck and silt, 15% gravel and rubble, 10% sand, 10% boulders.
Water - Moderately clear and extremely infertile. Winterkill may occur.
Vegetation - Moderate densities of submergent varieties in addition to some lily pads.

FISHERY
Species - Largemouth Bass, Bluegill, Perch.
Comment - Bluegill and perch are considered stunted.

LAKE MANAGEMENT
    Lake Investigation Data - None.
    Stocking - None.

FISHING TIPS — Wood and weeds provide the major fish holding cover in Langley. Work the shore, keying on logs, stumps, fallen trees, and weeds. Down-sized bass presentations (i.e., plastic worms, spinnerbaits, balsa minnows, jig n' pig, etc.) should take fish.

CONCLUSION — Langley offers some nice size bass in a rather scenic setting. Again, catch and release is encouraged.

TWIN LAKES (NORTH AND SOUTH)

LOCATION — In the central portion of the area, immediately west of Rhinelander and north of Highway 8.

ACCESS — **Type III (Public):** On the west side of the lake; take the Rhinelander-Oneida County Airport road north from Highway 8 for 0.3 mile to an unmarked paved road on the right. Turn right and proceed 0.2 mile to another unmarked road. Make another right onto this dirt/grass roadway and drive a short distance to the carry-in access.

SPECIAL FEATURES — Airport property adjoins the lake. A fishing pier is provided for shore anglers.

LAKE CHARACTERISTICS
    Size and Depth - 8 total acres. North Twin has a maximum depth of 34 feet and South Twin has a maximum depth of 14 feet.
    Water Source - Seepage lakes: No inlets or outlets.
    Shoreline - Primarily bog with limited upland areas around North Twin Lake.
    Bottom - Mostly muck with some firm material (sand, gravel, rock) found in North Twin.
    Water - Highly infertile and very clear.
    Vegetation - All varieties are scarce.

FISHERY
    Species - Largemouth Bass, Bluegill, Pumpkinseed.

LAKE MANAGEMENT
    Lake Investigation Data - None.
    Stocking - None.

CONCLUSION — Twin Lakes has the ability to produce some nice fish with good catches of panfish reported by local ice fishermen. Angler harvest can greatly impact the quality of fishing in a lake of this size and fertility. Keep this in mind as major fluctuations in fishing success can occur.

HANSON LAKE

RHINELANDER-ONEIDA Co. AIRPORT

LEGEND

Marsh	P. Peat	Br. Bedrock
Spring	Mk. Muck	B. Boulders
Intermittent stream	C. Clay	Stumps & snags
Steep slope	M. Marl	Rock danger to navigate
Indefinite shoreline	Sd. Sand	T. Submergent vegetation
Dam	St. Silt	Emergent vegetation
Dwelling	Gr. Gravel	Floating vegetation
Resort	R. Rubble	Brush shelters
		Log Crib

to N. RIVER Rd

HANSON LAKE

LOCATION — In the central part of the book area, immediately west of Rhinelander and south of Highway K.

ACCESS — **Type I (Public):** On the south end of the lake; drive 0.2 mile west from Highway 47 on North River Road to the intersection with Hanson Lake Road. Continue straight 0.2 mile to an unmarked gravel road. Turn right and follow this rough road 0.2 mile to the gravel landing. This unimproved access is recommended for carry-in boats (canoes) or four wheel drive vehicles with small trailers.

SPECIAL FEATURES — A good little fishing lake uniquely situated near the end of an airport runway.

LAKE CHARACTERISTICS
Size and Depth - 36 acres and 25 feet.
Water Source - Seepage lake: No inlet or outlet.

Shoreline - Mainly upland with only a minor wetland on the northwest side.
Bottom - 35% sand, 25% muck, 20% gravel, 20% rubble and boulders.
Water - Quite infertile and very clear. Dissolved oxygen concentrations are sufficient at all depths.
Vegetation - Generally scarce.

FISHERY
Species - Largemouth Bass, Perch, Bluegill, (Muskie), (Walleye).
Comment - Muskie were introduced in the 60's in an attempt to control excessive numbers of stunted panfish. Few muskie are thought to be present now.

LAKE MANAGEMENT
Lake Investigation Data - None.
Stocking - None recently.
Treatment - Old records indicate that log crib fish shelters were installed in the past.

FISHING TIPS — Submerged wood comprises the main source of fish holding cover. Work the wood for bass with spinnerbaits, 6" plastic worms or crankbaits. Also look for a few muskie to be suspended off the first break.

The clear water requires the use of down-sized tackle and lures... also try low light periods for best results.

CONCLUSION — If you are interested in small water bass fishing, Hanson Lake is definitely worth trying. Bass up to 20" have been recorded. Keep in mind that catch and release is essential in maintaining quality fishing on this type of water.

LILY LAKE (LILY BASS LAKE)

LOCATION — In the south central portion of the book area, south of Highway 8 and east of Emma Lake.

ACCESS — **Type III (Public):** On the south shore of the lake; take South River Road 3.9 miles south from Highway 8 to Cook Drive. Turn right onto Cook Drive and immediately make another right onto the narrow unmarked access road. A short carry-in down a moderately sloping bank is required.
Note: Please be respectful of the adjacent private properties.

SPECIAL FEATURES — A small picturesque lake with an interesting and diversified fishery.

LAKE CHARACTERISTICS
Size and Depth - 42 acres and 28 feet with an average depth of 8 feet.

LILY LAKE
(LILY BASS LAKE)

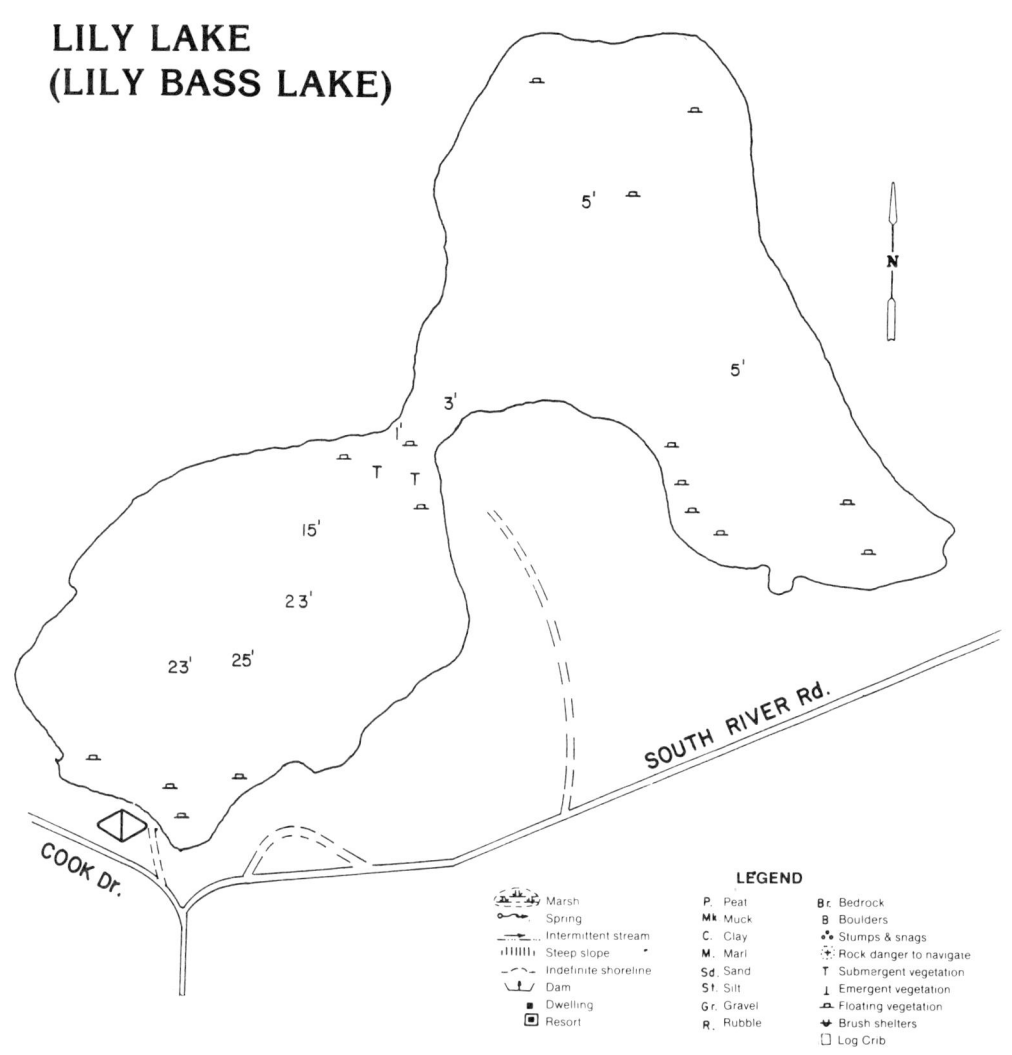

Water Source - Seepage lake: No inlet or outlet. However, during high water conditions a small channel to Emma Lake exists.

Shoreline - 70% bog and shrub type wetlands. Entirely private, except for the small access area.

Bottom - 65% muck, 20% sand, 15% gravel and rubble.

Water - Quite infertile and light brown in color.

Vegetation - Moderate densities of floating varieties surround the lake. Heavier growths are found at the narrows between the north and south basins.

FISHERY

Species - Muskie, Northern Pike, Walleye, Smallmouth Bass, Largemouth Bass, Perch, Crappie, Bluegill.

Comment - The small connecting channel to Emma Lake permits the movement of fish between the lakes. This has resulted in a very diverse fish community for a lake of Lily's size.

LAKE MANAGEMENT
Lake Investigation Data - None recently, but an old seine survey indicated that good natural reproduction was occurring for largemouth bass. The vast majority of fish sampled during the survey were young-of-the-year panfish.

FISHING TIPS — As is typical of the many small area lakes, submerged wood and the weed edges are the spots to concentrate your efforts. The south basin of Lily is significantly deeper than the north basin and holds the most fishing potential.

Ice fishing is also quite popular on Lily - try early ice for good results on gamefish and panfish alike. Crappie will provide action during the 'late ice' period...small minnows are suggested.

CONCLUSION — Lily is small water that has the potential to produce some large fish. Year-around action from a variety of species can be expected. Again, catch and release of larger gamefish is essential to good fishing in the future.

EMMA LAKE

LOCATION — In the southern part of the area, immediately southeast of Crescent Lake.

ACCESS — Type I (Public): To the east side of the lake; drive 3.9 miles south on South River Road from Highway 8 to Cook Drive. Turn right and follow Cook Drive 0.4 mile to this roadside access. The shallow gravel landing has parking for 1-2 rigs.

LAKE CHARACTERISTICS
Size and Depth - 223 acres and 17 feet.
Water Source - Seepage lake: No inlet or outlet, but a small channel leads to Lily Lake.
Shoreline - Predominantly upland and private.
Bottom - 65% sand, 25% muck, 10% gravel and rubble.
Water - Light brown in color and very infertile.
Vegetation - Moderate densities of lily pads and emergent types are found along the shore. Submergent types are also found throughout most of the lake basin.

FISHERY
Species - Walleye, Northern Pike, Largemouth Bass, Smallmouth Bass, Perch, Crappie, Bluegill, Rock Bass, Pumpkinseed, (Muskie).
Comment - Walleye are reported to be modest in number. Numerous small perch and bluegill are present. Crappie are currently the main panfish in the lake.

LAKE MANAGEMENT
Lake Investigation Data - None recently, but old records indicate that walleye growth rates are slightly below the area average.

EMMA LAKE

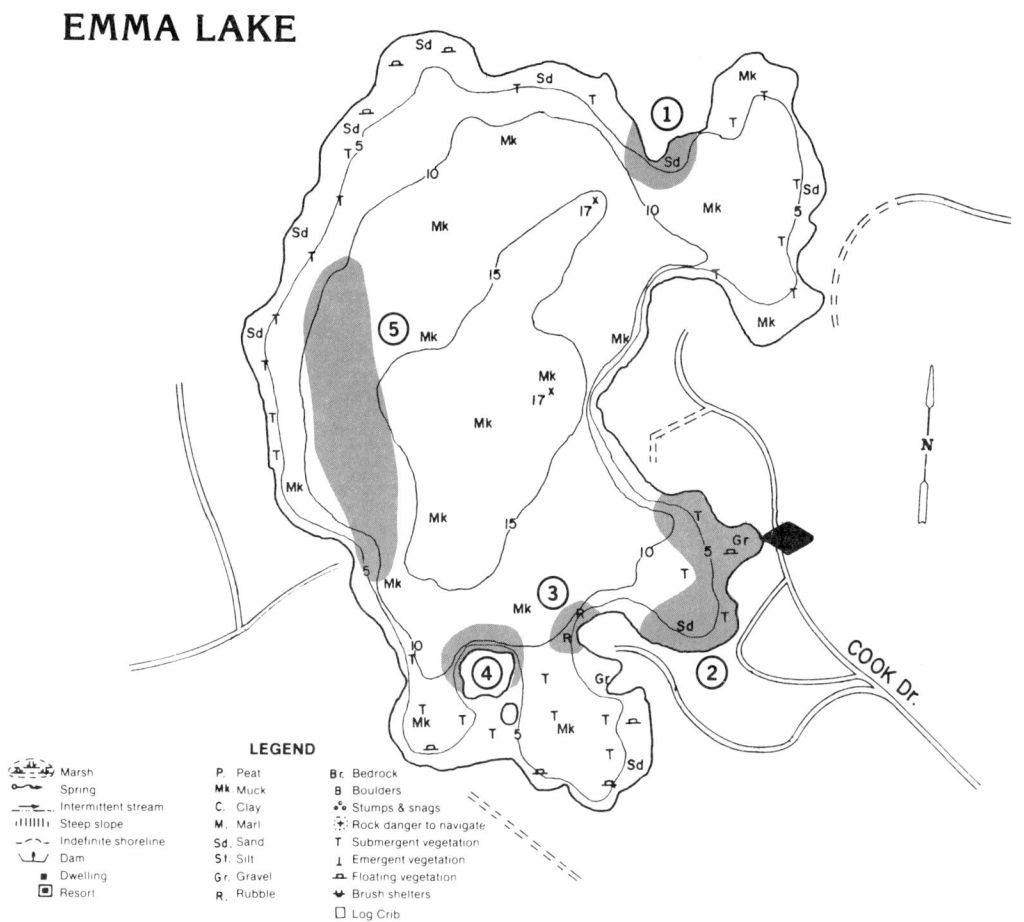

Stocking - Most recently, 11,000 three inch walleye were planted in 1983. Prior to that walleye and muskie were stocked in alternating years during the 1970's.

Treatment - None.

LAKE SURVEY MAP — Fishing Areas Shaded

Area (1) This point on the north shore holds walleye through May and into June. Jigs tipped with minnows or leeches are standard selections.

Area (2) Work around the bay in front of the landing for bass and pike. A few panfish can also be expected.

Area (3) Walleye will relate to this rocky point in spring and early summer. Try along the transition zone where the rock gives way to muck.

Area (4) The north side of the island attracts walleye throughout the year. Various live bait rigs will produce...leadhead jigs, floating jigs, and slip bobbers are all good selections.

Area (5) This stretch along the west side is a very popular ice fishing area for walleye and northern pike. Tip-ups rigged with large shiners or suckers are the preferred method.

FISHING TIPS — Concentrate your walleye efforts to the shoreline areas during the early part of the season. Later, also look for summer walleye over the mid-lake mud flats. Drifting with slip sinker/floating jig combos will cover large areas quickly. Use crawlers or leeches to tip the jig.

Shoreline weeds and cover provide the best opportunities for largemouth bass action, especially during the evening.

CONCLUSION — The infertile water of Emma Lake supports only a modest fishery. State walleye stocking has maintained only marginal opportunities for this species... excessive angler harvest may be a factor. The few northern pike and largemouth may add a little interest.

CRESCENT LAKE

LOCATION — In the southwestern part of the book area, west of Rhinelander and south of and adjacent to Highway 8.

ACCESS — Type I (Public): On the north side of the lake, take Highway 8 west from Rhinelander approximately 5 miles to the wayside/access facility on the south side of the road. A concrete slab landing, paved ramp, and parking for about 10 rigs are provided. Picnic and toilet facilities are also available.

RELATED SERVICES
    Boat Rentals - Yes.
    Bait Shops - Yes.
    Resorts - Yes, several.
    Public Parks - Yes, a picnic area at the access.
    Campgrounds - None.
    Guide Services - Yes.

SPECIAL FEATURES — Crescent Lake supports an excellent fish population.

LAKE CHARACTERISTICS
    Size and Depth - 612 acres and 37 feet deep. 46% of the lake has depths greater than 20'.
    Water Source - Spring-fed lake: An outlet, Crescent Creek, is a tributary of the Wisconsin River.
    Shoreline - Predominantly upland and completely private, except for the access.
    Bottom - 30% sand, 25% gravel, 20% rubble, 20% muck, 5% boulders.
    Water - Slightly fertile and clear. Moderate algae blooms have been known to occur.
    Vegetation - Moderate amounts of submergent varieties with lesser quantities of emergent and floating types. Most weeds are found

in the north side near the landing and in the bays on the south end. Pickerel weed, coontail, cabbage, and water lily are the most common types.

FISHERY

Species -
   Primary - Walleye, Perch.
   Secondary - Muskie, Smallmouth Bass, Bluegill, Crappie.
   Limited - Northern Pike, Largemouth Bass, Pumpkinseed, Rock Bass, Burbot.
Comment - All species have average or above average growth rates and are in good condition. Rusty crayfish are abundant but have not dramatically impacted the fishery.
Forage - Bluntnose minnow, mimic shiner, and young-of-the-year perch.

LAKE MANAGEMENT

Lake Investigation Data - The results of a comprehensive fyke netting survey are listed below. As seen, the dominant predator species are walleye and muskie, while perch are the primary panfish.

SPECIES	NUMBER	SIZE RANGE	AVERAGE LENGTH
Walleye	804	7 1/2"-25"	14 1/2"
Muskie	23	15"-51"	31"
Northern Pike	7	9"-23"	19"
Smallmouth Bass	6	11"-18"	13"
Perch	482	4"-11 1/2"	6"
Crappie	1	8 1/2"	8 1/2"
Bluegill	36	4"- 6 1/2"	5"
Pumpkinseed	2	3 1/2"-4"	4"

The study also indicated that walleye growth rates were above the area average during their first 5 years of life, but displayed average growth after year 5. The total annual mortality rate (deaths from natural causes and fishing harvest) for walleye larger than 15" was 49.3%. This figure is slightly lower than those for other area lakes. An electrofishing survey in the fall of 1980 was conducted to assess walleye natural reproduction. The data showed walleye reproduction was adequate, according to the state "to maintain a satisfactory walleye population."

Stocking -

YEAR	SPECIES	NUMBER	SIZE
1980	Muskie	1,200	8"
1982	Walleye	30,000	2"
	Muskie	200	11" (Private)
1984	Muskie	780	8"
1986	Muskie	1,200	11"

CRESCENT LAKE

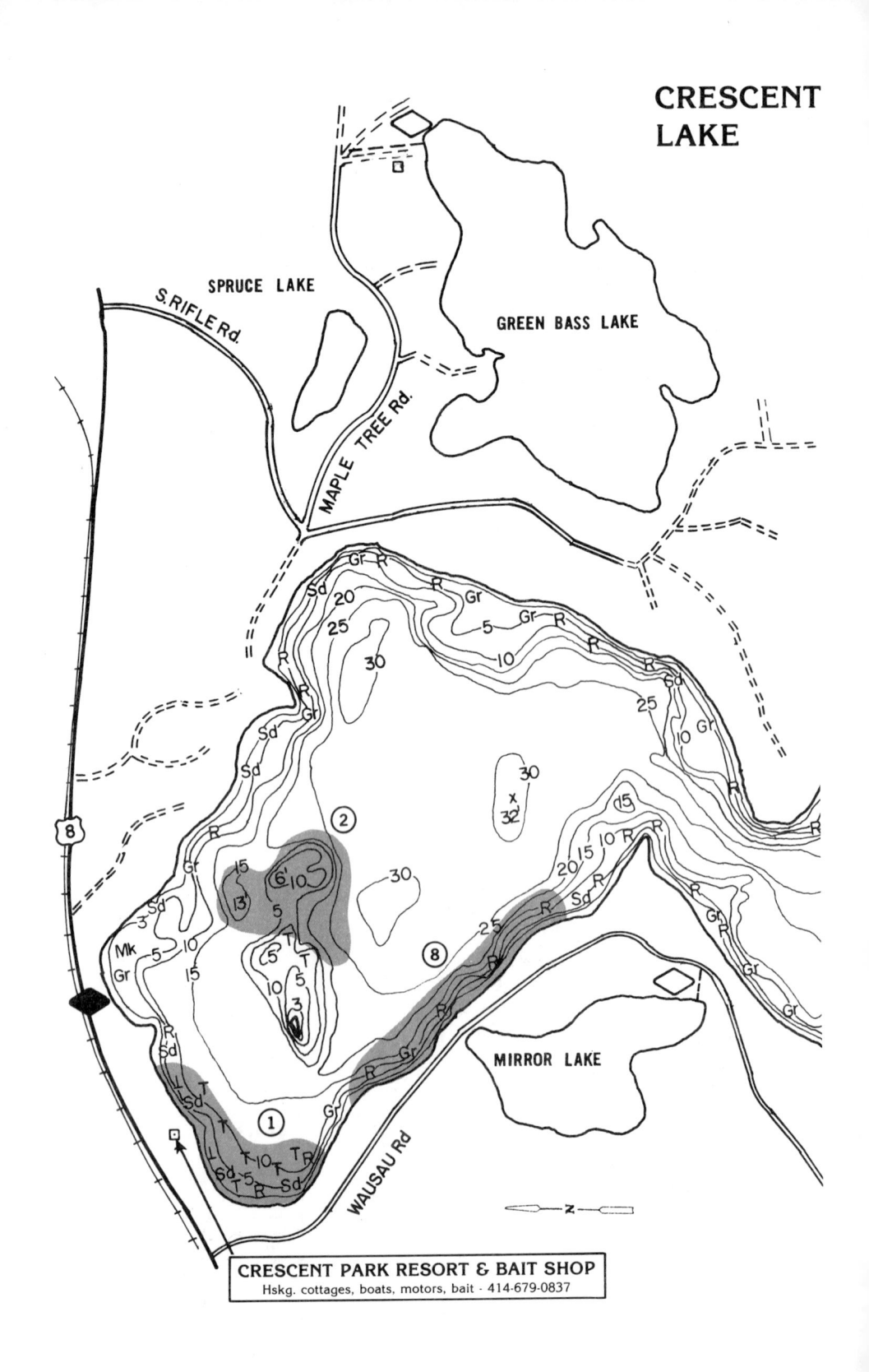

CRESCENT PARK RESORT & BAIT SHOP
Hskg. cottages, boats, motors, bait - 414-679-0837

119

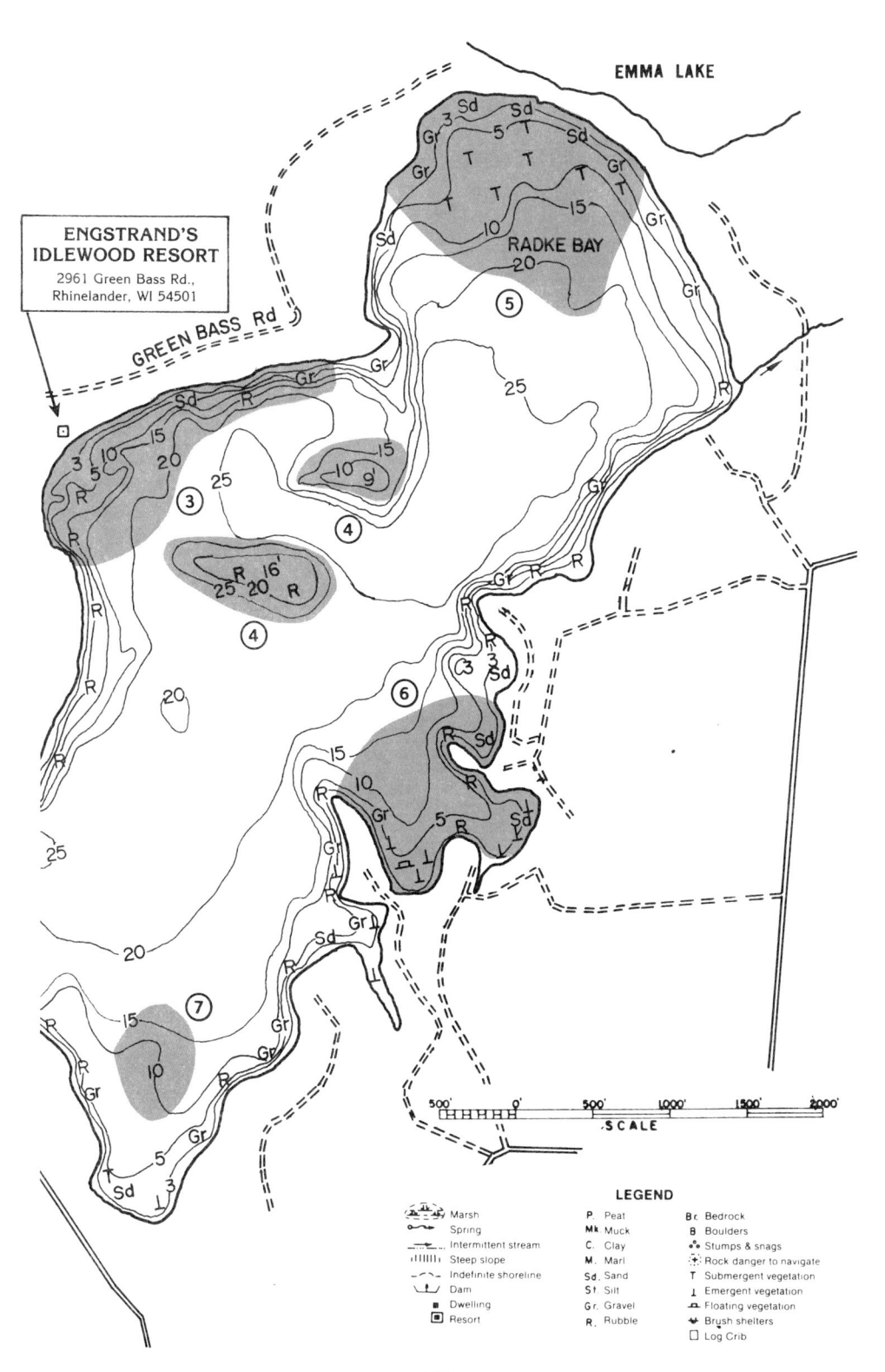

LAKE SURVEY MAP — Fishing Area Shaded

Area (1) The drop-offs adjacent to the weedline in the northwest corner will attract walleye. Try jig/live bait combinations.

Area (2) Both walleye and muskie inhabit this region of weeds and irregular bottom. In particular, cast for muskie around the 6' hump.

Area (3) This portion of the east shore features an unevenly contoured bottom, and provides excellent habitat for fall walleye. Remember to work your presentations parallel to this rocky shore.

Area (4) These two mid-lake humps should be fished for walleye and muskie throughout the season. A weighted black bucktail with a silver blade has been effective for local muskie fishermen. Walleye are taken on a variety of live bait presentations.

Area (5) Early spring action for walleye, muskie, and panfish can be can be found in Radke Bay. The water warms fast and stimulates early weed growth. Use slip bobbers or jig combos to take walleye from the weeds. Near the outer weedline, a number of irregular fingers form a series of peaks and valleys. Try these for walleye... working the peaks early in the season, the valleys later on. Closer to shore, fish perch with crabtails all summer long and again through the ice.

Area (6) Heavy weed growth near shore holds panfish and muskie during summer. Smitty's shallow running crankbait or a Suick are both good choices. Also concentrate on the sharp breaks off the weed edges for walleye and perhaps a muskie.

Area (7) 'Hard water' fishermen should try here for walleye and perch through the ice. Jig a Swedish Pimple with a perch eye for perch. A golden shiner rigged below a tip-up is standard fare for walleye, which use this area all year... so try again when the season reopens.

Area (8) The irregular shoreline along the northwest side produces muskie and walleye.

FISHING TIPS — When fishing drop-off areas for muskie, use weighted bucktails or crankbaits. Also, work the many sharp drop-offs for walleye... evening is especially productive.

Only a portion of the many fishing areas are detailed here. Use your depthfinder to locate the numerous other spots that will hold fish. Underwater points, bars, 'benches', deep weedlines, etc. are all worth trying.

CONCLUSION — Crescent Lake has plenty of walleye habitat and supports a good population of this popular gamefish. Large walleye are rare... the bulk of the action is provided by numerous smaller sized fish. However, Crescent Lake remains a quality fishing lake and will provide action for a variety of species throughout the year.

GREEN BASS LAKE

LOCATION — In the southwest segment of the book area, immediately east of Crescent Lake.

ACCESS — **Type IV (Public):** To the northeast corner of the lake; take South Rifle Road south off Highway 8 for 0.5 mile to Maple Tree Road. Turn left and continue about 1/2 mile to the end of the road. The 66' wide access strip is on the south side of the road just east of the adjacent blacktop driveway. The access runs nearly due south from the road for about 450' to the lake and is heavily wooded and steep. There is no trail or road leading to the water. (See Crescent Lake map for approximate location).

LAKE CHARACTERISTICS
Size and Depth - 68 acres and 26 feet.
Water Source - Seepage lake: No inlet or outlet.
Shoreline - Mainly upland with only minor wetlands.
Bottom - 45% gravel, 35% sand, 10% rubble, 10% muck.
Water - Light brown in color and rather infertile.
Vegetation - Quite sparse, with some floating types present along the shoreline zone.

FISHERY
Species - Largemouth Bass, Panfish, (Muskie).
Comment - Information on the fishery is extremely minimal as a result of the difficult access situation.

LAKE MANAGEMENT
Lake Investigation Data - None.
Stocking - None recorded.

FISHING TIPS — Since it's nearly impossible to get even a canoe over the public access land, consider wading the shoreline or using a 'belly boat' to fish this lake.

CONCLUSION — Years ago, when easier means of access where available, local fishermen reported taking nice catches of largemouth and even a few muskie. However, current information is limited, but suggests that some decent action can still be expected if you're willing to get to the lake.

MIRROR LAKE

LOCATION — In the southwestern part of the area, immediately west of Crescent Lake.

ACCESS — **Type III (Public):** On the northeast side of the lake; take Wausau Road south from Highway 8 for 1/2 mile to where the road right-of-way meets the lake. Safe roadside parking is not available - this access is not recommended.

Type IV (Public): To the southeast corner of the lake; drive south on Wausau Road for approximately 1.0 mile to the unmarked subdivision type access. A 60' strip of public property leads to the lake through the woods. This is a difficult access. Note: See Crescent Lake map for approximate location.

LAKE CHARACTERISTICS
Size and Depth - 17 acres and 16 feet.
Water Source - Seepage lake: No inlet or outlet.
Shoreline - 80% upland, 20% wetland. Mostly private.
Bottom - 100% muck.
Water - Highly infertile and clear. Summer dissolved oxygen levels are adequate at all depths.
Vegetation - Moderate densities of floating types around the perimeter.

FISHERY
Species - Northern Pike, Largemouth Bass, Bluegill, Pumpkinseed.
Comment - Low fertility has resulted in stunted populations of bluegill and pumpkinseed.

LAKE MANAGEMENT
Lake Investigation Data - None.
Stocking - None.

CONCLUSION — Not much is known about the fishery of Mirror Lake. However, the water chemistry suggests a very limited fishing potential.

-LAKES LIMITED IN ACCESS OR FISHERY IN SECTION 6-

ALICE LAKE
COOK LAKE
FLAG LAKE
HOIST LAKE
JOHN LAKE
LOON LAKE
PERCH LAKE (S5, T36N, R8E)
PRUNE LAKE
ROUND LAKE
SHADOW LAKE
SPRUCE LAKE (S16, T36N, R8E)
SPUR LAKE
VICKS LAKE

LOCATION — In the west part of the book area, south of Highway K and west of Highway 17.

ACCESS — None public, except for Vicks Lake and Flag Lake which have difficult wilderness type access.

LAKE CHARACTERISTICS
Size and Depth - These small lakes, 4-50 acres in size, range in depth from 6'-26'.

Water Source - Seepage lakes: No inlets or outlets.

Shoreline - Completely private except for public lands along Vicks Lake and Flag Lake. Mostly uplands.

Bottom - For lakes of this size considerable areas of firm bottom are present. However, Alice Lake, Spruce Lake, and Hicks Lake are entirely muck.

Water - Quite infertile and clear. Only Alice Lake and Vicks Lake have a brown color. Winterkill has been known to occur in Loon Lake and Spruce Lake.

Vegetation - Sparse to moderate in density. Floating species are most prevalent.

FISHERY — The entire group of lakes contains a largemouth bass/panfish fishery. In addition to bass and panfish, Spur Lake is reported to have northern pike.

CONCLUSION — This group of essentially private lakes has nothing to attract the fishing public. Again, low fertility and stunted panfish highlight most of these waters.

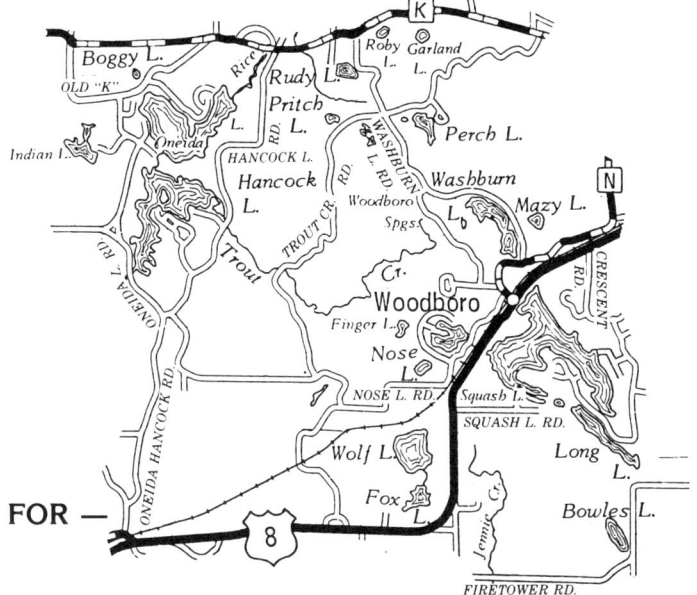

SECTION 7

SECTION MAP FOR —
Hancock Lake
Oneida Lake
Perch Lake (S2, T36N, R7E)
Washburn Lake
Squash Lake
Bowles Lake
Finger Lake
Fox Lake
Garland Lake
Indian Lake

Long Lake (S30, T36N, R8E)
Mazy Lake
Nose Lake
Pritch Lake
Roby Lake
Rudy Lake
Wolf Lake

HANCOCK LAKE

LOCATION — On the extreme western end of the book area, directly south of Oneida Lake and Highway K.

ACCESS — **Type I (Public):** To the southeast corner of the lake; travel south from Highway K on Hancock Lake Road for 2.4 miles to Dombrowski Road. Turn right and continue 0.2 mile to the marked access road on the right. A gravel approach, concrete plank landing, and loading pier are provided by the township.

RELATED SERVICES
- **Boat Rentals** - Yes, at resort.
- **Bait Shops** - None.
- **Resorts** - Yes, one.
- **Public Parks and Campgrounds** - None.
- **Guide Services** - Yes.

SPECIAL FEATURES — One of the more fertile lakes in the area. Known for providing good action for a variety of species.

LAKE CHARACTERISTICS —
- **Size and Depth** - 259 acres and 22 feet.
- **Water Source** - Drainage lake: An inlet (Rice Creek) from Oneida Lake, another inlet (Trout Creek) on the southeast side. A 6' head dam controls the southwest side outlet (Little Rice Creek).
- **Shoreline** - Mainly upland, although significant areas of bog are present. Mostly private.
- **Bottom** - 50% muck, 30% sand, 10% gravel, 5% boulders, 5% rubble.
- **Water** - Light brown in color with moderate fertility. Summer dissolved oxygen levels can be inadequate for gamefish below 11'. Thermal stratification during summer does not occur (no thermocline). Dense summer algae blooms have been documented in the past.
- **Vegetation** - Emergent and submergent forms are found throughout most of the lake with dense growths in the shallow bays. Arrowhead, water lily, and pondweeds are the common types.

FISHERY
- **Species**
  - **Primary** - Northern Pike, Largemouth Bass, Bluegill.
  - **Secondary** - Muskie, Crappie, Pumpkinseed.
  - **Limited** - Walleye, Smallmouth Bass, Perch.
  - **Comment** - Muskie are sustained by the State's stocking program. Walleye are few in number but above average in size.
  - **Forage** - Bluntnose minnow, common and golden shiners, juvenile panfish.

HANCOCK LAKE

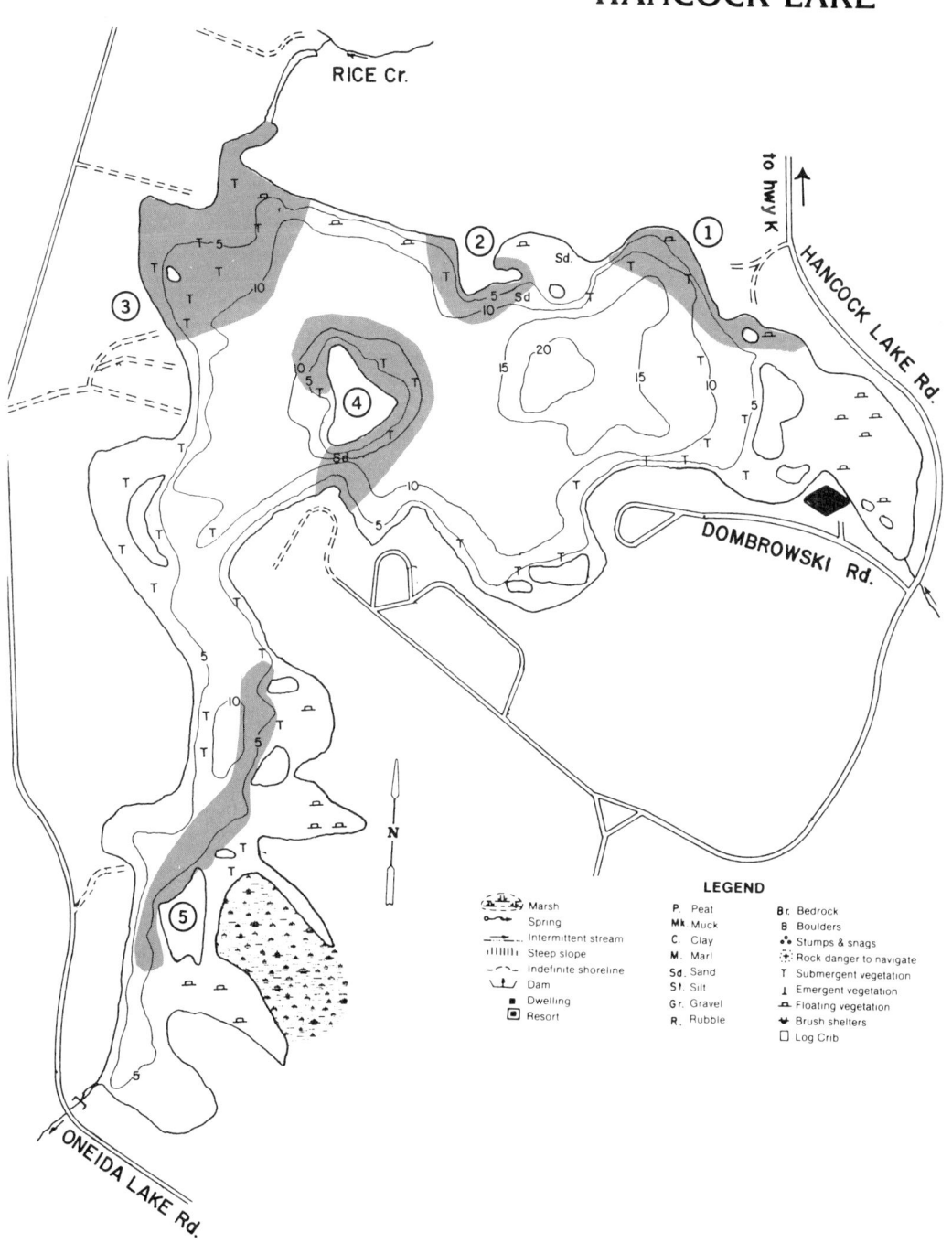

LAKE MANAGEMENT

Lake Investigation Data - An old fyke net survey showed good populations of northern pike and largemouth bass. The results indicated both good size and numbers of fish present.

SPECIES	NUMBER	SIZE RANGE
Northern Pike	98	10"-33"
Muskie	2	20"-27"
Largemouth Bass	31	7"-17"
Smallmouth Bass	1	8"
Walleye	10	13"-28"
Crappie	330	7"-14"
Bluegill	1,881	2"- 9"
Pumpkinseed	90	2"- 7"
Perch	24	5"- 9"

Additionally, spawning habitat for walleye and smallmouth was determined to be poor. However, spawning habitat for largemouth and northern was good - both species are sustained by natural reproduction. Also notice the unusually high number of largemouth bass caught. Largemouth tend to avoid entrapment in nets, yet 31 were captured. This suggests that a strong population of bass exists - reports from local anglers support this contention.

Stocking - Walleye and muskie have been stocked in the past, recently only muskie are being planted.

YEAR	SPECIES	NUMBER	SIZE
1982	Muskie	500	10"-12"
1984	Muskie	375	10"-12"
1985	Muskie	515	10"-12"
1986	Muskie	500	8"

LAKE SURVEY MAP — Fishing Areas Shaded

Area (1) Work this portion of the north shore for northern pike and bass. Weedless spoons and spinnerbaits have been productive.

Area (2) Early season walleye are attracted to the small point on the north end. A jig and minnow or slip bobber rig are a good bet.

Area (3) The inletting waters of Rice Creek provide another good spot for early season walleye. Northern pike and muskie can also be taken here. Panfish are available too.

Area (4) The area around the large island in the center of the lake holds a number of species. Again, try for early walleye off the north and south ends. Fish the weed edges and pockets for bass, pike, and muskie.

Area (5) This zone in the southern end of the lake can be fished through the ice and again in early spring for walleye and panfish.

FISHING TIPS — The extremely heavy weed growth restricts most fishing activity to early spring, fall, and winter since summer weeds choke

most of the lake. Good weed fishing techniques are the key to success on Hancock. Look for pockets in the weeds and weedlines, emphasizing both inside and outside turns. Also, work back into the 'slop' for bass.

Muskie fishermen should plan on using surface baits, especially during the summer when the weeds are thicker.

CONCLUSION — Hancock is a fertile and productive lake offering excellent opportunities for pike and largemouth. Walleye and muskie can also produce some action for those who can find them.

Above average populations of panfish add to this lake's appeal. Panfish and northern pike are also popular during the winter with ice fishermen.

The only problem with this lake is the heavy weeds which can hinder both navigation and fishing.

ONEIDA LAKE

LOCATION — In the very western portion of the area, about 9 miles east of Rhinelander and south of Highway K.

ACCESS — **A Type I (Private):** On the north side of the lake; take "Old K" south off Highway K (just west of Horsehead Lake Road) for 0.9 mile to Oneida Lake Road. Turn left and go 0.2 mile to the Alpine Resort/tavern facility. A concrete landing with ample parking is provided. Permission from the owner is required PRIOR to using this landing. Boat gas, oil, and food can also be purchased.

B Type III (Public): On the west side of the lake; take "Old K" south from Highway K for 1.3 miles to Oneida Lake Road. Turn left and proceed 0.6 mile to a three-way intersection. Turn left onto Schmidts Drive and travel 1.0 mile to the unmarked access on the right. This old town-owned access facility is on a steep bank and can be difficult to find. This access is not recommended.

RELATED SERVICES

Boat Rentals - Yes, at resort.
Resorts - Yes.
Public Parks and Campgrounds - None.
Guide Services - Yes.

LAKE CHARACTERISTICS

Size and Depth - 255 acres and 34 feet.
Water Source - Drainage lake: An inlet (Rice Creek) on the northeast side and a controlled outlet on the southwest end to Hancock Lake.
Shoreline - Chiefly upland and completely private except for the access.
Bottom - 35% sand, 30% gravel, 15% rubble, 15% muck, 5% boulders.

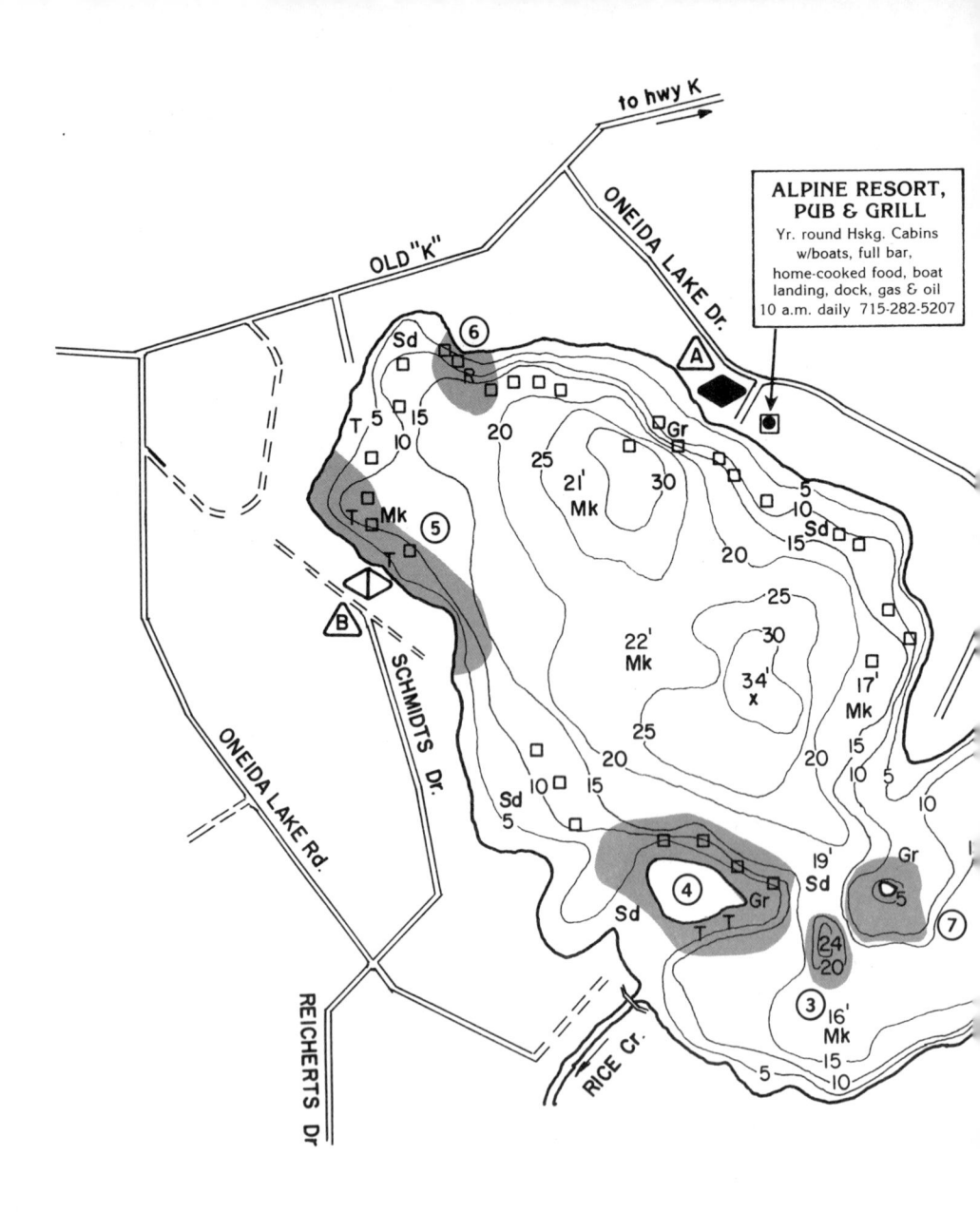

Water - Slightly fertile and clear. Dissolved oxygen levels are insufficient for gamefish below 25'.

Vegetation - Sparse growths of submergent types in addition to some lily pads and arrowhead. Moderate growth occurs near the inlet stream. A heavy summer algae bloom is an annual occurrence.

ONEIDA LAKE

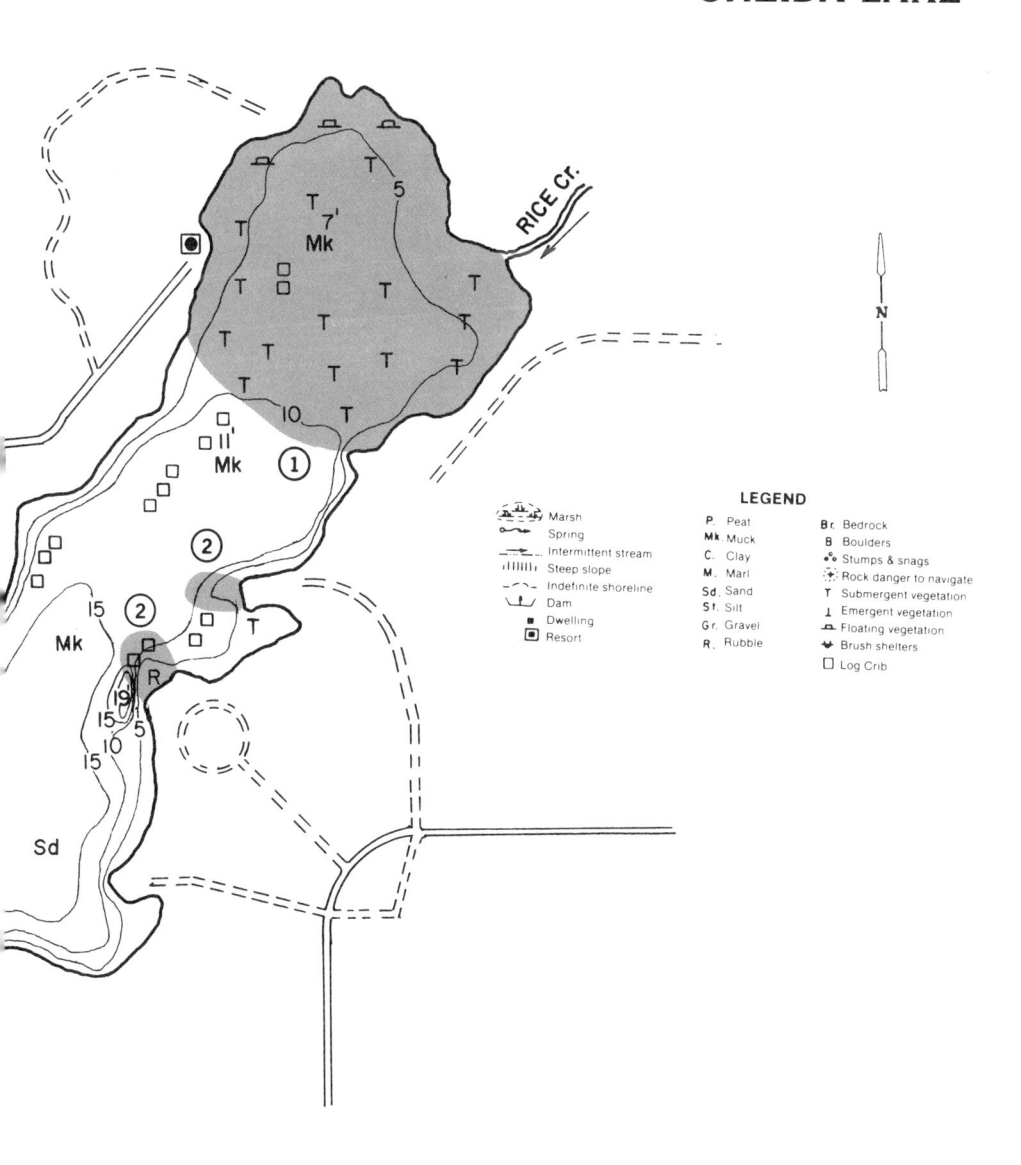

FISHERY
Species
Primary - Walleye, Bluegill, Rock Bass.
Secondary - Muskie, Northern Pike, Crappie, Pumpkinseed.
Limited - Largemouth Bass, Smallmouth Bass, Perch.
Comment - Walleye and muskie numbers are maintained by state stocking.

LAKE MANAGEMENT

Lake Investigation Data - Although no surveys have been conducted recently, an old study using fyke nets resulted in the following data:

SPECIES	NUMBER	SIZE RANGE
Muskie	10	15"-31"
Walleye	43	11"-25"
Smallmouth Bass	2	13"-21"
Crappie	25	9"-15"
Bluegill	48	6"- 9"
Perch	3	7"- 9"
Rock Bass	97	5"-10"

Problems associated with the rusty crayfish began to develop in the early 1960's. Since that time dramatic reductions in weed-bed areas has occurred. In an attempt to control excessive crayfish numbers, the State periodically planted smallmouth bass throughout the 1960's and 1970's. Increased commercial harvest (trapping) of crayfish was also encouraged. These measures had little, if any, impact on crayfish numbers.

Stocking -

YEAR	SPECIES	NUMBER	SIZE
1980	Muskie	500	8"
1983	Walleye	13,000	3"
1984	Muskie	425	10"
1986	Muskie	500	12"

Treatment - The Oneida Lake Association installed 44 log crib fish shelters from 1974-1976. The cribs were placed in 10'-12' of water. See map for location.

LAKE SURVEY MAP — Fishing Areas Shaded

Area (1) The inlet bay on the northeast side is one of the best "Hot Spots" on the lake. Post-spawn walleye are attracted to this area early in the season. Walleye are taken here through the ice too. Also, work surface baits and jerkbaits over the weeds for muskie.

Area (2) Two small rocky points on the east end are excellent spots for walleye. Rock and scattered brush will hold fish throughout the season. Use a slip bobber rig to keep your bait just above the snags.

Area (3) Fish this 24' hole for summer walleye with a jig and crawler or jig and leech.

Area (4) The region around the larger island can provide good muskie and walleye action. Concentrate on the northwest side for walleye...the weeds on the south side for muskie.

Area (5) Cast for muskie along this stretch of shore. The scattered weeds and irregular drop-off should be fished early in the morning for best results.

Area (6) This subtle rock point on the north end can hold both walleye and muskie.

Area (7) Early season walleye can be found on the gravel areas around the small island. Jig and minnow combos are suggested.

FISHING TIPS — Oneida Lake walleye can be unpredictable and are often found where you would least expect them. Don't overlook the shallows...even in mid-day during the summer months. Rocks, wood, and the deep holes should all be fished when looking for active fish. Be sure to work the wood...especially in the evening. Natural colored jerkbaits have been particularly effective for muskie on this water.

CONCLUSION — A quality lake that both walleye and muskie anglers should try. It's small enough to learn quickly, yet large enough to support a diverse and balanced fishery. Catch and release is advised to maintain quality gamefish populations.

PERCH LAKE (S2, T36N, R7E)

LOCATION — On the west central end of the book area, south of Highway K and east of Oneida Lake.

ACCESS — (A) **Type I (Public):** To the northwest corner of the lake; follow Washburn Lake Road south from Highway K for 1 mile to Trout Creek Road. Turn left and continue 0.2 mile to the marked access road on the right. The landing is a short distance down this road. In addition to a dock, a gravel ramp, landing, and turn-around are supplied by Oneida County.

(B) **Type III (Public):** On the east shore of the lake; take Trout Creek Road 0.4 mile east from Washburn Lake Road (0.2 mile beyond access road described above) to the marked entrance road. Turn right and continue 0.2 mile to the county-owned picnic area.

SPECIAL FEATURES — Shore fishing opportunities are available at the county picnic area. Perch Lake is the only lake with a stocked trout fishery in the book area.

LAKE CHARACTERISTICS

Size and Depth - 23 acres and 21 feet.

Water Source - Seepage lake: No inlet or outlet.

Shoreline - Mostly upland with some wetlands on the north and west sides. Significant public ownership in the form of Oneida County Forest lands.

Bottom - 40% muck, 25% sand, 20% gravel, 15% rubble and boulders.

Water - Very clear and quite infertile.

Vegetation - Sparse and limited primarily to lily pads. Moderate growths of filamentous algae occurs.

PERCH LAKE

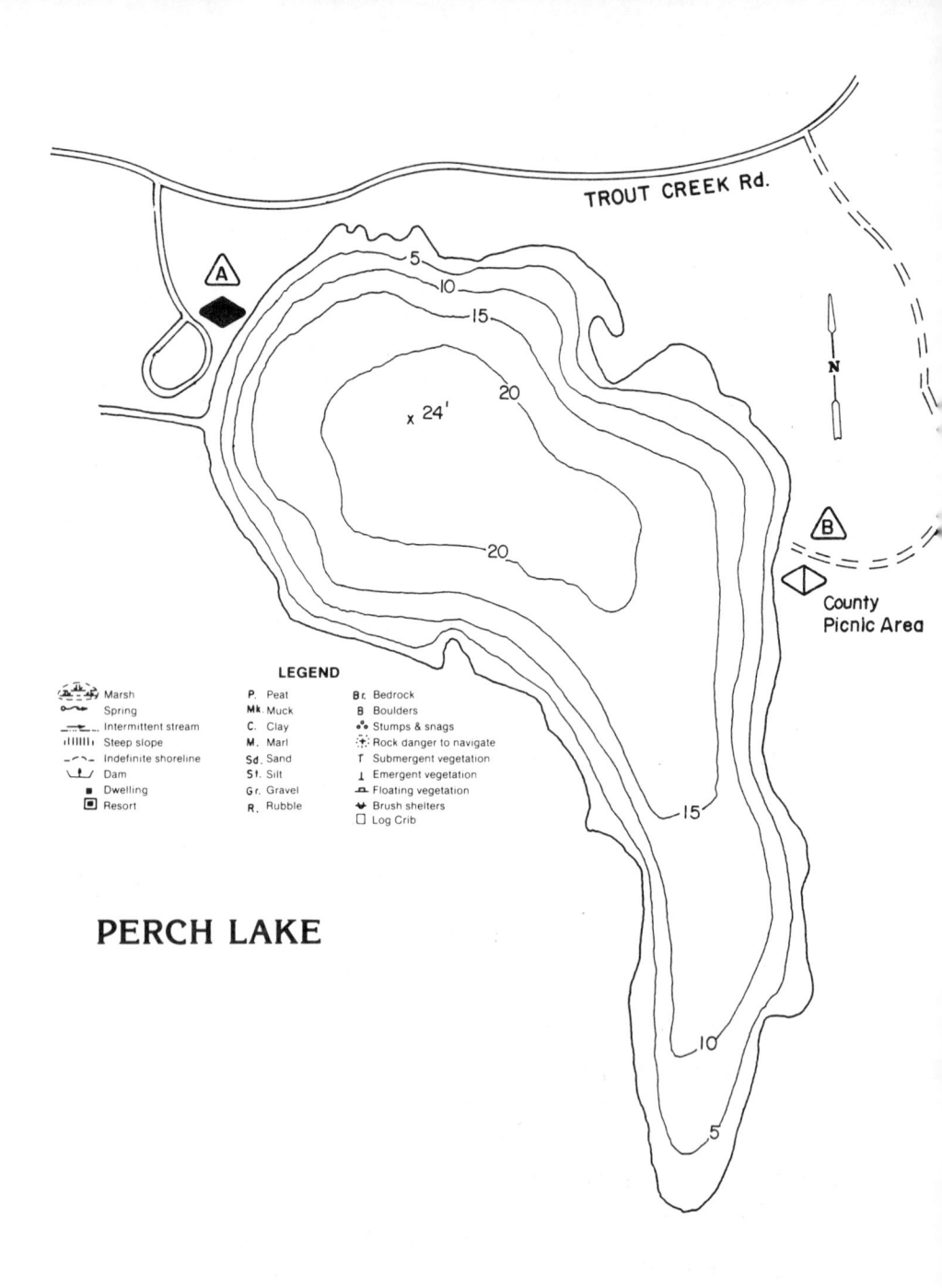

FISHERY

Species - Rainbow Trout, Largemouth Bass, Bluegill, (Brook Trout), (Perch).

Comment - Annual plantings of catchable size trout sustains the fishery.

LAKE MANAGEMENT

Lake Investigation Data - In 1986 a survey was performed to evaluate the trout stocking program. Variable mesh (experimental) gill nets were used. The nets were fished for 2 days and captured the following fish.

SPECIES	NUMBER	SIZE RANGE
Rainbow Trout	2	13"-13 1/2"
Largemouth Bass	2	7"- 7 1/2"

As might be expected, the researchers suggested that an alternative method be employed for future surveys on this lake to avoid such a small and unrepresentative sample.

Also, angler interviews were conducted during the study and reported that trout up to 24" have been caught.

Stocking - Annual plantings of 3,000 rainbow trout have occurred throughout the 1980's. A long history of trout stocking exists, dating back to 1967.

Treatment - The trout fishery was established following chemical eradication of undesirable populations of stunted panfish in 1966.

FISHING TIPS

Trout are the main attraction here and are taken on a variety of standard offerings. Crawlers, worms, and minnows are preferred live bait selections. Small spinners, spoons, or floating minnows are productive artificials. Some anglers suggest that corn, marshmallows, and cheese can also take fish.

Remember to use light line... 4# or less. Also tie your hooks and lures directly to the line - don't use a snap swivel. Fly fishermen should work the shoreline areas during the evening hours.

CONCLUSION

Perch Lake is an enjoyable lake to fish for those interested in trout. It has a history of providing good angler success. This fishery is obviously dependent on state stocking and as long as it continues, so should the good fishing.

WASHBURN LAKE

LOCATION — In the southwest segment of the book area, just north of Highway 8 and Squash Lake.

ACCESS — **Type I (Public):** To the southeast corner of the lake; follow Highway N north from Highway 8 for 0.7 mile to Washburn Lake Road. Make a left, the landing is a short distance down the road on the left hand side. A rough gravel/sand landing with roadside parking is available. The access is best suited for smaller-sized rigs.

LAKE CHARACTERISTICS

Size and Depth - 80 acres and 25 feet.
Water Source - Seepage lake: No inlet or outlet.
Shoreline - 65% upland, 35% bog. Mostly in private ownership.

WASHBURN LAKE

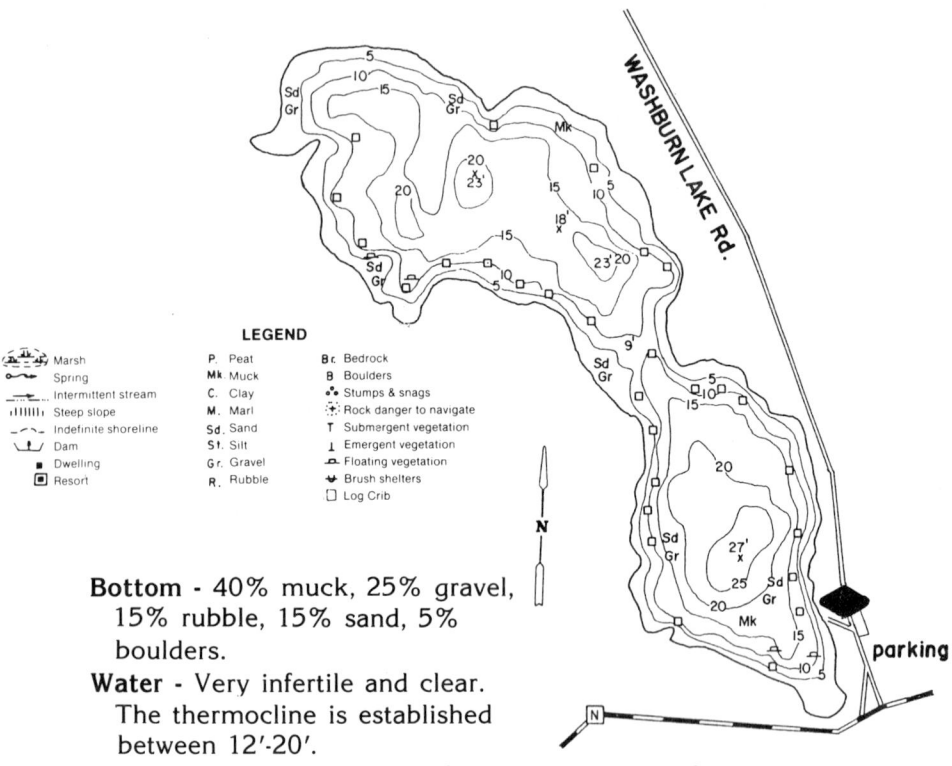

LEGEND

Marsh	P. Peat	Br. Bedrock	
Spring	Mk. Muck	B Boulders	
Intermittent stream	C. Clay	Stumps & snags	
Steep slope	M. Marl	Rock danger to navigate	
Indefinite shoreline	Sd. Sand	T Submergent vegetation	
Dam	St. Silt	Emergent vegetation	
Dwelling	Gr. Gravel	Floating vegetation	
Resort	R. Rubble	Brush shelters	
		Log Crib	

Bottom - 40% muck, 25% gravel, 15% rubble, 15% sand, 5% boulders.

Water - Very infertile and clear. The thermocline is established between 12'-20'.

Vegetation - Dense growths of both emergent and floating species around a narrow shoreline fringe.

FISHERY

Species

Primary - Bluegill, Crappie, Bullhead.
Secondary - Largemouth Bass, Northern Pike, Pumpkinseed.
Limited - Perch, (Walleye), (Muskie).

Comment - Largemouth and pike keep the panfish in relatively good balance with decent populations of average size fish.

LAKE MANAGEMENT

Lake Investigation Data - The figures listed below are the results of an old fyke net survey conducted to assess the status of the fishery.

SPECIES	NUMBER	SIZE RANGE
Largemouth Bass	9	4"-13"
Northern Pike	7	14"-27"
Walleye	2	21"-22"
Bluegill	199	4"- 7"
Crappie	127	4"-11"
Pumpkinseed	48	3"- 6"
Bullhead	67	5"-11"

As can be seen, the panfish species (bluegill, pumpkinseed, crappie) are numerous with both crappie and bluegill reaching desirable size. Largemouth bass are actually more abundant than the data shows since bass are difficult to capture with this type of sampling gear.

Stocking - None recently. The last effort occurred in 1970 when muskie were planted.

Treatment - Thirty brush shelters were placed in the mid-60's.

FISHING TIPS — Washburn Lake is known best for panfish and northern pike action. Good catches of average size panfish are taken from the many shoreline weed areas. Try the north end for bluegill and crappie early in the season. Use worms or waxies for bluegill... small minnows or Twisters for crappie. During summer try small leeches for the bigger bluegill. Look for these fish off the deeper weedlines.

Fish the outside weed edges for pike and bass. Spinnerbaits and floating Rapalas will take both species.

Ice anglers also report decent catches of panfish and pike.

CONCLUSION — A good panfish lake to consider for a family outing — both crappie and bluegill will keep the kids happy, while pike and bass can add to the family fun. Don't expect big fish... good numbers of 'average' size fish will provide the bulk of the action.

SQUASH LAKE

LOCATION — In the southwestern part of the area, south of Highway 8 and west of Crescent Lake.

ACCESS — **Type I (Public):** On the south side of the lake; take Crescent Road south off Highway 8 for 1.8 miles to Long Lake Road. Turn right, and continue 1.5 miles to the "Gudis Landing" sign on the right. This narrow, steep access has a concrete plank landing with a blacktop approach and is provided by the Hodag Sports Club and the Town of Crescent.

RELATED SERVICES
  Boat Rentals - Yes, at resort.
  Resorts - Yes.
  Public Parks and Campgrounds - None.

SPECIAL FEATURES — From 1971-1982 a 2# 4 oz. bluegill from Squash Lake held the Wisconsin state record for that species.

LAKE CHARACTERISTICS
  Size and Depth - 392 acres and 81 feet.
  Water Source - Seepage lake: No inlet or outlet.
  Shoreline - Chiefly private except for the access. Primarily upland.
  Bottom - 40% sand, 35% gravel, 15% rubble, 10% muck.

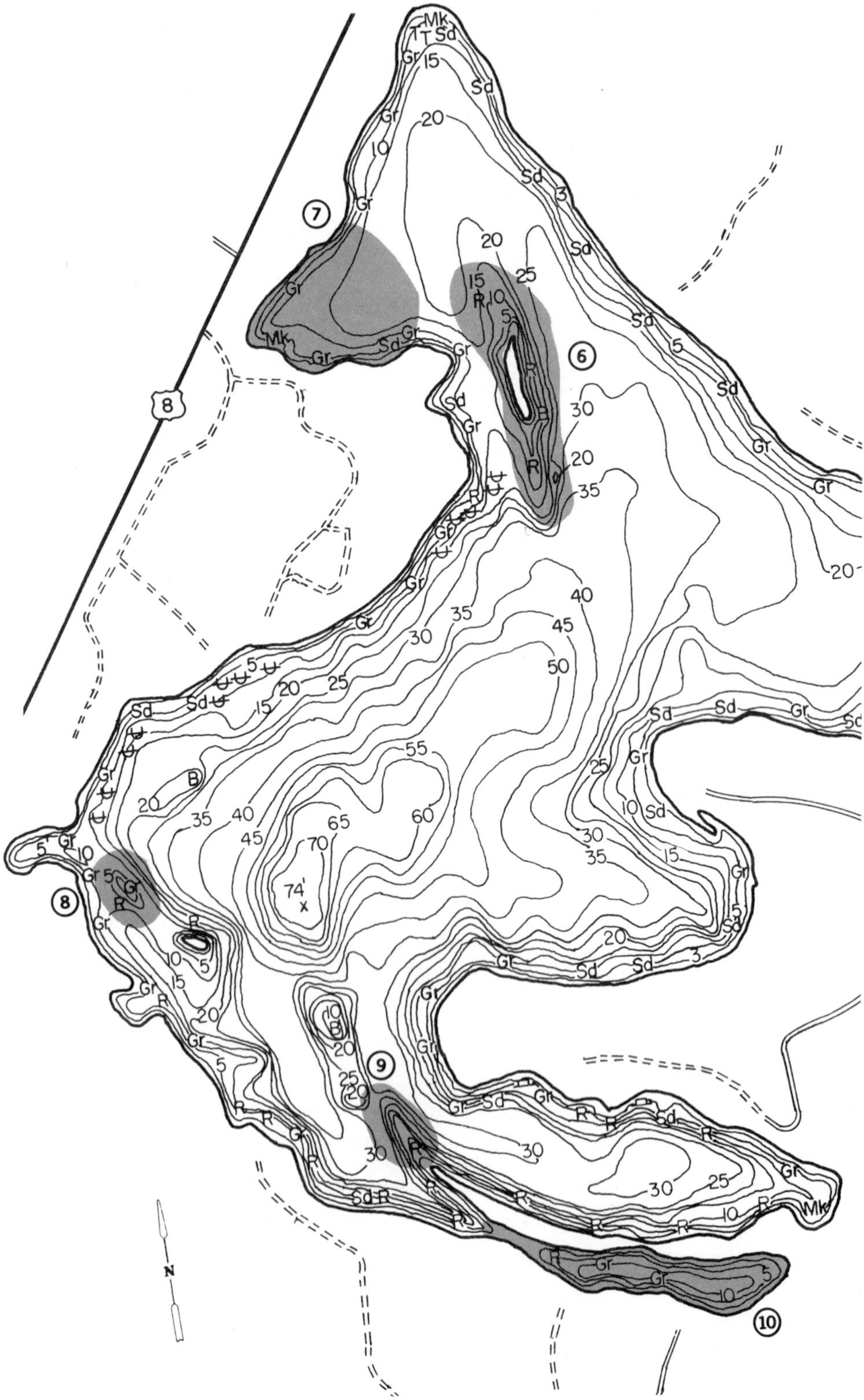
7
6
8
8
9
10
74'
N

SQUASH LAKE

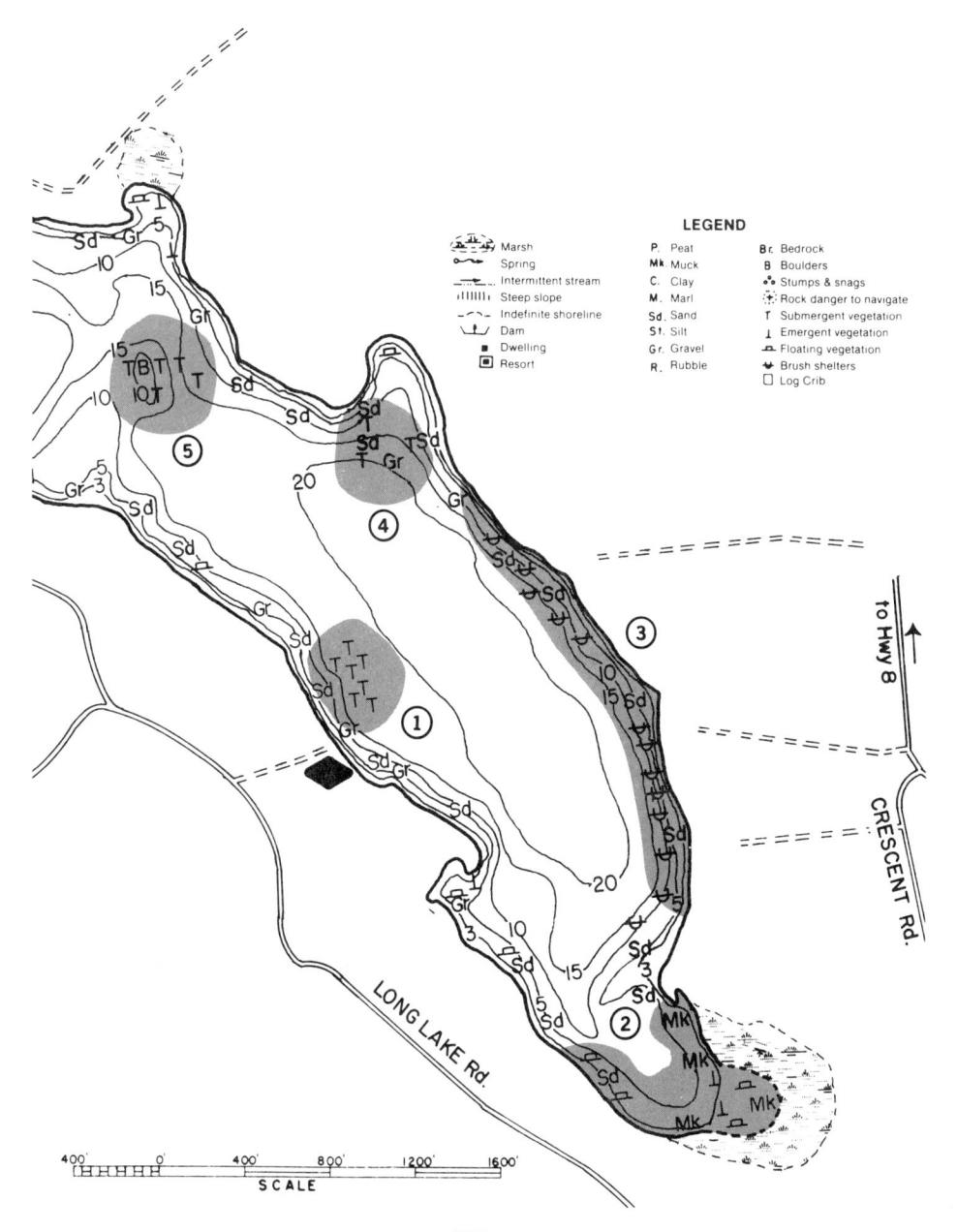

Water - Quite clear and infertile. The thermocline zone extends from 25'-35'.

Vegetation - Rather limited with lily pad, pickerel weed, pondweed, elodea, and coontail being most common.

FISHERY
Species
Primary - Walleye, Smallmouth Bass, Bluegill.
Secondary - Northern Pike, Perch, Rock Bass.
Limited - Largemouth Bass, Brown Trout, Crappie, Pumpkinseed, (Cisco).

Comment - The State rates the walleye population as "excellent" in terms of both numbers and natural reproduction. The status of brown trout could be upgraded due to future state stocking plans.

Forage - Bluntnose minnow, common shiner, mimic shiner, an abundant white sucker population is present.

LAKE MANAGEMENT
Lake Investigation Data - The results of an old fyke net survey are shown below.

SPECIES	NUMBER	SIZE RANGE
Walleye	350	9 1/2"-30"
Northern Pike	16	13"-41 1/2"
Smallmouth Bass	17	11 1/2"-15"
Crappie	6	6 1/2"-10"
Perch	23	4 1/2"-14 1/2"
Rock Bass	4	3 1/2"- 8 1/2"
Bluegill	164	3"-10"

The survey indicated that early life growth rates for walleye are similar to other Northern Wisconsin lakes. However, growth rates are above average for walleye beyond the age of four. All fish sampled appeared to be in good condition... that is good body weight for a given length.

In late summer of 1985 a survey was conducted to evaluate walleye natural reproduction. Researchers electrofishing the shoreline areas concluded that good levels of natural reproduction were evident for the years 1983-1985.

The rusty crayfish was found to be quite abundant, but less numerous than in the past.

Stocking - 10,000 brown trout were planted in 1988 to establish a two-story fishery.

Treatment - Brush shelters were installed in the past.

LAKE SURVEY MAP — Fishing Areas Shaded
Area (1) North of the landing is a deep weedbed that attracts walleye and northern pike. Try white or blue leadhead jigs tip-

ped with a minnow for walleye. Cast deep diving crankbaits and spinnerbaits for northern pike.

Area (2) To the south, the bay at the end of the lake is a good spot for northern pike. Spoons or Shad-Raps are good choices.

Area (3) Old brush shelters along this sharp drop-off may hold a few jumbo perch and perhaps a smallmouth.

Area (4) A small weedbed is found at the mouth of this north side bay. Silver or perch colored crankbaits worked over the weeds will take summer walleye. Also try jig/crawler combos.

Area (5) Work this area of coontail for "weed walleye" throughout the season. A small jig tipped with a redtail chub is a good bet, as is a leech or minnow worked below a slip bobber.

Area (6) Rocky underwater extensions of this island provide good habitat for smallmouth bass and walleye. Traditional presentations will produce spring walleye. A variety of 'plastics' are very effective for smallies...4" plastic worms, Twister Tails, or Reapers are suggested.

Area (7) Debris from an old sawmill now provides the premier "Hot Spot" on the lake for smallmouth bass. Spinnerbaits, crankbaits, and plastics will all take fish.

Area (8) Walleye and smallies can be caught on this small rocky hump.

Area (9) This long narrow bar provides the classic rocky habitat for smallmouth bass. Try dragging a lively crawler over the rocks.

Area (10) Scattered weeds in this shallow, narrow bay attracts Squash's large bluegill. Worms and crawler pieces are always a good bet.

FISHING TIPS — Periods of low light will be most productive due to Squash's high water clarity. Try early morning, evening, and after dark...also cloudy days. The scarcity of vegetation and clean hard bottom places a high value on any available cover. Try anything that would appear to provide some cover...'drowned wood', docks, weeds, etc. Old brush shelters will still hold and concentrate some fish.

CONCLUSION — Typical of most deep clear lakes, Squash can be difficult to fish, but will produce if you take the time to learn the lake and fish it correctly.

The addition of brown trout should expand the fishery potential of this fine lake.

-LAKES LIMITED IN ACCESS OR FISHERY IN SECTION 7-

BOWLES LAKE	MAZY LAKE
FINGER LAKE	NOSE LAKE
FOX LAKE	PRITCH LAKE
GARLAND LAKE	ROBY LAKE
INDIAN LAKE	RUDY LAKE
LONG LAKE (S30, T36N, R8E)	WOLF LAKE

LOCATION — In the west and southwest portions of the book area.

ACCESS — None public, except for Roby which has a difficult wilderness type access over county forest land. An access that was once considered public on Nose Lake is currently posted as private.

LAKE CHARACTERISTICS

Size and Depth - As a group there is a size range of 7-88 acres with maximum depths from 4-28 feet.

Water Source - Seepage lakes: No inlets or outlets.

Shoreline - Mostly upland, yet Garland Lake, Mazy Lake, Pritch Lake, and Wolf Lake are surrounded by wetlands.

Bottom - Predominantly muck, but Long Lake has significant hard bottom areas.

Water - Quite infertile. Indian Lake, Mazy Lake and Wolf Lake are subject to winterkill.

Vegetation - Most have moderate to heavy growths of floating types - mostly lily pads. Densities of submergent species vary dramatically from lake to lake.

FISHERY

Species - Largemouth Bass, Panfish.

Comment - Most of these waters are bass-panfish lakes, except Long Lake which has a diverse fishery...including smallmouth bass. Typical of the other small private lakes in the area, little data is available on these waters.

CONCLUSION — Again, the absence of adequate public access curtails any fishing activity. However, the water chemistry suggests that only a limited fishing potential should be expected.

GLOSSARY

BIOMASS - A biological term to describe the entire amount of fish of all species in any given lake.

BREAKLINE - A length or distance along a lake's bottom where the drop-off changes to a steeper gradient. Often this occurs at a specific depth of water.

EDGE - The border or fringe of any fish-holding habitat - weeds, wood, brush, rock breakline, etc. Traditionally a good place to fish.

FERTILITY - The biological productivity of the water in a lake. A high fertility usually results in a quality fishery due to a well developed food chain. However, it can also lead to overly dense vegetation and algae blooms. A lake with extremely low fertility often has stunted fish populations.

FISHERY - All the species of fish that inhabit a lake.

GAMEFISH - The group of fish sought by anglers, including muskie, northern pike, walleye, largemouth bass, smallmouth bass, and trout.

HABITAT - A region to which fish relate and can often be found. Usually associated with some form of structure - bottom, weeds, wood, etc. Providing either cover and/or food.

LAKE TYPES -
   SPRING - Always a substantial outlet, but rarely an inlet. Most of the water supply comes from ground water. Usually the most fertile type of lake, with the most varied fishery and greatest fish population.
   DRAINAGE - Has at least one inlet and an outlet. Water supply comes from stream drainage and direct runoff. Usually very fertile, with a diversified and quality fishery.
   DRAINED - Has a "small flow" outlet, but rarely an inlet. Water supply comes from ground water sources. Usually moderately infertile with bass and panfish the main fishery.
   SEEPAGE - No inlet or outlet (landlocked). Water supply comes from ground water sources. Usually very infertile with only bass and panfish populations. An exception would be a large seepage lake with a stocked fishery.

LITTORAL ZONE - The shore area of the lake. Usually out to the 5 foot depth or the outside edge of the shoreline weeds. This zone is referred to in the discussion of bottom materials.

PANFISH - The group of fish sought by anglers including perch, bluegill, crappie, rock bass, pumpkinseed, and bullhead.

PRIMARY BREAK - Usually the most pronounced drop-off to deeper water, often adjacent to a submergent weedline and always a key location for finding fish.

STATE - Reference made to the Department of Natural Resources (DNR).

STRUCTURE - A distinguishing break or change on the bottom of the lake that separates it from the surrounding bottom.

STUNTED PANFISH - A panfish population that does not maintain an average rate of growth. These populations are associated with lakes of low fertility, where food supplies are inadequate. There are many lakes in Northern Wisconsin that have this condition.

THERMOCLINE - A layer of reasonably well oxygenated summer lake water that displays a rapid drop in temperature from top to bottom. This water will range from 45 degrees F. to 65 degrees F. and will hold fish preferring cooler water. This layer prevents the wind from circulating warmer surface water into the cold lake bottom water.

"TWO-STORY LAKE" - A lake that supports a warmwater fishery in its upper levels and coldwater (trout) fishery in its lower levels. This is accomplished only when lower levels have cool, well oxygenated water and abundant food supplies.

YEAR CLASS - The group of any particular species of fish in a lake produced in any given year.

NOTES:

FISHING HOT SPOTS SUPPORTS CATCH AND RELEASE

TIPS ON RELEASING FISH

1) After the decision is made to release a fish, do not play it to a "state of exhaustion." If you plan to release a fish try to keep the time from hooksetting to release at a minimum.

2) If at all possible, do not remove your fish from the water, release it in the water where its body is supported.

3) Remove hooks with long-nosed pliers. If hook removal is difficult and may cause injury to the fish, cut the hook off with wire cutters or else cut the line. Do not attempt to remove hooks from fish that are deeply hooked.

4) Care should be taken not to remove the fish's protective body mucous.

5) A dry hand, contrary to popular opinion, reduces the amount of pressure required to restrain the fish and therefore, decreases the chance for internal injury. If at all possible, avoid handling the fish. A landing net can save a large fish from injury and help restrain the fish while removing the hook.

6) When landing a fish use a net rather than a gaff. If you decide to net your fish be careful so it doesn't thrash around in the boat and injure itself. If hook removal is done inside the boat, lay your fish on a wet, soft surface like a wet gunny sack. Don't hold the fish up when removing the hook.

7) With a squirming, hard to handle fish the natural reaction is to slide your hand forward until pressure is placed on the gill covers. Do not hold a fish by the gill covers, as undue force may result in injury to the gills. Remember, never hold a fish by the eye sockets or gills.

8) Hold your unhooked fish horizontally and righted in the water with both hands - one supporting the belly and the other holding near the tail. If the gill covers are not moving, gently move the fish back and forth in the water to facilitate breathing. Hold your fish until it can remain in an upright position and swim away by itself.

9) If the fish must be out of the water for any length of time, cover the head with a wet cloth (i.e., gunny sack) to help prevent drying of the eyes and gills.

10) Never release a large fish, such as muskie, pike, or bass over deep water. An exhausted and stressed fish is incapable of adjusting to the pressure of deep water.

11) A quick and accurate method for measuring fish is marking foot and inch increments on the side of the boat or by taking a wooden ruler and laying it next to the fish in the water.

12) Do not weigh or take pictures of your fish hanging from a scale, stringer, or being held by the gill covers if you intend to release it. This will put unnecessary strain on the delicate supportive and connective tissues between the head and body, as well as the vertebrae.

Tips and Illustration Courtesy of Muskies, Inc.

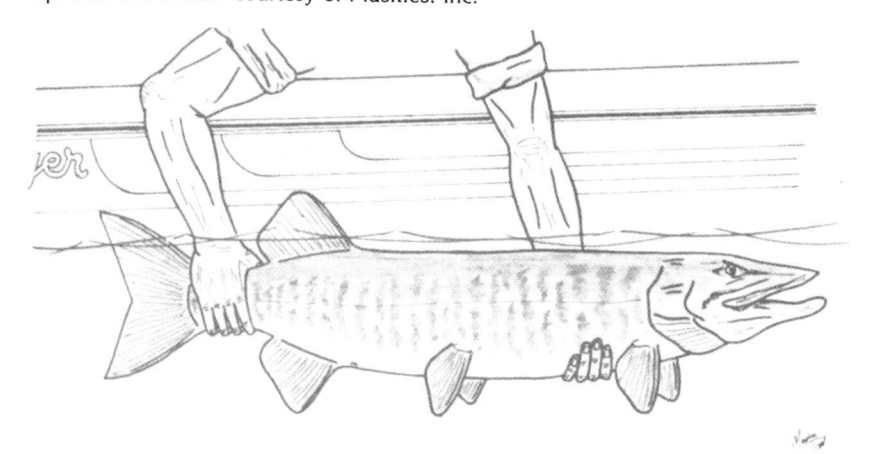

WE CAN SHOW YOU WHERE AND HOW TO CATCH MORE FISH

We Guarantee it!

Fishing Hot Spots CLUB

Join the midwest's **only** "informational" fishing club today. You will increase your catch, learn about the hottest producing lakes and rivers, and save time and money along the way.

Sound exciting? It is if you enjoy catching fish!

Don't delay! Write or call for more information:

FISHING HOT SPOTS CLUB
1999 RIVER STREET
RHINELANDER, WI 54501
715/369-5555